FULL COURTROOM PRESS

A Novel

by

Martin Lion Aronson

Nancy and Eric, June 2022

Here's the legal quasi thriller that no doubt will make Grisham and Turow envious! I can dream, can't I?

A fun project during this stage of my life.

Ellen and I so value having such a wonderful connection with the two of you.

Warmly,
Marty

*Enjoying the slow sunset of an amazingly joyful life
not the least of which joy was the writing of this book.*

DEDICATION

Ellen Sax, my inspiring wife, editor of each and every
draft, and voice of encouragement throughout the years
I spent writing this novel;

Tracey Aronson and Jennifer Parker, my extraordinary
daughters whose love and very presence in my life is an
inspiration;

Eric Parker, my son-in-law whose astute mind and wit
keeps all of us laughing;

Nathaniel Burke, Georgia Parker, Caroline Burke,
Myranda Parker, our talented and loving grandchildren.

IN MEMORY

Myrna Aronson, my prior wife and mom of our children, who was taken from us at a very young age.

CHAPTER ONE
MIKE

MARCH 1972

"SHOOTER, SHOOTER…GET DOWN…DOWN," Boston trial lawyer Mike Lyons shouted as he and his client were walking toward the front entry of the Suffolk County Courthouse. A gunman, face covered with a black ski mask, stood poised at the Corinthian columned entryway.

Mike dropped his briefcase, wrapped an arm around his client Danielle Webb's waist and maneuvered her to the pavement. Instinctively, he positioned himself on top of her prone body in an effort to protect her.

Staying upright is crazy…so much more vulnerable than hugging the ground, he thought.

Mike turned his head toward the gunman. He recognized the weapon. *Glock 22. That means eight rounds. Oh, please, God, no more ammo on him.*

"Mike, what in hell's happening?" Danielle Webb screamed, raising her head.

"Crazy man. He's got a gun. You're safe. You're going to be okay. Stay calm," he answered while lowering the side of her face onto the pavement.

Did I say calm? Jesus, this is scary, Mike said to himself. *Christ, there must be twenty people out here on the square.* Two shots blasted the air.

"We gotta get out of here," Mike heard a lawyer scream whose face was contorted with terror. He watched the lawyer grab his client and start to run.

"NO, NO" Mike screamed. "HIT THE GROUND."

Two more volleys rang out. The bullets ricocheted off the pavement, dangerously close to the running lawyer.

"If you're a believer, Mrs. Webb, please start praying."

"I'm not a believer, but I'm sure as hell praying. I've got two kids. This is terrifying."

People were running haphazardly, clutching briefcases and handbags, stumbling in panic.

"Oh, my God," an elderly man cried as he hobbled a few feet, then collapsed to his knees. He had not been shot. Fear tightened his chest and shortened his breath. Mike observed a young woman shimmy to his side. She spoke confidently, "I've got you, sir."

Smart. Gutsy. Kind. I'd want her next to me in the trenches. I hear sirens. Jesus, get here fast. Son-of-a-bitch has four more rounds. I hope that's it.

Mike craned his neck and noticed a couple, alarm and confusion on their faces, hunched over and lurching laterally toward Mike's position.

Another pair of volleys in rapid succession. They smacked the cobblestone area just a few feet from Mike and Mrs. Webb.

Holy shit. Is this guy gunning for us?

He bellowed at the hunched-over couple, "GET DOWN! DOWN!"

"Mike," his client mumbled, "it's getting tough to breathe down here."

"I'm sorry, but this guy's gunning in our direction. If we get up and run, we'll just be making it easier for him. Hug the ground. We'll ride this thing out. You're going to be okay."

The nearby couple had not yet sprawled onto the pavement. Mike made eye contact and slapped his palm against the ground, again pleading, "DOWN."

Too late. Mike could hear the thud of deadly rounds tearing into the couple. As they collapsed to the pavement, the color of their clothing transformed to crimson. *Oh, my God. Bad. They've been hit bad. But that's it...that's the last of the rounds,* Mike thought. He rolled off Danielle Webb and reached toward the downed couple. Korea came racing back. This was all part of an infantryman's training when anyone close to him was hit. You go to them. The horror of that war always lurked in his subconscious. He looked in the direction of the gunman. *Please be done, you bastard. Please, dear God, no more ammo.*

The shooter had fled.

Six Days Earlier...

"My mother was Irish Catholic!"

"Spare me, big guy. You've told me that a zillion times," Mike's wife, Alison, quipped.

"Well, you asked me last night why I wouldn't wear a condom," said Mike.

"Last night? Oh, did something happen last night?" Alison quipped. She turned and threw an arm across Mike's chest.

"No time. Trial today—gotta get moving," said Mike.

He jumped out of bed, pulled on his boxer shorts, leaned down and pressed a cheek to his wife's sleepy face.

"I'll take the dog out, get the kids up, make some coffee," he said. "And you, madam school psychologist, better start to shake it."

"I know, I know," she replied. "It's only six. I've got another fifteen. I'll take the kids to the bus. You just get yourself organized."

Mike slipped into a pair of sweats, a ski sweater, grabbed his jacket, and knocked on each daughter's door.

"Okay, Dad. I hear you." Hillary, the eleven-year-old, was always easy to rise.

"Hey, Michelle—time. Michelle?" He rapped on the door again. Finally, his ten-year-old's scratchy voice managed a response. "Okay, Dad, okay."

They'll never know how much I adore them. Growing up too damned fast. Can't stand it, Mike thought.

Off he went for his early morning walk with Macbeth, the smartest and most stubborn standard poodle who ever roamed the backyards of the bedroom town of Sudbury.

When he returned, Mike completed his morning hygiene and put on his lawyer uniform of the day. Pinstripe navy blue suit, white oxford cloth button down shirt, midnight blue tie with an easy pattern of subtle white lines—definitely trial attire. He plunked down his mug of half-consumed coffee on the kitchen counter.

"Ali, I'm off—have a good one," he shouted from the bottom of the stairway of their four-bedroom contemporary Cape. The house was situated on a knoll in a cul-de-sac.

"Okay," she yelled. "Did you make coffee? Good luck today."

"Are you kiddin'? Best damned cup of coffee in Sudbury. See you tonight."

Mike opened the garage door and paused a moment as he put his briefcase onto the back seat of his Mercedes. *Me—Mike Lyons—kid from the Brighton projects—now a house in the 'burbs...a Mercedes Benz. Okay, car was three years old when we bought it, but such a luxury.* Shaking his head, he patted his briefcase. "Bring me luck today, pal—bring me lots of luck." It was a daily ritual.

* * *

Michael Arthur Lyons was the son of a mixed marriage. His mother was Catholic, his father, Jewish. Mike's dad struggled with a series of low-paying jobs until he finally realized his dream. Mike was eleven when his father became a police officer. His parents were very much in love and earnestly set about saving so that before too long they could free themselves from the low-income housing project where they lived in the Brighton section of

Boston. It had been passable when they moved in, but gradually disintegrated into a place rife with drugs and gangs.

"Out. We're getting out of here. This is no place for us—no place for Mike. I'll grab as much overtime as I can. We'll keep stashing away what we can and before too long we'll have enough for a down payment," Mike heard his dad lament to his mother on more than one occasion.

And then the nightmare. Mike's dad's Achilles tendon snapped while chasing a couple of drug dealers across railroad tracks near Fenway Park. He catapulted onto the tracks. A train was coming. Mike's dad was unable to scramble to safety. Mike, an only child, was just fifteen.

His mother was an RN. The medical staff at Beth Israel Hospital had nothing but accolades about her work. Patients benefited from her kind bedside manner as well as her professional expertise. The Chief of Medicine encouraged her to take advantage of a hospital program that would help finance medical school, but before she had a chance to seriously consider such an opportunity, she lost the love of her life. She was never the same. Depression set in. She was prone to melancholia and mood swings, all of which kept her from working on a regular basis. They were stuck in the projects.

Two police officers, loyal to the memory of Mike's dad, served as mentors and kept the teenager on a steady course. He was a natural athlete and while playing basketball for the high school team garnered the attention of an alumnus of Northeastern University who had played ball there. He introduced Mike and his mother to Joe Zabilski, the school's head coach.

"You're a hell of a good basketball player and your grades are excellent. I'm not only going to recommend that you be admitted, but I'm going to see to it that you get some scholarship assistance," Coach Zabilski said. He turned to Mike's mother, "I think your son would be a good fit at Northeastern and a strong contributor to our basketball program."

Mike matriculated in the fall of 1951. A preseason knee injury kept him from playing basketball most of his freshman year. And he found the academics at Northeastern murky. The school emphasized engineering, which wasn't a comfortable fit. There were, of course, other subjects offered, but after all was said and done, Mike was just not ready for the transition to college. Confused and muddled about what he wanted from life, he listened to the macho side of his brain. He left Northeastern at the conclusion of the fall semester, joined the Marines and served with distinction during the Korean War as a combat infantryman.

The war, as it did with so many young men, impacted the depth of Mike's being. Like most people who served in combat zones, he seldom talked about his experiences. But during one of his pre-marriage dates with Alison, she asked about Korea and his decision to go on to college after serving.

"Going into detail about what the war was like isn't something I'm ready to talk about. Suffice it to say, each day was an eternity. But the Marines I served with were the very best men I will ever know. In boot camp we were just a bunch of rudderless kids. In combat, we had each other's back. We were no longer kids. I thought that if I get through this hell, I'm going back to school… make something of myself. I owed getting an education to my mom and the memory of my dad. I left the nightmare of war ready for college."

Mike served in the First Division. Lt. Colonel Walter Pastel, one of its heroic leaders, took an interest in Mike. He admired the infantryman's toughness, courage under fire, and leadership ability. The Lt. Colonel was a Dartmouth College graduate. After the war ended, Pastel was assigned as an NROTC instructor at his alma mater. He spoke with Mike about Dartmouth, and after Mike returned home, he took him to Hanover, New Hampshire to visit the college. Mike was instantly impressed and felt that it would be a haven after his hellish experience in Korea. The "GI Bill of Rights" for Korean War vets would provide the means to attend college. Mike was admitted and he pursued the academic and athletic opportunities with verve, excelling not only in the classroom, but also on the basketball court. He was the Ivy League's top point guard.

His mom, whose moments of pleasure were rare, watched proudly as her son was singled out at graduation for his "service to our country, academic excellence, leadership, and stardom on our varsity basketball team for three years." Tragically, one month to the day of his graduation, Mike's mother died of a massive heart attack.

He would always miss her. Not a day would go by that he didn't think about his parents. *Strange,* he thought as he readied himself for law school, *I'm actually an orphan.* But Mike was resilient and self-contained. He attended Boston College Law School's night program while working myriad jobs during the day, including as a law clerk for a firm that would hire him as an associate upon graduation.

* * *

The forty-five minute drive to the Norfolk Superior Court in the Town of Dedham, a suburb about twenty-five miles south of Boston, was spent in silence. No radio. His mind raced through his list of witnesses, their anticipated testimony, his opening statement to the jury, and cross-examination of the defendant's witnesses. It was a civil trial involving personal injuries sustained by his client when a defective diving board in a neighbor's swimming pool snapped loose and pummeled his client's head, rendering him unconscious while in the water. Fortunately, friends pulled him out. He suffered a serious concussion with long-lasting symptoms.

Despite the immediacy of this case, Mike couldn't keep his mind from darting to another vastly more significant matter scheduled for trial in the federal court in just a month. It was his biggest case to date. His client, Bobby Farrington, had ingested a drug prescribed for his lupus erythematosus. The drug damaged his retina, leaving him legally blind. The drug manufacturer, Mike alleged, was well aware of the dangerous side effects, but nevertheless failed to provide warnings about the potential risk as well as any advice for the user to have periodic eye exams. Mike asserted that such examinations would have revealed any early signs of the onset of chloroquine retinopathy and at the very least would have given his client a chance to save his eyesight. Mr. Farrington's condition was now irreversible.

Trial lawyers, like Mike, have a heavy caseload and must train themselves to shift seamlessly from one matter to another, often within short time periods. This includes concentrating upon new cases. Mike had said it more than once: "A trial lawyer simply never knows what kind of situation is about to step off the elevator and suddenly consume his/her life."

And indeed, a pair of new intriguing cases was about to descend upon him. One would walk into his office later in the day. It would involve an alluring woman named Danielle Webb who would appear at his office with a prominent black eye, courtesy of her husband, descendant of an old-line wealthy Boston family. The other matter that would unfold in a matter of weeks would concern the emotional destruction of a young sister of the church by an older priest who had served as her mentor.

It was endless for trial lawyers—the challenge of juggling multiple dramas, constant inner conversations, constant reminders, constant coaching. He had learned his craft well but the competitor within him felt he still had rungs to climb before reaching the top. Nevertheless, as self-critical as he could be, Mike knew that his trial skills were well honed. He had earned the respect of the more senior trial lawyers because he had stood up in courtrooms and, as some put it, "been counted." Consequently, he was a frequent invitee to speak at continuing legal education programs. He wasn't what was known in the practice as strictly a settler. He was a true litigator. There were masters at negotiating excellent settlements and rarely going to court. Mike tried to learn from them as well.

He appreciated the value of settling cases short of trial but was always ready to go the distance in the courtroom if need be.

"Make us fear you," an insurance claims supervisor had advised Mike when he was a neophyte in the litigation business. "Go to trial. Show us that you've got the stuff to go at it in the courtroom. Then you'll start getting much more generous offers to settle."

Mike Lyons heeded that advice, mixed it up in the courtroom with several jury trials, always ready to try them to a verdict, but never hesitant to settle when he thought doing so was in his client's best interest. It wasn't long before he started getting larger offers to resolve cases short of full-scale trials.

The thrill of the kill—standing up for my client in a courtroom—that's why I became a lawyer. But if there's a strong offer on the table, I'm not going to be a fool. Client comes first. If it makes sense, we'll settle. But always be ready to go the distance.

The handsome thirty-nine-year-old litigator pulled into the parking lot behind the Norfolk Superior Court and stepped out of his car. At six feet even, dark luminous eyes, Mike managed to maintain his athletic build. He brushed a hand through his thick black hair, pointed an index finger skyward, and, as he did most every day, thanked his mom and dad. He reached for his briefcase.

He hesitated before walking toward the Greek Revival courthouse built in the 1820s, a place where many felt a great injustice occurred back in 1921: the conviction (and subsequent execution) of two Italian immigrants, Nicola Sacco and Bartolomeo Vanzetti, for the murder of two men during an armed robbery. Many felt that the evidence against them was questionable, that the jury was prejudiced because they were immigrants. Eventually in the 1970s the Governor issued a proclamation that Sacco and Vanzetti had been unfairly tried and convicted.

"Counsel." It was the voice of today's adversary, Bill O'Leary. "You must be doing very well these days. Very slick wheels."

"It's hot, Bill. Stole it right off a Mercedes lot," Mike quipped, extending his hand. He smiled easily.

"I'm holding on to my wallet, Counsel."

"How's Rose these days? Still tolerating you? Good thing she's such a fine painter…nice escape from putting up with your antics."

Bill O'Leary slapped a hand across Mike's back.

"You've got a good memory. She's having an exhibition soon at one of the galleries on Newbury Street. I'll send you and your brave wife an invitation to the opening," O'Leary said. "I'm proud of her, Mike. Be sure to stop by."

"Absolutely. I'll be able to buy a couple of her paintings after I clean house with you on this case," Mike said with a smile.

"Dream on, Counsel, dream on. Your client was drunk as a skunk. That's why he couldn't get out of the way of that diving board. Major mitigation factor," said O'Leary.

"Two beers, Mr. Defense Lawyer. And I'm bringing that out during my opening and during direct. I'm not letting you hammer him on cross-examination."

"Takin' the wind out of my sails. You don't play fair, Lyons."

"I wish you luck, my friend. I'm not talking about this case. I'm talking about the judgeship. Hope it works out," Mike said.

The lawyers touched fists as they entered the courthouse. Mike thrived on the competition in the courtroom and valued the camaraderie among fellow trial lawyers. He and O'Leary walked down one of the corridors. There was a natural elegance about the way Mike Lyons moved.

"There you are, handsome man. Let me have a quickie."

Mike chuckled. "Donna Stephens, you are big trouble. And you got it all wrong. I'm slow and easy. No quickies for this stud."

Attorney Stephens poked her index finger at the dimple in Mike's chin and then ran it along the faint scar on his right cheek. It was the remnant of a shrapnel wound during the fighting at the Chosin Reservoir, North Korea.

"This is what I'm talking about, Big Shot. Not a roll in the hay. Last time I did this, it brought me luck," she said playfully.

She slapped Mike on his rear.

"Did you see that!" Mike shouted, looking at no one in particular. "Sexual harassment!"

"See yah, handsome."

The jousting was all part of the courthouse banter. There was an understanding among trial lawyers. One couldn't describe the thrill, the stress, the all-consuming challenges to those who didn't experience the competition of the courtroom. It was the warriors who actually went at it in the courtroom multiple times, who lived the incredible highs and devastating lows—who really knew just what it meant to be a *trial* lawyer. Mike was proud of the badge and of having earned the respect of his colleagues.

He needed to put the pharmaceutical case aside and concentrate on the diving board trial. He made his way to the hallway just outside the courtroom, where he greeted his client.

"Josh, great to see you," Mike said. "How're you feeling?"

"A little nervous, Mr. Lyons. But after our prep session the other day, I think I'm ready."

"Josh, you're going to be great. Just remember, stick to the truth and the truth only. It'll all come racing back to you as I ask my questions—just as we went over in the office. When I ask about drinking, don't hesitate...not for a second. If you do, the jury will be suspicious. You told me that you had a couple of beers within an hour of going into the pool. That's what I want to hear in front of the jury. Clear and straightforward. They know that young people your age at a summer pool party are going to drink. They'll respect your honesty."

"I understand, Mr. Lyons."

"And having a couple of beers had nothing to do with that diving board becoming unhinged and slamming down onto your head."

"It was a shocker, Mr. Lyons."

"I expect that the other lawyer and I will be summoned into the judge's lobby before we actually get started."

"Lobby?"

"Just a word we lawyers use to describe a judge's office. Some people even refer to it as chambers."

Josh nodded.

"As I mentioned the other day, judges like to see if they can get the lawyers together and settle," Mike said.

"Mr. Lyons…"

"It's Mike. No formal stuff, except in the courtroom."

"Do you think they might settle?"

"Tough to say, but at the moment we've got to stay focused on getting into the courtroom and going to trial. As I mentioned before, many cases get resolved during trial. I like to get started and show the other side that we're ready to go all the way," said Mike. "That way we'll maximize any settlement efforts on their part."

"Counsel on *Merrill vs. Aquatic Industries*. The Court will see you in chambers," a court officer announced.

"Okay, Josh, that's our case. The judge's going to meet with the lawyers…probably explore possible settlement. We'll see how it plays out. I should be out in about a half hour. I suggest you grab a coffee while I'm gone." Mike gave his client a reassuring pat on the shoulder. "We'll talk after this conference. I'll let you know exactly what went on."

Mike and Bill O'Leary went into Judge Boudreau's chambers. Well, "chambers" is a bit of an exaggeration. Two thread-worn faux Oriental rugs covered much of the uneven wood floor. The judge sat behind an old oak desk. There were a few straight-backed wooden chairs, their backs against windows in dire need of washing. One of the walls was covered with black and white photographs of judges and politicians, including one of Judge Boudreau with President John Kennedy.

"Gentlemen, have a seat, please." The judge extended his hand. "Good to see you, Mike. You did a hell of a job at trial last week for that poor fellow with a drinking problem. And, Bill, you look as distinguished as ever. I hear it looks pretty certain you're going to be joining us on the bench."

Bill O'Leary smiled. "I hope so, Judge. Fingers crossed."

"Well," said Boudreau, "you'll be a hell of an asset. Don't you think so, Mike?"

"Absolutely, Your Honor. Bill is right at the top, sir. In fact, we could put him over the top if he'd get sensible and persuade his insurer to come up with a decent settlement of this case."

Gotta let the judge know I'm an open guy—always willing to talk settlement. But actually I'd like to try this one to conclusion. I like my chances. And I think any jury will like my client. Likability. Funny, but so often much of it comes down to which lawyer, which client the jury likes...and believes.

O'Leary sprung open his briefcase and removed his file. "I'm afraid not. I think we're going to have to try this one," he said. It was the usual posturing of a defense lawyer in the personal injury business. Although the named defendant was technically their client, it was the client's insurance company that controlled the payment of any compensation. And it was the insurance companies that issued the marching orders to their trial lawyers. The mantra of many claims supervisors: "Even if we're eventually going to settle, don't let on at the outset. Play hardball. Make the claimants sweat. No easy settlements. Low-ball any offer. Then, depending upon the facts and quality of the plaintiff's lawyer, we can raise the ante."

It's all part of the dance, Mike thought to himself. *And it just repeats itself, case after case. In a couple of seconds, the judge will say, "Well, come on gentlemen, let's talk about this."*

"Well, come on, gentlemen, let's talk about this," Judge Boudreau predictably said.

Boudreau's a good man. He knows the two of us and he knows we both can try a case. He'll navigate through the posturing, get a good idea of what he thinks makes sense about a potential settlement, and then apply just enough pressure to try to make each side bend and then fold. But, hey, this could be one where we just don't get together and then we'll hammer it out before a jury, Mike thought.

"So, Mike, as the plaintiff's lawyer, you've got the laboring oar. Tell me what you've got," said the judge. "And then, Bill, I'll of course hear why you can't pay a dime."

"Well, Your Honor..." Mike started.

But Mike was interrupted by a court officer who had partially opened the door and leaned into the room, "Your Honor, sorry to interrupt, but the clerk's office just received an emergency call for Attorney Lyons. Shall I have it transferred here?"

Emergency? Accident? Ali? The kids? Oh, my God.

CHAPTER TWO
MIKE

"Transfer the call here, please," said Judge Boudreau.

"I hope nothing crucial with your family, Mike. Bill and I will step out so you have some privacy."

"Hello."

"Mike, it's Paul Melrose."

Mike uttered a major sigh of relief, a lawyer on the phone, not family.

Paul Melrose was "The Chairman of the Board." He was Boston's finest civil trial lawyer, earned the respect of every trial judge and was plugged into the Boston political world. Now in his seventies, Melrose was past president of just about every legal organization, earned and enjoyed eminent success as a lawyer for the injured for the past fifty years. His charming manner before a jury had "winner" indelibly stamped across his suit jacket. He was one of Mike's courtroom heroes. He was also Mike's adversary in the Farrington product liability case. For reasons unclear to Mike, Paul Melrose, usually a lawyer for victims, was representing the pharmaceutical company that manufactured the medication that rendered Mike's client virtually sightless.

"Mr. Melrose? I can't tell you how relieved I am. The court officer said it was an emergency…"

"Oh, Jesus, and you of course thought it was something personal, your family. Didn't he tell you that it was me? I'm sorry you were alarmed. Clumsy of me."

"No problem," Mike lied. Family anxiety was relieved but now a different concern set in. *Something blow up with the Farrington case? Something about the trial date? Or is Melrose looking for a continuance?*

"You'd better let me talk with Boudreau and apologize. Your secretary…Jane, is it?"

"Yes, Mr. Melrose. Jane Donnell," Mike responded.

"She told me that you were out there in Dedham about to get started with a trial. Who's on the other side? Were you guys conferencing with Boudreau? Good judge. Fair…honest."

"I'm going up against Bill O'Leary," said Mike, knowing that this call had to have something to do with his major case against Intercontinental Pharmaceutical.

"Bill! I should speak with him as well. This will be his last trial. The Council has approved his nomination to the bench."

Paul Melrose…the kingmaker…always in the know.

"That's great news, Mr. M. They both stepped outside. Hold on, I'll get them," Mike said.

"No, no. Wait a minute, Mike. Let me talk with you first, then I'll get on the phone with them."

This is really weird. Is it some kind of tactic? Here I am about to get started with a trial and then this. No other lawyer could get away with this…interrupting a conference with a judge…telling somebody in the clerk's office that it's an emergency?

"Mike," Melrose started, "Listen, I'm calling about your man Farrington. I screwed up. I owe you a thousand apologies. I got a call Wednesday from the bastards on the other side of your Farrington case, my not so distinguished clients, and totally forgot to let you know that one of their VPs is coming to my office this afternoon to talk business."

"Bastards? My not so distinguished clients?" Cute tactic. Suddenly my adversary and I are partners going up against his client. Clever. I'm gonna put this one in my playbook.

"What kind of business?" Mike replied.

"Settlement, Mike. They're here to put this case to rest. I'll get Boudreau to release you. Come directly to my office. The pharmaceutical company is self-insured for a lot of dough. And if we need to choke them for more, their excess insurer will pony up. I can get this son-of-a-bitch to loosen the coffers."

"Mr. M, this is really strange. This case has been pending for three years. All kinds of pretrial machinations, but not once has your client even asked what I'm looking for, let alone come forward with an offer. And I know you came into the defense recently, but I have a suggestion. Why don't you wrestle with your client, get a figure that they consider fair and then we can talk once I finish this trial." Mike guessed that this wouldn't fly, but he didn't want to let on how ruffled and anxious he was. He tried to come over as cool and take the initiative.

"I hear you, Mike. And I respect exactly what you're saying. Believe me, I'm not playing games and you know that I wouldn't insult you. But they're genuinely…well, I can't reveal why the urgency…at least not until after we've put this thing to bed. I can't guarantee anything, but they wouldn't send one of their major players unless they're serious about settling this case, Mike. I'm not messin' around. You know I'm a straight shooter. I've urged that they come up with a strong number. It's in your best interest to get here while they're here. And you'll be doing me a favor. I promised you'd be here. I'm embarrassed that I just plain forgot to call you right away on Wednesday."

This could be a trap. Raise my expectations. Set me up for a fall. Settling cases is tricky business. It's an art. A negotiator has to be tough, persuasive and reasonable. Knowing when it makes sense not to try to be a hero and go to trial, but to settle at a compromising level. Paul Melrose is the master…in and out of the courtroom. He'll be using his charm…try to get me to accept something far less than good value to take care of my client's needs. Catch me off guard while my head is filled with the case I'm about to try out here.

"Okay, Mr. M, you win this round. I'll take the bait. But I'm a stubborn guy. And I'm looking forward to getting tossed around in that courtroom by the very best ever."

"Flattery always works with me, Mike. Remember what I once told you: too stressful to try more than two substantial plaintiff cases a year. The trick is to keep the 'enemy' from knowing whether or not the case he has with you is the one you're going to try or settle. Settle this one. It's too risky to try. I'll get you the right figure."

"Mr. M, your persuasiveness permeates these phone lines. But you're aware that I'm about to get started with a trial out here."

"Let me speak with the 'boys.' I'll get you out of there pronto," Melrose said.

Power. Just like a Marine Corps CO. Connections. Earned respect.

After a brief conversation among Paul Melrose, His Honor, and soon-to-be-judge Bill O'Leary, all parties agreed upon a continuance.

The behind-the-scenes machinations of the power boys, Mike thought to himself.

Hiding his angst, Mike stepped into the hallway and explained the necessity of a continuance to his client, who was relieved that he wouldn't have to take the witness stand for another few weeks. "And the truth is," Mike added, "we'll kick their butts. Thanks for your understanding, Josh. I appreciate it. Whether we go through a full trial or settle your case, I'll express my real thanks and adjust my fee to less than a full third called for in the Contingent Fee Agreement."

They shook hands. "I'll be in touch next week," said Mike.

Mike Lyons seldom got thrown...not after what he had been through in his young lifetime. But this unexpected turn of events took him totally by surprise. The Bobby Farrington case was major. The man's family and future were relying upon Mike to achieve a substantial monetary result to provide financial security. Legally blind and suffering with lupus, Mike's client's earning capacity had been washed down the drain because of a drug that was a huge profit maker for Intercontinental. The medication was properly prescribed to help control the systemic lupus erythematosus with which Bobby Farrington suffered, but some people who ingested that drug developed irreversible retinal vascular disease. Mike was prepared to prove that Intercontinental was aware of the potentially dangerous side effect and failed to properly warn doctors and users.

Expect the unexpected. One moment I'm about to dive into a swimming pool accident trial and then, on a dime, I'm shifting gears to deal with the biggest case of my career, Mike thought.

* * *

Mr. Melrose's secretary greeted Mike. "Cold enough for you, Mike? How about a cup of hot coffee?"

Florence Morse had served Paul Melrose faithfully for forty years. She knew almost as much about Paul's cases as he did. And she knew that Mike Lyons was one of her boss' favorite young lawyers. He had offered Mike a position with his elite boutique firm just five years ago but Mike had his heart set on going out on his own. He had been with a fifteen-lawyer firm and had tired of its politics. He wanted to get out and be beholden just to himself and his clients. Florence Morse came to know Mike when he and her boss met to discuss a possible working relationship. And, like her boss, she admired and respected Mike.

"Here you go, Mike. Black, one sugar. I remember from the last time." Mrs. Morse smiled and returned to her desk. "Oh, this is the packet that your secretary sent over." Mike opened the sealed envelope containing his summary file. There was honor among the quality trial lawyers. He had zero concern that anyone in Paul Melrose's firm would attempt to open, read, and then reseal the contents.

Mike stretched his legs after taking a seat in the waiting area. *Christ,* he thought, *how could Mr. M have forgotten to call me? These matters don't just pop up out of nowhere. This is probably a*

setup. If Melrose forgot, sure as hell Florence wouldn't have
slipped. She would have reminded him to call me.

"Wow, this is fabulous coffee, Mrs. Morse. What did you
spike it with?"

"A wee bit of Scotch," she said.

Mike chuckled. "Trust me, Florence Morse, when I get home
tonight, I'm having one tumbler full."

"Well, maybe you'll have something to celebrate," she said
putting her hand over her mouth.

"Looks like our friend, Mr. M, is starting to lose the hop on
his fastball. Totally forgot to call and give me any advance notice?
That's not like the master." Mike raised an eyebrow.

Florence Morse looked down at her desk and pretended to
busy herself. She knew that Mike suspected that it was an
uncharacteristic tactic, last-minute notice, but she was also aware
that Paul Melrose was beginning to become forgetful. She was
embarrassed for him.

"Mike, Mr. Melrose has the highest regard for you. He never
would have asked you to come into the firm if…he's…well, I
really shouldn't be talking like this. How's your family, Mike?"

I guess maybe he really did forget. Some of the other trial
kings of Paul's vintage are also starting to slip a bit. They're in
their seventies. Even the sharpest start to lose their edge after so
many stressful hours in the courtroom. Wonder how long I'll be
able to handle the pressure before I lose my full court press?

"Oh, they're great. Thanks for asking. My daughters are
doing fine. I'm hoping to grab some family time during one of
their vacations. The trial of this baby will be over. And then my
wife and I and the kids will head for someplace fun. As I
remember, Mrs. Morse, you and your husband are fellow Red Sox
fans. Hard to believe that the Sox opener is just days away."

"Even harder to believe that it's five years since the Sox
Impossible Dream team in '67. What do you think about the
trade?" Florence asked.

"I guess they're looking for some hitting. Danny Cater's been a good one, but he's getting up there. And not really a power guy. I'm excited about their young catcher, Fisk. We'll just have to see how it all plays out."

Paul Melrose made his entrance. The man took over a room with his presence. His aura was electric. Perhaps it was the constant twinkle in his blue eyes, or his elegant silver hair, or his movie star Nordic good looks. He was brilliant, crafty, and had an air of kindness.

"Hey, Mike, thanks for breaking away from court and racing in here."

They clasped hands. Paul Melrose tipped his head slightly to the right and fixed his smiling eyes upon Mike.

"Come in, come in." Melrose's hand was on Mike's back ushering him toward his office.

"After you, please, Mr. Melrose."

"Cut that Mister crap. You young bastards try to make an old man of me. Well, I've got that *International* bastard in the library downstairs. I think…"

"Intercontinental, Mr. M," Florence corrected her boss.

"International, Intercontinental, what the hell's the difference," Melrose said, exchanging a wink.

Mike sat on the other side of Melrose's desk. Friends…a mentor-mentee kind of relationship. But on this matter they were adversaries. Paul Melrose, however, was fairly new to the case. Previous counsel had been fired. The drug company was tired of that firm getting beaten up by Mike throughout pretrial motions and discovery. When Mike learned that they had engaged Paul Melrose to represent them, he was surprised. Like Mike, Melrose was a plaintiff's guy.

"Mike, let's get this thing settled. I want you to be reasonable. It's in each of our best interests not to go ahead with a trial. Too much risk for each of us. But if we do try this case, you know I'll go all out to bury you. I don't want to do that. I also know you're no lightweight. You've stood up and been counted. Hell, I asked you to come into my firm because I know you've got the goods. You're smart, Mike, and you've already proven yourself as a damned good trial lawyer. This guy from *International's* a tight bastard, but I think I've got him positioned to come up with a strong settlement."

"Mr. M, it's Intercontinental, not International," Mike chuckled affably, knowing that Paul Melrose knew his client's correct name…and then some. *They call him the Silver Fox for a reason,* Mike thought.

"I don't get it, Mr. M," Mike replied. "How come all of a sudden, out of the blue, they want to do business? I know that you just stepped into this case a few months ago but I've been at this with depositions and motions for three years without a peep of interest from them about settling this case. Why now? Your magic?"

Paul Melrose smiled, got up from his high-back chair, unbuttoned his gray suit jacket, came around and leaned against the front corner of his desk. He enjoyed the compliment. Despite all his years of success in obtaining large verdicts, the seventy-two-year-old warhorse still loved hearing that he was good…even magical. The needy ego of many a trial lawyer.

"The Chairman of the Board of Intercontinental and I serve together as trustees at Northeastern University. He's worked with me in helping to get some underprivileged kids into Northeastern with scholarships."

"That's impressive. You guys have some serious clout," said Mike. "So, the Chairman asked you to take over for the defense of this baby?"

"He told me he needed a favor. He knew defense work wasn't my choice, but asked that I take a hard look at the case from all angles. I did and advised him that he's got some serious exposure and should think seriously about settling this case," said Paul. "And I also told him how highly I think of you."

"So, suddenly some big shot VP drops out of the sky to write a check?" Mike asked, raising his eyebrows. "Tells you on Wednesday that he's coming in Friday and wants to do business?" Mike chuckled, got up and walked over to the window.

He turned and faced his elder adversary. "It doesn't add up."

"Mike, there's something going on at the company that I simply cannot reveal. Confidential information is just that. But he's here to try to settle this case. I'll introduce you. He's pompous. Let me take the lead," said Melrose.

Paul Melrose started toward his door. He stopped. "And don't blow your cool. Don't forget, Mike, if we try this baby I'll take you to the cleaners. There's no such thing as a perfect case. I'll make things rough for you and your client. He's not as blind as you may think."

Son-of-a-bitch. My adversary is making like we're best pals and then he lobs a hand grenade at me. Is this going to be a "good cop, bad cop" routine? And what does he mean: "Not as blind as I think?" I know that Bobby tried to do some roofing work on his house with one of his pals, but couldn't handle it. They no doubt have been keeping a close eye on him. Wouldn't be surprised if they've got video of him mowing his lawn or maybe even that time he climbed up a ladder. And do they know he and his wife sometimes go to the movies? Bobby can barely make out what's on the screen, but he likes going. Likes the smell of the popcorn. "Makes me feel normal," he told me. What the hell am I worried about? When we go to trial, I'll bring this stuff out myself. The truth is the truth and no way will it sink our ship. Will it? I've got outstanding experts…strong evidence to prove that the drug did my guy in. They'll make noise about all the other meds in Bobby's life that could have caused the loss of eyesight. Standard fare. But I know…and they know it too…I've got a damned strong case.

Preston Bradford, a vice president at Intercontinental Pharmaceutical, was introduced. A thin, wiry man, he extended his hand toward Mike as though it would surely fall off should they connect. In fact, he closed his eyes when they actually shook hands. Arrogance was written all over his face. Bradford sat on the couch and commenced to regale Mike with the virtues of Intercontinental and the great service it had rendered with the development of "a true wonder drug for providing relief for so many thousands of victims of malaria and lupus." He was careful not to say a word about the relief it had provided the bank accounts of his company's hierarchy.

"I hope you understand, Mr. Lyons, that my being sent here to meet with you and Paul is highly unusual. And I don't intend to waste a lot of time." Bradford did not make eye contact with Mike.

Melrose is right. This guy is smug. He's got that look on his face as if someone just threw up on his shoes. Suit looks too tight for him…just like his personality.

Mike smiled and nodded.

Melrose stepped to the center of the room. "Mike, we know that your man alleges that he took the drug…"

"Alleges! Hell, Paul, I provided you with copies of all the doc's prescriptions. We're well past *alleges*," Mike burst out.

Keep your cool, Mike. But that was okay…a shell across the bow lets Bradford know I mean business, Mike thought to himself.

Bradford started: "You've got an uphill fight in this case. - We've got video of your man climbing up a ladder to get to his roof…and smoking. And there's clear evidence that he failed to go for the prescribed eye checkups once he started taking our chloroquine compound."

"Mr. Bradford, surely you're aware that at the time your drug was prescribed for my client to treat his lupus there was no warning issued whatsoever by Intercontinental about the danger of damage to the retina and the necessity that the patient should have eye checkups. Internal memos show your people were clearly knowledgeable of the dangers at the time Mr. Farrington was prescribed your drug. Warnings, such as they are, came after, sir. Perhaps you weren't there at the time, but I've got solid evidence to prove that during the five years that RETLU was taken by Mr. Farrington there were no warnings of its dangerous potential side effect of causing irreversible damage to one's eyesight. Nothing whatsoever to doctors or the patients about any need to have frequent eye checkups. Sir, that all came after my client stopped taking the drug and was already condemned to irreversible retinopathy. Intercontinental, sir, used false and misleading marketing to push RETLU. It prioritized distribution and profit over public health."

Bradford postured as though he hadn't heard Mike.

"And our experts will have a field day with your guy's medical history. So many other meds he took that might well have brought on damage to his retina…and the booze," Bradford added. He plastered a smirk across his face as though he had just conquered Mount Everest. He was wrong.

Mike responded: "You both know what I've got. And that's one hell of a strong case. The evidence is patently clear that your drug was prescribed by Bobby Farrington's doctor. A first-rate physician, Johns Hopkins Medical School, who will testify to the truth. He'll tell the jury that your detail men who introduced the doctor to the drug said nothing to him about potential adverse side effects that destroyed Mr. Farrington's life. And they said nothing because even they were kept in the dark by your company about the danger of ingesting RETLU. And you're well aware that I have an eminent expert, chief of the Department of Medical Research at one of your major competitors and formerly with the FDA and NIH, who will testify about the industry's knowledge regarding the potential danger to a patient who takes RETLU and that during the time period Bobby Farrington was taking the drug, Intercontinental knew of the serious side effects. Mr. Bradford, let's face it…the evidence is overwhelming that your people knew of the risks…there's a trove of internal memos that acknowledge the problem…but they failed to issue reasonable warnings. No warnings until well after my client ingested your drug. You think this isn't enough to carry the day?"

Bradford's face turned the color of sunset red. Paul Melrose had to turn and look out a window to hide the pleasure he experienced with Mike's feisty delivery.

Mike continued: "Any jury in America would draw the quick inference that all Intercontinental was looking for was sales and profit. You think this isn't going to crush any defense you try to mount? Jurors don't like powerhouse corporations that cheat."

Melrose and Bradford exchanged meaningful looks. If Bradford wasn't aware before, he now surrendered to the idea that Mike knew exactly what he was doing.

"And I'll tell you something else," Mike said, gathering his papers while feigning that he was preparing to leave. "The jury's going to fall in love with my guy…and his wife. Churchgoing citizens, Little League coaches, lead the town blood-donor drive every year, and Bobby gives motivational talks for other vision-impaired people. Tell me something, gentlemen, are we actually here today to argue whether or not Bobby Farrington is permanently blind…irreversible macular degeneration…and that what he suffers is related to your drug? If that's the purpose of this meeting, we're wasting each other's time."

Mike added to his theatrics by getting up from his chair and extending the palm of his hand toward Melrose as if to indicate his willingness to end this conversation and leave. The tactic worked.

Paul Melrose smiled. He liked Mike's spunk, and he knew exactly the message Mike was sending to Preston Bradford: that if this case has to go to trial, Mike's more than ready to rise to the occasion.

"Mike, we're here to do business. We're three honorable men. Let's reason and see if we can get this thing resolved. I don't want you beating my brains out in a courtroom…" said Melrose. Bradford winced at the thought and was surprised to hear such a concession-like statement.

"But," Melrose continued, "I don't want to see you get the thrashing of a lifetime, either. We all know the risks of trial. We can both spill a lot of blood in that courtroom and neither side will escape unharmed."

The negotiators locked horns. There was more posturing.

"Climbing a ladder, Mr. Lyons." Bradford jumped in. "What the hell do you think a jury will do with that?"

"Rest assured, Mr. Bradford," said Mike, "Paul Melrose knows that I would never attempt to hide that stuff. I'll bring it out myself loud and clear during my direct examination of Mr. Farrington. We have nothing to hide. Keep you from scoring points by springing this on the jury during cross-examination. What will a jury do with that, you ask? They'll reward him for trying to do something useful with himself…attempting to help a friend repair his roof…for not just sitting around and vegetating. He'll testify how he tried to do chores, to get up on the roof with the help of a friend and fix some tiles, but that it was all for naught…because he couldn't see what he was trying to do."

Mike and Paul Melrose exchanged knowing glances.

"And how do you think, Mr. Bradford, a jury is going to take to your spies snooping around, ducking behind some damned tree or car and filming my client while he struggled to climb a ladder and tried to make himself useful? The man can't even recognize his own kids by sight unless they're right smack in front of him. For God's sake," Mike added, "all he's left with is distorted vision at best…and a dim future."

Bradford crossed his legs and stuck out his jaw. A look of surrender or was he waiting to get nailed again?

"Lyons, I'm here to write a check. Paul has persuaded me that's the thing to do in this case. I just want you to be reasonable. Don't try to break the bank," said Bradford. He leaned forward, the pomposity in his tone having mellowed. "Mike, tell us what you need. Don't give me a crazy number. We're not going to barter back and forth. We're willing to be generous…take care of your fellow's needs. You must be realistic."

"Mike, give us your absolute bottom take. Bradford and I are serious. And we've all done enough jockeying. Let's get down and settle this thing."

Mike responded quickly: "Five Hundred thousand. And that, gentlemen, is after I have trimmed down with my client."

After additional posturing, Bradford and Melrose tried to persuade Mike to accept a lesser figure.

"I guess I misunderstood," said Mike. "I thought that you wanted to avoid nonsense. I didn't start at a higher number expecting that you'd drive it downward. I took you at your word. I gave you my bottom line. Five hundred thousand, nothing less."

Bradford exploded, "A half a million dollars! I don't have that kind of authority. Would you excuse us, Mike?"

In a short while they beckoned Mike back into the room. He had already put on his coat and placed his papers in his briefcase.

"You're not going any place, Mike," said Melrose, a twinkle in his eye. He knew Mike's ploy. "Now take off that coat. We made the call to the CFO. She's familiar with the case. I know she'll be reasonable. Should hear shortly just how far they're willing to go," Paul said.

The atmosphere was somber. Big money was at stake.

They're gonna come back three-fifty and expect me to settle at three seventy-five, four. Mike thought to himself.

"Mr. M., gentlemen, the call is on line one," Florence Morse said.

Mike started to leave the room, but Paul put up his hand.

"Stay. I want you to hear exactly what her instructions are…directly from her. Let's put this thing on speaker," Paul Melrose said.

"Mr. Lyons, my name is Phyllis Atkinson. I'm the CFO of Intercontinental. Before Mr. Bradford left for this Boston meeting, we had in-depth discussions with our law department and claims supervisor. Our intent is to settle this case. But you're looking for a great deal of money, Lyons,'' the voice said. "We'll do three seventy-five...as in three hundred seventy-five thousand dollars. But let's structure it. It'll cost us less, protect the plaintiff from getting all of the money at once and have to ward off cousins he's never seen."

"I have no problem with setting up an annuity. But your offer...well...frankly it's insulting and below-the-belt negotiating. I gave Mr. Melrose and Preston Bradford my take number. And now you're attempting to shake me down. You're asking that I bid against myself. That's not how I do business. This is not negotiating in good faith. No deal," Mike said.

"Mr. Lyons, you're going to walk away from this over a few grand?" the voice said.

"Ma'am, I've not had the pleasure of meeting you nor have you met me. I've got some stubborn Irish blood in me. And I'm not walking away from a few grand, as you put it. It's not improbable that I end up with a verdict well in excess of a million. Mr. Melrose will tell you that the federal court juries here in Boston have been generous with their verdicts when a case is worthy. This case is more than worthy," Mike said.

Paul Melrose, after looking at Bradford who nodded his head, spoke up: "Mrs. Atkinson, let me speak with Attorney Lyons and we'll get back to you."

"Absolutely," she responded.

He turned toward Bradford: "Preston, give us a few moments?" The VP stepped out of the room.

"Mike, I'm not going to be obnoxious and creep up to four. Will you accept four hundred fifty thousand dollars? Give me something."

Mike countered: "For you, Mr. M, and only because it's you, I'll yield twenty-five thousand...reluctantly. Four hundred seventy-five. I'll make up the difference with my fee so that the Farringtons net the same as if we settled for the full half million."

"You drive a hard bargain, Mike. You're good. Let me go to work and see what I can do."

"Just remind Bradford and their money woman that their profits from this drug are in the hundreds of millions. And you know better than me...I'll be presenting all of the numbers during trial."

"You'll have to fight me to get that stuff into evidence," Melrose put a hand on Mike's shoulder.

Melrose advised Bradford to accept Mike's counter proposal. He agreed. They called the office and informed the "money woman" of Mike's new and absolute final figure.

"I feel like we're being strangled, Lyons. But you do have a strong case." The CFO paused. "I'm feeling generous. Deal," she said. "But definitely a structure."

"Annuity is fine," said Mike. "But present-day value of four hundred seventy-five thousand. I'll meet with my clients tomorrow. I'll recommend they accept. I have every reason to believe they will. Then we can each have our structured settlement people draft proposals."

"Done," said the voice on the phone, "but with one proviso."

"Confidentiality?" asked Mike.

"For certain," Bradford interrupted.

"No boasting, Mike. No publicity in *Lawyers Weekly*. You know how I loathe those plaintiff lawyers showing off their settlements in that paper's obnoxious brag sheet section," Paul Melrose said.

Mike said: " Mrs. Atkinson, gentlemen, compromise is in order. Limited confidentiality is as far as I go. My client and I will agree to keep the amount of the settlement absolutely confidential. But I won't agree to any kind of gag order regarding the law, facts, and evidence involved in this case."

"Well..." the voice on the phone started.

"Mike's got a good point," said Melrose. "The money we're paying is what we really want to keep under wraps. As a lawyer, I think we might be mucking around with the canons of ethics if we seek to enjoin Mike from sharing substantive information about the case. He's not going to seek any cheap publicity."

"Okay," said the CFO. "No revelation of the absurd payment we've agreed upon. Deal?"

"I'll confirm with Mr. Melrose just as soon as I sit down with my clients."

Mike felt triumphant, numb, happy and shocked at the day's turn of events. *In this business of litigation, always expect the unexpected,* the words of his one-time professor and now associate, Sean Murray.

"Hefty fee, Mr. Lyons," Bradford said sarcastically.

Mike bristled. "Sir, make no mistake. This is not about my pocket. This is about..."

"Gentlemen, we have an agreement. Let's shake," Paul Melrose cut off any potential deal-killing words and concluded the conference. "Mike, I'll wait for your call."

And with that, Mike Lyons stepped out into the brisk March early evening. He raced to the nearest pay phone and dialed Sean Murray.

"Sean! You'll never believe what happened today. I started to go for a swim in the Norfolk Superior Court..."

"Swim?" said the former professor. Then recalling the case, "Oh, the diving board case. How'd that go?"

"It didn't. I wind up the day settling the Farrington matter!"

Sean responded: "You *what*?! Settled Farrington? How in hell did that happen? How much? Where are you? This calls for a double!"

"I'm at a pay phone on Devonshire near the Old State House. Are you sitting down? Four hundred seventy-five great big ones!"

"Fantastic! With some decent investing, these folks'll be set for life," said Sean.

"That's the idea. And I'm going to shave the fee. I want them to net what they would if we got the full half million. I've got to get to the office. Jane'll go nuts. I'll call you as soon as I'm through wrapping up. Come out to the house with me. We'll have a mini celebration. Put some burgers on the grill. Jeez, Sean, this is *big*!"

"Great job, Mike. I can't wait to hear how this happened. Out of the…the fucking blue!" said Sean.

The professor hung up and walked over to the window of his small office, then opened a desk drawer and removed a bottle of his favorite Scotch. These past years he's regarded this liquid tranquilizer as a friend. Then he gazed at the photo of Adele and his boys. He slipped into a fog. Self-condemnation. The numbness never faded.

CHAPTER THREE
SEAN

TEN YEARS EARLIER

Twenty-one-year-old Romano DeAngelis was a handsome, tough, thick-skinned dyslexic hit man. The Mob referred to him jocularly as "Ass-End-To." Nevertheless, the Boston Italian Mafia, headquartered in the city's North End just a block from the historic residence of Paul Revere, loved Romano's lack of conscience and unwavering loyalty.

What a contrast: weapons in the hands of Boston's artisans and laborers fighting in the 1770s for our country's independence and freedom as opposed to weapons in the hands of sociopaths who killed mercilessly, not for country, but for what was known, among other appellations, as the "Organization."

The Boston Celtics were a tough, thick-skinned, but beautifully coordinated basketball powerhouse. Playing their home games on the idiosyncratic parquet floor of the Boston Garden, its dead spots known only to them, under the tutelage of Hall of Fame Coach Red Auerbach, the Celtics had won the National Basketball Association Championships from 1957 through 1962. (They would go on to win several more). Professor Sean Murray and a Boston College Law School colleague were sitting in the Garden the night of November 21, 1962 watching the Celtics take on the St. Louis Hawks.

Romano DeAngelis and Anthony Ricci, thirty years Romano's senior, were summoned by Mafia consigliere Norman Di Giovanni. The seven o'clock meeting venue was Stella's Restaurant. Opened in 1925 on Fleet Street in the North End, it reigned supreme among multiple Italian eateries in that section of

Boston. On any given night this popular and fashionable destination would host celebrities, politicians, people of all social and educational backgrounds, as well as the infamous. A private, soundproofed room was always in reserve for the "Organization."

As Professor Murray and his friend joyfully grabbed burgers and fries at a McDonald's near the Garden, the consigliere and cohorts DeAngelis and Ricci were indulging in Veal Scaloppini a la Marsala, Stella's signature dish.

Sean Murray had a passion for basketball and the Celtics. Like so many Boston sports fans, he was enamored with the prowess of Bob Cousy, Bill Russell, K.C. Jones, Tom Heinsohn, and rookie John Havlicek, each a future Hall of Famer.

If there was a Mafioso Hall of Fame, Romano DeAngelis and Anthony Ricci were about to blow whatever chance they may have had for induction.

"This is a most important assignment," the consigliere said. "I didn't call you together just to enjoy dinner. But you know that."

The two enforcers nodded as they finished their meal. Their facial expressions asked what was the assignment. They knew it would be for a hit but had not a clue about the target.

"You know that Lucia did something she never should have done. We all thought she had more brains than that," said the consigliere.

"Lucia! No way. We can't do Lucia," said Anthony.

"Not Lucia. She's already been—done. Incapacitated, shall we say."

The hit men exhaled, both out of relief and fear.

"Some prick excuse for a lawyer who the Don trusted did a very bad thing. I know the guy. We were sworn into the Bar together." The consigliere took a sip of wine.

"Fucked her? Fucked the Don's princess? Lucia!?" Romano said.

"I can't fuckin' believe this guy," said Anthony. "How fuckin' stupid can an asshole get?"

"And Lucia? She's lost her mind," Romano added.

In a sinister voice, the consigliere responded: "In a manner of speaking, the Don has seen to that."

Lucia was not the Don's wife. Thirty-five years younger than the Boston Mafia kingpin, this Hollywood look-a-like and one-time model was his property—his lover and only *his*. "Hands off" was like a code clearly understood by all who knew the Don. All, apparently, except a Newton lawyer, Saul Mendelson. Saul was a wannabe mafia criminal lawyer. But Saul made the mistake of thinking not with his brains. He erred when he acted upon Lucia's flirtations. He put a target on his own back.

"Listen to me very carefully," said the consigliere.

Romano took out a pen. His sidekick grabbed it and sneered at him.

"When the fuck will you ever fuckin' learn. We write nothin' down. You know that," said Anthony while slapping the younger enforcer on the side of the head.

The consigliere leaned forward, turned his head to both sides despite knowing that it was just the three of them and that the room was soundproof.

"The target's name is Saul Mendelson. He lives in Newton. Three Twenty-Three Waverly Avenue. Here's a map. Although I think you did a job out that way not too long ago, Anthony?"

"Fancy fuckin' town. Me and young Bibbo just a week ago got one of them slow payers to pick up the pace. Center Street, I think. I remember exactly how to get there."

Nevertheless, the consigliere, a cool operative who had a penchant for detail, opened a map of Newton Centre. It is one of thirteen villages in the City of Newton, a well-heeled Boston suburb.

Waverly Avenue, running off Ward Street, was outlined in red. The escape route to the parking lot behind the nearby elementary school was marked in blue.

"I remember Wahd Street. That guy Lepcio who used to play for the Sox back in the fifties married some rich Jewish dame who lived there," said Anthony.

"You go up Comm Ave., take a right on Hammond Street," said the consigliere, while running his finger along the route on the map.

"I remember," said Anthony. "We go left here onto Wahd and then down here we hook a right onto Waverly. Easy."

"You got it, Romano?" the consigliere asked.

"Got it," he said.

"And here's where you ditch the Roadmaster. Right behind the school. Sonny will be waiting for you. He'll be in a silver Lincoln Continental. Plates have been changed."

* * *

The full house in the Garden erupted when Havlicek stole the ball from the Hawks' Hall of Famer, Cliff Hagan. Bill Russell signaled and waited for Havlicek's pass.

Professor Murray slammed his friend on the back as Russell hooked a two-pointer.

The consigliere set fire to the map.

"What's the address?" he asked.

"Three twenty-three Wave Avenue," Anthony said."

"Waverly, not Wave," the consigliere corrected him.

"And you, Romano, what's the address?"

"Easy. Three twenty-three Waverly Avenue." He emphasized the last two letters in Waverly.

"Don't forget. When you go down Ward, you'll come to an island," said the consigliere. "That's where you take the right onto Waverly. Then take the first side street after the house. It should be quiet there. Everyone inside on such a cold night. Romano, you go out and do your thing. Anthony waits for you. Same plan the two of you have done before."

The Don's lawyer and trusted confidant in all things important paused.

"*Capisce?*"

"*Capisce*," the executioners said in unison.

* * *

Red Auerbach called a timeout. St. Louis had just gone on an eight to nothing run. "What are you guys forgettin' about? D…the Big D…you're lettin' them get to half court too fast. Gotta tighten up our defense…change the scheme. You guys know better than me…when they're runnin' up points…when we're gettin' hammered, time for full court press. Make 'em fight for everything. Tire them out. Understood?"

"Understood," the starting five said in unison.

"Anthony, the Don wants you behind the wheel. He worries sometimes that 'Ass-End-To' gets—gets a little, shall we say, excited when driving." The consigliere turned to Romano. "But he loves your finesse…the way you break in and the way you handle the twelve."

He was referring to the weapon of choice for this execution: twelve gauge shotgun.

"No worries," said Romano. "His fuckin' brains on the walls already."

"Mendelson's family has a routine. After dinner, Mendelson and his wife go into a den and watch TV. When you enter the back door go straight through the kitchen. The den's the first room on the right. The kids'll probably be upstairs," the consigliere instructed.

He added: "I don't have to tell you, Romano. Ski mask. We don't want the old lady or in case the kids are downstairs making any ID."

"I can't nail the kids and the old lady?" Romano asked, oblivious to any horror associated with such an action.

"No! You know the Don loves kids. And he wants the wife and kids to live to know just what an asshole shit-for-brains cheat her husband, their father, Mr. Don Juan, was. Just pump Mendelson and get the hell out of there. Quick and neat."

"Tonight? Tomorrow night? When's the Don want this guy removed?" Anthony asked.

"You know better than to ask that question." The consigliere placed his napkin on the table, signaling end of dinner.

"I got it," said Anthony. "Now. Tonight."

"Do your jobs. Call when completed. Once you dump the Roadmaster behind the school and haul your asses into Sonny's car, he'll drive west. He'll stop at a pay phone near the dance hall. Anthony, you make the call. 'The Celtics won' means mission accomplished," the consigliere completed his instructions.

"Dance hall? You mean the Totem Pole? I was fuckin' there last week with Connie. Fuckin' Jerry Grey's band. Jerry never forgets where he came from. But no fuckin' booze in that place— lot of high school kids," said Romano.

"You get this piece of crap Mendelson removed, Romano, you and Connie will be dancing at the Ritz," said the consigliere.

Professor Sean Murray was loving every minute of the game. But not to the exclusion of thinking about his wife and kids. He met Adele Lister when he had just turned forty. She was twelve years his junior. He had been invited to speak at a Bar Association conference. When it came time for questions, Sean was taken with the quality of an issue raised by Adele. And he was immediately infected by her adorable smile. He sought her out during the post-conference cocktail party. They talked nonstop for two hours. It was rhapsodic for him. And in Adele's own words, "It was magical. I fell madly in love." They married within six months of that first encounter and had two boys.

* * *

The black 1958 Buick Roadmaster turned right onto Waverly Avenue. It drove slowly past identical large brick Tudors and Dutch Colonials, some fronted with high hedges protecting the neatly trimmed lawns. Even in the dark of this November night there was a feeling of affluence and neighborhood calm.

"There it is. Three thirty-two," said Romano.

"Three thirty-two?" said Anthony. "You sure you ain't got the number twisted, Romano."

"Look, for chrissake, the fuckin' mailbox got his fuckin' initials SM. Saul fuckin' Mendelson."

"You're right. I see them letters, Romano. I'll pull around the corner, just like the Boss said to do," Anthony said.

After pulling to a stop on the closest side street, Anthony directed his cohort: "Put the fuckin' mask on. Don't slam the door. I'll be right here. Five minutes and I'm lookin' for you to hustle back here. Pick the back door, you hear? Through the kitchen, first room on the right and just blast the old man and screw. You got it?"

"For chrissake, Tony, it's not my first hit, you know. I ain't a rook no more."

With that, Anthony doused the lights of the Buick and parked between two houses. One was completely dark, the other had lights on at the back. What Anthony didn't see was that a teenager who lived a couple of houses from where Anthony parked, had just finished bringing rubbish from the house to the street. The youngster would later tell the police that he loved cars, looked and saw *"a beauty...Roadmaster...'58...they stopped making them when they came out with the Electra..."* He explained that he was about to go to the car "to take *a closer look* but I was concerned when I saw a man get out and start quickly toward Waverly. Looked like he was carrying something and he was wearing a mask. I got nervous. I ran in the house and told my dad. He looked out the window and then called the police."

Within a minute of that phone call, Romano broke into number three thirty-two. It was the wrong house. It was the house in which Sean Murray and his wife and children lived. When the assassin stormed into the den, he saw Adele and her two boys. She screamed. Romano yelled: "Shut the fuck up. Where is he?" Adele grabbed her sons, pulled them toward her and barely managed to say "he's not home… he's…"

Romano responded: "You're a fuckin' liar, lady." With that, Sean's older son lunged at Romano. The gunman panicked. He emptied the shotgun, killing all three—just like that. In a matter of seconds three innocent, beautiful human beings were murdered. The assassin ran outside and dashed to the Buick.

Sean was at the Boston Garden. Unbeknownst to him, his life was incinerated.

A faint siren could be heard.

"Did you do it?" Anthony asked as Romano jumped into the back of the car.

Sirens were getting louder.

"Go, just fuckin' go. The fuckin' cops."

Anthony proceeded straight on Bracket Rd. "Did you nail him?" he asked, sweat streaming down both cheeks.

"He wasn't fuckin' there. Holy shit, Tony, they're up there. They're fuckin' blockin' the goddamn street. Turn the fuck around."

"What do you fuckin' mean, he wasn't there," Anthony screamed as he spun the steering wheel. "I heard the fuckin' blast."

Anthony tried a U-turn, but the car's wheelbase couldn't navigate it with one turn. He had to stop and put it in reverse. Quickly, Newton police surrounded the stopped Buick. The heartless assassin bent down to remove a revolver that had been strapped onto an ankle. The move didn't elude the police officer who swung open the back door. He reacted and fired twice directly into Romano, fatally wounding him. Anthony emerged from the car, arms extended upward. He would die in prison.

* * *

When Professor Murray arrived at his house, an ache set in that would never leave. Simply seeing the police cars messaged terror. He didn't know at that moment the unspeakable extent of the tragedy. This marvelously gentle man has no memory whatsoever of the hours and days before the family funeral. And his brain was completely numb during the service.

Mike Lyons, having graduated from law school a year earlier, and his wife Alison, were there every painful step of the way. They begged and cajoled and finally succeeded in having Sean Murray move into the guest room of their apartment. Mike took care of all the details regarding the myriad entanglements that result when not only a spouse dies, but one's children as well. Sean Murray never stepped foot in his former house from the moment he arrived that night.

After a number of weeks the professor felt the need to allow Mike and Ali to live without his depressing presence. He felt he could handle living on his own. And he wanted privacy to imbibe freely in Scotch, his favorite crutch. Ali found an apartment for Sean in Brookline Village.

The professor medicated himself with alcohol. He stopped teaching. In fact, for weeks he stopped everything. After moving from their home Ali and Mike organized a few of the professor's colleagues to assist with visits and providing groceries and home-cooked meals. Mike was in daily contact, including getting Sean to his and Ali's apartment at least once a week for dinner.

Somehow Sean began to heal as the summer arrived. He retired from his teaching post at the law school. Sean adopted Mike's suggestion of creating a bar review course. He was brilliant, a master of the law, and a crisp lecturer. In addition, Mike arranged with the law firm he was working for to make space available for Sean. "For you, Professor. You can operate your bar review business out of this office. Jane Donnell, my secretary, is more than willing to be available. And it would be a godsend to me if you would help out with some of my cases—memoranda, research, briefs. You know I can *tell* a story, but my *writing* is less than quality."

As the post-tragedy months unfolded, Mike remained patient with the alcoholism and erratic behavior that beset his deeply wounded friend. He understood Sean's inconsistency and lapses and need for one-night stands. There were times when Sean was so inebriated that he couldn't deliver a scheduled bar review lecture. Mike stepped in. It would be awhile before the professor began to think he might have a right to actually try to enjoy life, although he would always be plagued by understandable guilt. "If only I hadn't gone to that game."

Mike and Sean never once spoke of any of the specifics of the destruction of Sean's family. There was simply nothing to be said. Since meeting as one of Sean's students in law school, Mike revered the connection. Sean was eternally grateful for the support and gift of friendship from Mike, Ali, and Jane.

CHAPTER FOUR
DANIELLE

"The First Time Ever I Saw Your Face." An elated Mike
Lyons heard himself sing Roberta Flack's new recording as he
made his way to his office in the Ames Building, located at One
Court Street in the heart of Boston's financial and law office
district. The Romanesque style building is a Boston landmark,
reflecting some of the manufacturing days of the city as it was in
the early 1900s. When completed in 1893, it housed the Ames
family's agricultural tool company. The personality of the area,
similar to many other cities, changed and by the 1950s the building
became home to many law firms. When Lyons decided it was time
to leave the litigation firm where he had worked since graduating
from Boston College Law School in 1962, he seized upon an
opportunity to lease a suite on the seventh floor. His secretary and
assistant, Jane Donnell, wanted to join Mike as well; her loyalty
and friendship with him motivated her to take the financial risks
involved in opening a new practice.

It was Friday after six p.m. when Mike bounded into his
office suite, early departure for most of the city's lawyers. Some
headed for a last weekend of skiing, others for R & R at home.

"Jane, what the devil are you doing here so late? I thought
you and Phil were heading to Rockport this afternoon." Mike
lowered his briefcase onto his secretary's desk, snapped it open
and reached for some papers.

He was oblivious to her pointing toward his office and that
she was whispering.

"For God's sake, Mike, I wasn't going to leave until I knew
what was going on. Got a call from Mr. Melrose telling me that it

was urgent that he get a hold of you. Obviously, I knew something was hopping with the Farrington case. But…"

"We've got a great offer to settle the case," he said.

Aware that he hadn't heard a response from his secretary, he glanced up.

Once she had his eye, Jane nodded to the left, toward Mike's office. "New client," she whispered. "Insisted on waiting for you…in there. Tell me about Farrington."

"What's she doing in my office? Why isn't she out here?"

"She ushered herself in. Couldn't get her out," Jane said, still whispering.

"Terrific, just what I need." He paused, dismissed his sarcasm and shifted gears back to his settlement triumph. "Got four hundred seventy-five thousand for the Farringtons. Properly managed and it will take care of their needs for life."

"Did I hear you right? Did you say four hundred seventy-five thou…?" Jane mouthed.

"I did, indeed. This is a great settlement, Jane. See if you can get them on the phone, please, and ask what's a convenient time for me to stop by their place tomorrow. Don't say anything about the proposal. They'll get understandably anxious. Just tell them there's a matter I want to discuss; that I'll give them a call later tonight."

Jane nodded.

Gesturing toward his office, Mike said: "I'll make short order of this one."

"Mr. Lyons, is that you?" The client, an attractive woman with a Nordic face and sharp cheekbones, was standing on the threshold between Mike's office and the reception area. She removed sunglasses and revealed a left eye nearly swollen shut, with its surrounding area a distorted mixture of blue, black, and yellow.

"I'm Danielle. Danielle Webb." There was a slight Scandinavian accent. An air of sophistication as she extended a hand.

Tall, trim, fair-skinned, blonde hair…early thirties. She wore a white blouse, the top three buttons unfastened. A necklace with a gold crucifix rested on the revealed cleavage. A gray pleated wool skirt had the look of Boston's fashionable Newbury Street.

Jane gathered her purse. "Can't begin to imagine how thrilled the Farringtons are going to be. Here are your messages. Alison called. She wanted to remind you that the kids are having friends over tonight. Although it's cold, Ali said she hopes you won't mind doing burgers on the grill for the kids." Mike's loyal secretary and friend raised her voice an octave. "She'd like you to get there ASAP." She turned to the client.

"Goodbye, Mrs. Webb," a curl in Jane's voice. "It was nice to meet you."

"Yes." The client kept her eyes focused on Mike.

Mike gestured toward his office and Danielle Webb sat on a chair opposite the lawyer's mahogany desk, the surface of which was covered with small decks of files and standard desktop accoutrements.

"Mr. Lyons," it was Jane's voice. She was opening the reception door leading to the floor's central hallway.

"Excuse me." Mike got up.

"Jane?"

She shrugged a shoulder motioning him to come out into the hallway.

She whispered: "I don't like this one."

"That's obvious. It's written all over your face."

"She's snooty and brazen. I couldn't get her out of your office. Get rid of her. Go home. I think the shiner's probably fake…or, better yet, justified," Jane said.

"You're the best." Mike leaned forward and kissed his secretary of several years on the cheek.

"I mean it, Mike. She's a phony. And your kids are waiting for you."

"I will, I will. Ten minutes. Have a great weekend. And don't forget to remind Phil that he and I are on for the Celtics game on the twenty-fifth."

"I don't have an awful lot of time," Mike started, trying to be stern, as he came back into his office. But something about the potential client piqued his interest.

"Yes, of course. I heard. You're wanted home." Danielle Webb pulled at her skirt and crossed her legs, knees bare. Mike was aware. He forced himself to focus on her face.

"What happened? That's quite a black and blue…mark."

He sat on his leather desk chair and reached for a legal sized pad.

"*Mark*? Is that what you call it? Where I grew up, Mr. Lyons, it would be called one hell of a shiner."

Mike leaned forward. Staring at the wound, he said: "It's swollen. This was recent."

"Today."

"Tell me about it. But wait one second. Let me make a quick call."

As Mike was explaining to his wife that he would be slightly delayed (not the first time she had heard this lament) and that Sean would be joining them, he saw tears roll down his potential client's cheeks. He wondered about the authenticity. He gestured to a box of Kleenex resting on the nearby radiator cover. Mike never got used to clients' tears.

A smile no longer on Danielle's face, she blew her nose and wiped at the running mascara. *Interesting,* Mike thought to himself, *no makeup covering that shiner.*

She was mindful of his stare. "It hurt too much when I tried to camouflage it with concealer."

"Mrs. Webb, let me get some preliminary information."

She lived in Louisburg Square on Beacon Hill. Born in Sweden, she came to this country in her early teens. Her family bought a farm in Wisconsin. She met her husband seven years ago at Charles de Gaulle Airport. "I was traveling. I noticed a distressed looking guy. His luggage was lost. He seemed like a little lost boy, but tall…I thought rather interesting looking. I speak French, so I helped him with the authorities to locate his bags. He was grateful. I could tell that he was shy, so I suggested lunch together. Things moved very quickly and two months later we married."

"*The* Webb family?" Mike asked.

"*The* Webb family," she replied.

"International underwater cables?"

"That would be correct. Money not an issue."

"Do you have children, Mrs. Webb?"

"Two children, three and five. Live-in nanny. I do some volunteer work. Family sold the business. Very large dollars involved. Brooks is a chemical engineer. He works for a small company in Cambridge. I'm never certain exactly what it is they do. He doesn't need the money and until recently seemed to enjoy his work," she said.

Mike resented the Brahmins. Envisioned the elite living luxurious and self-centered lives…playing tennis, screwing each other's friends, cocktails at five…living off the proceeds of their ancestors' ill begotten fortunes.

"Okay. So tell me. Who did it? What happened?"

Mike, his brain celebrating the unexpected turn of events in his day, stretched back and beckoned with his hand.

This is amazing. I get up today all set to go ahead and start my diving board accident trial…then whisked away totally by surprise to Paul Melrose's office…think it's a setup of some sort…and wind up settling the biggest case of my career…close to a half a million…and now I'm looking at one of the wealthiest

women in Boston with one hell of a black and blue shiner...and
sexy at that.

Danielle Webb gained her composure. She leaned forward,
aware that she was exposing her upper breast area and that Mike
strained to keep his eyes on her face. He maintained a professional
course.

Mike stared at his pad and gestured for her to start.

She shifted and recrossed her legs. "I was in the apartment. It
was around one o'clock. I was going to make sandwiches for the
children. They were out with our nanny. My husband came home."

"Was that usual? Did he join you for lunch on a regular
basis?"

"No. He usually doesn't get home until around six. Some bad
things happened at his lab and he was in a foul mood. He has a
nasty disposition. I tried to mollify him but he just kept sounding
off as if what happened at work was my fault. I was just trying to
help him, Mr. Lyons."

The tears cascaded once again.

"I'm so sorry. Please forgive me."

"No, no, not at all. Please..." Mike gestured again toward the
Kleenex. He got up from his chair and started to walk around his
desk. He rested a hand on her shoulder, trying to be human, to be
reassuring.

She reached and touched his hand. "You're very kind. I'll be
brief. I know you've got to get home."

Are we signaling each other? Am I feeling something I
shouldn't be feeling? Careful.

Mike went back to his yellow pad. "You had words."

"It was awful. He has a terrible temper. He's hit me before
but this time it was really hard. I fell back against the wall. I was
so startled."

"That's terrible. He has no right. He's done this before?"

"Oh, Mr. Lyons, I don't know what I should do. I'm so
afraid."

"I'm asking you, Mrs. Webb, has this happened before?"

She nodded, bringing Kleenex to her eyes.

"Not good," said Mike. "We've got to get him out. What happened after he hit you?"

"He left. He stormed out of the apartment. I haven't heard from him since."

"He could be dangerous. Who's with the kids?'

"The nanny. God love her. She's just so wonderful with the children."

"Has he ever been physical with the children?"

"I don't think so…"

"Mrs. Webb, I know this is upsetting. But it's important that you be forthright. Now, has he ever hit your children?"

"Not that I know of, but…"

"You must not hold back. Have you contacted the police?"

"Oh, no. I don't want the police involved. The family name, publicity…"

"Mrs. Webb, for your safety, for the safety of the children. You must go over to the station on Sudbury Street and file a complaint."

"Mr. Lyons, I don't want to do that. What I want is a divorce. I'm frightened. If I get the police involved, there'll be recriminations. These are the Webbs."

"I don't care who he is. This man has no right hitting you. I want you to seek a criminal complaint for assault and battery. If you like, I'll accompany you. Now."

"I hear you. But that's not necessary. I'll go myself. I'll take your advice. You're very kind. It's late and your family's waiting for you. May I come back Monday and make arrangements to retain you? I'm serious about getting a divorce. And I want my children."

She stretched, raising her shoulders and thrusting her breasts forward.

My, oh my. She is sexy. Fidelity. Keep your ticket. Keep your hands off. Mistake enough that you patted her shoulder.

Mike placed a legal pad and pen in front of Mrs. Webb.

"There are some steps I want you to take right away," Mike said pointing to the pad. "Arrange to see your doctor. And if he or she's not available…"

"I've already done that. I saw my ophthalmologist before I came here. Her office squeezed me in when I told the receptionist what happened. The doctor wants to run some tests next week."

"Let's hope nothing serious," Mike said. "I'm glad you've sought medical care. And her record will be useful in your case. Okay. Next. As I said, I advise that you to go to the police station and file a complaint. I'll make a call in advance to a friend. If he's on duty, he'll make things go quickly. There won't be an arrest unless you insist upon it. But it's important this be documented with the police. After that, I'd like you to go to my photographer. She's not far from where you live, so it'll be convenient." Mike dictated the name and address.

"I suggest that you come in Monday at 9. We can be in court for an emergency hearing no later than Wednesday afternoon to get an order removing your husband from the apartment. If anything serious happens between now and then, we'll contact the police and they'll get a warrant to arrest him. This is no time for discretion, Mrs. Webb. This is a time to take care of yourself and your children."

"Arrest? Okay, I hear you. Police station, photographer. I'll be here first thing Monday. Thank you so much."

"And one more piece of advice. Contact a locksmith and change the locks." Mike said. Mrs. Webb's mouth dropped open.

"If he complains, you blame it on me."

Mrs. Webb nodded, stood up and gathered her handbag.

Mike accompanied his new client to the elevator. *Jane is wrong. This is a nice person. Sexy, sure. But a decent woman. Her husband is a bully. I'll straighten out that bastard. Webb? I don't give a crap about that blue blood bullshit. This one's going to be fun. I don't give a damn if he's the President.*

"And Mr. Lyons," she said as she stepped onto the elevator, "don't worry about your fee. Whatever it is, I'll pay it. I must get out of this marriage and have custody of my boy and girl."

The elevator door closed.

CHAPTER FIVE
DANIELLE

MARCH 1972

Danielle Webb stood in the hallway outside the locked law offices of Attorney Michael Lyons, holding a cardboard tray with coffee and pastries when Jane Donnell stepped off the elevator searching for her key.

"Good morning, Jane."

Startled, the secretary looked up and then peered back into her handbag. "Oh, oh. Hello, Mrs.…ah, here it is." She held up the office key. "Do you have an appointment with Mr. Lyons today?"

Mrs. Webb, her eyes covered with sunglasses, answered: "Yes, I do. When I met with him Friday, after you left, we talked for a short while. He instructed me to get some pictures taken of my eye. I told him I wanted to hire him…to get divorced…so he asked that I come in this morning."

After Jane unlocked the door to the office suite, Mrs. Webb extended the cardboard tray toward Jane's desk.

"May I?"

Jane nodded.

"A couple are black, a couple with cream. I wasn't sure who might like what. And I've got some of their fabulous coffee rolls."

"Thank you. That's very thoughtful." Jane's voice was cold, her demeanor business-like. "I just finished having coffee, but I'm sure Mr. Lyons will enjoy. He takes his coffee black. He should be arriving most any minute." She gestured to one of the waiting area chairs.

"Jane, please forgive me." Mrs. Webb's voice soft, demure.

The secretary looked at her quizzically.

"For my behavior Friday. I had no business planting myself in Mr. Lyons' office. I should have waited out here."

"Well," Jane responded while smoothing the rear of her skirt preparing to sit behind her desk, "it was a little unusual."

"Most unusual, I'm sure. And very ill-mannered." Changing the subject, "I sense a strong relationship between you and Mr. Lyons." She offered one of the pastries to Jane, whose fair complexion turned pink at the word "relationship." No longer the shy woman who spent her early years in Rumney, New Hampshire, a town with a population of less than one thousand, she was nevertheless flustered by what she read as a suggestion that she and Mike were intimately involved.

"Relationship? Oh, I can assure you it's nothing personal, Mrs. Webb…"

"Forgive me. I'm afraid my wording was awkward. Oh no. I didn't mean that." Danielle Webb waved her hand across her face. "I mean in a professional sense. When I was here Friday, I picked up the vibes of an attorney and secretary who respect and enjoy working with each other."

"Mr. Lyons and I have been working together for several years now." She was pretending to busy herself shuffling some of the papers on her desk. "I think he's a great lawyer…and a wonderful man. A real family man, you know."

"I gather that." Mrs. Webb removed a package of L&M's from her purse, gesturing toward Jane.

"No, thank you. I don't smoke."

"I was in a bad state when I was here Friday. No excuse, of course, but if I could have arranged an execution of my husband over the weekend, I would have done it. What is that you're wearing, Jane? It smells so refreshing."

Uncomfortable with the compliment and confused by the three hundred and sixty degree turn in attitude by the brazen and haughty woman who appeared just three days ago, Jane was about to respond when Mike Lyons arrived.

"Morning, Jane."

"Morning, Mr. L."

The lawyer exchanged greetings with his new client.

Mrs. Webb stood and Mike pointed toward his office. She scanned his desk, leather chairs, thick pile carpet, and large oil seascape. Her eyes focused on a photo on a credenza.

"Your girls?"

"Yes."

"Beautiful."

"Thank you. They're absolute gems. So, did you reconsider and file a complaint with the police? I know that you had the photos taken...got a call from the photographer," Mike said.

"Mr. Lyons, I thought about it...I understand your advice, but I just don't think it's wise to get the police involved. As I said, the family..."

"Your choice, Mrs. Webb. All I can do is offer my best advice that it would enhance your case and frighten your bully of a husband. I assume nothing happened over the weekend?"

"No. We kept our distance. Here are the photos." She handed Mike a clasped envelope, which he quickly opened.

"Terrific. Oh...no...not the fact that you got..."

"I know what you're saying, Mr. Lyons. The photos don't lie."

"Would you mind removing your sunglasses?" Mike asked. She obliged.

"The discoloration and swelling have improved since Friday, but still plainly visible," Mike said.

"I didn't put on any makeup. I thought you'd want to see the damage once again."

Mike nodded.

"Mrs. Webb, I'd like to get an overview of your marriage...your life with Mr. Webb. Just speak as openly and candidly as you can. If necessary, I'll interrupt with questions."

"Oh. Where to start?" And then she started.

Mike listened to a lengthy tale of verbal abuse, insensitivity to her needs, inattention to her and the kids, arguments about money and investments, and two episodes where Brooks Webb's temper led him to "smack me around. He's a self-centered bully." No matter how many times Mike heard these stories of abuse, they never failed to anger him. *I'll never get used to these bastards, whacking their wives, controlling the show with their money and muscle.* Toward the end of their conference, Mike raised the issue of fee. Before he uttered a word about an amount and terms, his client withdrew a checkbook from her handbag.

"Mrs. Webb…"

"I've asked that you please call me Danielle. Beneath this pretense is a regular gal." Her smile was infectious and like so much of her, sexy. "Have one of these cinnamon buns, Mr. Lyons." She paused. "They're soft and fresh." There was a decided emphasis on the "…sh."

Mike could feel himself getting aroused but was intent on establishing a professional relationship. *"If you're going to do any divorce work,"* Professor Sean Murray, had admonished, *"remember the 'tweeners': keep the desk between you and your client, and if it's a female, don't do your thinking with that thing between your legs. Use what's between your ears."* Blunt, sound advice.

Mike brushed aside the sexual tension. "Although there are never any guarantees, round one should be easy. Once he sees the photos and hears what happened, I fully expect that the judge will order your husband to vacate the family home. The courts don't take kindly to abusive men. I'm assuming that if you don't hire me, you'll be getting somebody to represent you. My point is, I don't advise going forward with something like this without a lawyer. It doesn't have to be me. But you will need representation."

"Mr. Lyons, as I said on Friday, I want to hire you. I want to proceed as quickly as possible." She uncrossed her legs, leaned back, and smiled as she removed her sunglasses.

Mike said: "I'm happy that you got the pictures taken. Clear and convincing evidence. As far as paying me, please take this written Fee Agreement home. Read it carefully. If you're content with all the terms, bring it back Wednesday morning signed. You can pay your retainer then and I'll get you prepared for the afternoon hearing. Assuming that I'll be representing you, I'll see to it that your husband is served with papers today informing him that there'll be an emergency hearing this Wednesday for the purpose of getting him out of the house as well as awarding you temporary custody and child support."

She stared directly into his face. It was not just the gaze of a client needing help, but a human being signaling for something more.

Careful, Mike. Be very careful. Too many of my fellow lawyers have taken advantage...bitten the vulnerable apple...and blown up their lives.

Mike stood and gestured toward the door. "We'll talk more when you come in Wednesday. You're not losing any time. As I said, I'll have him served at his lab this afternoon. Should you need me in the meantime, please don't hesitate to call. And if it's after six, just leave a message...my answering service knows how to get hold of me...and you have my home number."

"I'm really afraid, Mr. Lyons."

"Then please go ahead and change the locks, Mrs. Webb. Blame it on me."

"I hear you, Mr. Lyons. But I'm afraid that'll make things even worse."

Mike's facial expression signaled that he understood. "Mrs. Webb, just blame it on me. Is the nanny at home...working today?"

She nodded.

"Good. Contact a friend...have her go to the apartment with you. And ask the nanny to sleep over tonight. As long as you're not alone, you and the children will be safer."

"Thank you," Danielle said, acknowledging that she would follow that advice.

Not unexpectedly she called late that afternoon. "Mr. Lyons, I'm frightened. He was served with the papers. Came home in a hissy fit, handed me his lawyer's card. He was straining to control himself. I'm doing my best to stay clear of him. Mr. Lyons, I've signed the Fee Agreement and sent it via messenger together with a retainer check. Please..."

"Has he threatened you?"

"Well, not really. Just had a menacing look on his face...shoved the card at me."

"Don't leave the apartment. He or his lawyer could be cute and may be prepared to change the locks. It's your home. You stay. And his lawyer, I'm certain, has advised him to be a good boy...keep his hands to himself...otherwise, the judge on Wednesday will toss him into the Charles Street Jail. Just keep your distance...have dinner with the kids...read to them...tuck them in...in other words, your usual routine."

"Thank you, Mr. Lyons. You're very reassuring."

"Let me have the name and number of his lawyer. I'll call and see whether or not we can resolve this peacefully and have your husband agree to vacate. I doubt that'll happen but one never knows. In any event I'll see you in my office Wednesday morning at ten. I'll get you prepared for the hearing. And, again, you have my home number. If he raises a hand, tell him you've been instructed to call the police. He'll back off...then call me."

"Thank you." Mike heard the tears.

Danielle Webb showed up on Wednesday as directed. Obviously agitated, she avoided any niceties. "Did you speak with his lawyer?" she asked.

"Sit, sit, Mrs. Webb. Yes, I called Attorney Vasquez."

"And…"

"And I told her we'd be in court this afternoon to seek an emergency order to have your husband vacate the apartment."

"So, he's obviously said that he won't volunteer to leave? I told him that it would be best for everybody…for our children…if he would go without the necessity of having a judge order him to go. I thought he was going to hit me again," she said.

'He raised a hand?"

"Yes." She didn't look at Mike. Instead, she turned and gazed out his office window.

I wonder if that redness creeping up from her neck into her face is telling me something? Fear? Lying? Exaggerating?

"Show me. Tell me exactly where you were standing, sitting when he threatened you. The details are important. Although today's procedure is somewhat informal, the judge may ask you to take the stand. The judge will be *very* interested in each and every detail. We're going to go over everything now…from the time he came home on Friday…"

Mike was a zealot for preparation. As he explained the procedure he was aware that his client was not making eye contact. She sat staring out the window, seemingly detached.

"Mrs. Webb, I appreciate your retaining me. And I know how upsetting all of this must be, but we're not going to get very far if you don't focus and listen."

"Mr. Lyons, please forgive me. And I much prefer that you call me Danielle. I'm a simple person, Mr. Lyons."

Mike tipped his head to the side and frowned a frown signaling doubt.

"Really, I am. I'm just a farm girl. Born in Sweden, moved to the USA, raised on the family farm in Wisconsin. And I have a long history of spacing out when I'm about to deal with something unpleasant. But trust me, I've heard every word of your advice."

Danielle removed her sunglasses, raised her eyebrows pleadingly, and her cool blue eyes beamed directly into his rugged handsome face. Mike studied this beguiling client, but not for the reasons she might have been suggesting.

It had been five days since Danielle's husband punched her in the left eye. Mike observed that the swelling had reduced considerably and there was just a remnant of discoloration. *Not to worry. I've got those photos and they tell the whole story. If this one isn't a walk in the park, it's awfully close,* he thought to himself.

"When we're in that courthouse this afternoon I want those glasses off…"

"But…"

"No 'buts.' You don't need them. You're healing well. A judge will see them as an affect."

She put the sunglasses back on. "Just until we get to the courthouse. Please." She pouted, tilting her head to the side.

She's playing me, goddammit. Fresh coffee buns. That was cute. Hey, couldn't provocation be a defense? In court maybe, but not on the home front. And that's where my supreme court is…home sweet home. Don't be a fool. Keep it in your pants and stay the course.

"And remember, above all else, don't say a word. From the moment we walk into that courthouse…and I don't mean just in the courtroom…I mean that building…be sure to remain silent until you're asked questions. You never know who's listening. And when we're before the judge, just be yourself. Say not a word until he or I ask you a question. And your answers are to be what?"

"The truth. Just stick to the truth and everything will be all right." She recited Mike's mantra, which he had delivered multiple times during their prep session.

"It's not like the movies. Mess around with the truth and the judge will pick it up in seconds. He's an experienced judge. And like most of them, doesn't take kindly to exaggeration or bullshit. And he hates men who are quick to use their fists."

"You've made your point. I'll be the perfect client. May I call you Mike?"

He avoided the question, checked his watch. "Time to go."

* * *

It was a perfect March day. The bulk of the winter had passed and there was a crisp smell of spring in the air as they made their way up the hill known as Pemberton Square, leading to the partially cobblestoned courtyard-like setting in front of the Suffolk County Superior and Probate Courts.

They were approaching the front steps to the courthouse. *She's a good person,* Mike thought. *Sexy. A flirt, but not all wrapped up in herself. Probably a damn good mother. This Brooks Webb's gotta be one nasty prick. I'm gonna nail him. I love it…all this court stuff.*

"Hey Mike, how's it goin'?" a colleague asked. Like Mike, he was another litigator, grinding it out day-to-day. No lucrative corporate retainers, no big time transactional work. Like Mike and many of the ethnic lawyers of the sixties and seventies, divorce cases, injury cases, arrested hookers, drunk drivers filled their calendars and paid their bills.

"Fine thanks, how about you? HOLY SHIT! SHOOTER, SHOOTER…GET DOWN…DOWN," Mike yelled, dropping his briefcase. He wrapped an arm around his client Danielle Webb's waist and quickly but gently lowered her, face down, onto the pavement.

CHAPTER SIX
MIKE

There must have been a dozen people in the square within the shooter's range. Slowly, the survivors got up, began to collect themselves. Mike assisted his client to her feet. She was trembling, short of breath, tears streaming down her face. Scores of office workers poured out of the buildings; some wanted to help, others just voyeuristic.

"It's okay, it's okay. You're going to be okay. He's gone." Mike tried to reassure Danielle, pulling her close to his body. He could feel her heart pounding. He could smell her fear as well as a gardenia-like cologne. He thought, *how weird that at this kind of moment I'm aware of the scent of her perfume.* He gestured to a nearby ambulance attendant. It didn't take any persuasion to convince Danielle of her need to be taken to a hospital. Mike climbed into the back of the same ambulance. When they arrived at Massachusetts General Hospital (MGH), his client, physically shaking, was attended to immediately. He waited until Danielle adjusted to the sedative administered in the ER. She declined a wheelchair. Mike guided her from the ER into a hallway.

"Wait for me. I'm going to call my wife. Then I'll go outside and get you a cab."

"Your jacket, your pants...there's blood all over them." Danielle gagged.

"It's from when I went over to the couple who got hit. Just horrible. I hope the man is able to survive...his companion, unfortunately, must have died instantly." Mike peeled off his jacket.

"Mike," Danielle said, "they were so close to us."

"Scary, Danielle. We were awfully lucky."

She burst into tears and leaned into him, clinging until he slowly moved her. "You're going to be okay. The meds will soon start to take effect. I heard the doc say they injected a pretty good dose. You're going to sleep," Mike said.

"Here, over here, you sit. Deep breaths." Mike demonstrated. "As soon as you get home you'll be out like the proverbial light," he said.

Mike pointed to a bench on the wall opposite a row of pay phones as they left the emergency room. The dreary beige-colored walls on either side of the hallway were in dire need of a facelift. Light bulbs needed replacing. Relatively calm, Danielle sat, her head bowed, hands on either side of her face. Mike ultimately got through to Alison.

"Ali, have you heard? Do you know what happened?"

"What, Mike, what are you talking about?"

"Hold on Ali, wait just a second."

"Dave...Dave...it's me, Mike, what can you tell me?"

Detective Dave Driscoll, longtime friend, was on his way out of the ER and headed for one of the hospital exits. He looked grim as he turned toward the pay phone. "Mikey, two dead. We think the shooter's an ex-cop. Got a couple of good IDs as he was high-tailin' it down Cambridge Street after he stashed the mask and Glock. An ex-cop, Mikey." His voice was uncharacteristically flat.

"Oh, my god. A cop? Who?"

"I haven't got a name yet. I'll let you know." The detective turned and continued on his way. Then suddenly, he stopped. Mike had just started to get back on the phone.

"Mike, you? You okay?"

"Thanks, Dave. I'm good. Just a wrecked suit." He gestured as if to wipe the blood away. "And I'm shaken, that's for sure. It was as close as it gets."

Mike could hear Alison calling out his name on the phone. He picked up the receiver, turning to the detective and said, "Catch you later?"

"You bet. One of us will get in touch with you…need a statement." Detective Driscoll turned his head back toward the exit. "Son-of-a-bitch. A cop." The detective's voice dropped as he swung through the exit.

Mike got back on the phone.

"Mike, what's happening? Who's dead? I heard you talking to someone."

"Dave Driscoll"…Mike swallowed, trying to keep the tears from bursting out.

"Your detective friend. But why? Mike, you don't sound…"

"Ali, you're talking to one lucky guy. And I think I'm gonna lose it…just hearing your voice." Mike inhaled…slowly exhaled. He related the entire horrific happening.

"Oh, my god, Mike. Are you okay? Are you hurt? Your client okay?"

"I'm fine, Ali. My client's just a bit bruised and understandably shaken. I'm going to put her in a cab. They've given her a good dose of Valium," Mike said. "At least in Korea, I had a vest and a helmet. This fucker came awful close, but I'm fine. Neither of us was hurt. She's fine."

"Thank God. Oh, Mike…" Ali broke down.

"It's okay, Ali. It's okay. I'm alive. Shaken, but alive."

"I'm sorry, Mike. It just sounds so awful. I think you should come home."

"After I put Danielle in a cab, I'll go back to the office and then head home. I want Jane to know that I'm okay. Do you think…"

Mike's peripheral vision caught the sight of a figure hovering over his client. An unusually tall man, black hair slicked back, Valentino style. He was wearing black slacks and a black leather jacket. The man turned his head slightly in Mike's direction, still bent over in front of Danielle. His face was pockmarked. His expression was one of concern.

His eyes? Something strange.

"Of course, Mike. I'll leave work right away," Ali said. "Take a cab back to the office, Mike. I'll pick you up there."

Mike, puzzled about this stranger, could feel the reaction of the shooting begin to set in…nausea starting to creep through his gut. Split-second scenes of Korea wouldn't stop.

"Ali, that's a great idea, but I need some fresh air. The walk will do me good."

"Give me an hour," she said. "I'll be in front of the office. Go slowly. Deep breaths."

"See you in an hour. Please don't race, Ali." The lawyer leaned against the wall. He sucked in a big breath and then exhaled slowly. *Christ, did that really happen? I'm so, so lucky. Those two people, so close, they got hit instead of me. No different from the Chosin Reservoir bloodbath in Korea…fellow Marines just a few feet away…it's all so random.*

It felt good to hear the sound of his wife's voice. Mike was weak and vulnerable, but the deep breaths helped. He turned. The tall man was headed toward an exit. *Seems that Danielle knows him. Do I know him? He's leaving.*

Danielle was frowning. She looked disturbed. *But why shouldn't she,* Mike thought. *Hell, we were in harm's way. Damned lucky.*

The man disappeared.

Danielle remained sitting on the bench. She looked the way she felt…groggy.

"How're you doing? Are you okay? Someone you know?" Mike asked.

"I'm rotten. Shit, this was just awful. I can't believe it. Did it really happen? Am I dreaming, Mr. Lyons? Are those people going to be okay? My head feels so weird."

"It's the shock of it all…and the sedatives they shot into you. To answer your question, tragically, they were killed."

"Oh, how horrible. I don't ever want to hear that word 'shot' ever again." She managed a brief smile.

Danielle pulled a package of cigarettes from her purse. Mike noticed that her knees and one shin were scraped. Nothing serious.

He extended his hand and guided his client from the bench. "Time for you to get home. They gave you a good dose of Valium. You'll need to sleep it off." Mike took the cigarette from her. "Not in here. The gentleman who was with you a moment ago…somebody you know?"

She stopped for a moment. She started to reach for his arm.

"The man, the tall gentleman…" Mike started.

"Some other time."

"No secrets, Mrs. Webb."

"No secrets, Mr. Lyons."

* * *

Dazed by the entire experience, the two of them left the hospital. Mike signaled a taxi. He opened the door. As Danielle started to get in, she turned to him.

"Please. Ride with me. I'm, I'm…afraid."

Am I nuts? How can I be thinking about sex? I damn near got killed. But here I am gawking at that body. This is absolutely crazy. I need to get home…hug my kids.

"Is your nanny home?" he asked.

"Yes."

"Excellent. Then you won't be alone and your children will be taken care of while you sleep."

There was a pull to go with her. But he knew that would be dumb…no way to rationalize as part of his role, even under these unusual circumstances. It could easily be the prelude to something he would regret for the rest of his life.

"Call my office tomorrow afternoon. I should know by then just when the court will start business again. Get some sleep." With that he closed the taxi door. She did not return his wave.

Mike saw a figure down at the corner of Cambridge Street. *Is that the same guy? If not, it's one hell of a coincidence…two six-foot-six men dressed in black leather jackets, black slacks hanging out at the MGH?* Mike headed toward the stranger but before he reached the corner the mystery man craned his neck, glanced at Mike, then ducked into a taxi.

Something about this guy's look. Mike shook his head, reminding himself of his standard poodle emerging from a dunk in the ocean off the coast of Wellfleet. *I need fresh air. I need to walk.*

This is unbelievably surreal. Here I am, walking up Cambridge Street, toting my briefcase, looking like god knows what, and just an hour ago I damn near got killed. And this client. Have I lost my mind? She's beautiful, but...maybe that's how we humans get through this kind of stuff: think of the absurd.

By the time he arrived at his office news of the shooting had spread. Jane reached for him. They stood looking at each other. She cried. They consoled each other with a long, warm hug.

"Hey, I'm fine. I'm much too tough to be taken down by some nut. Bastard ruined a perfectly good suit."

Jane reached out and affectionately patted the gauze covering the burn on his cheek. She told him that the word was that it was a crazed retired police officer.

"Maybe the woman right near me, the one who got killed, was his wife. Were they getting a divorce? What did you hear? I bumped into Dave Driscoll at the hospital. He told me that the shooter was an ex-cop."

Jane filled him in on the rumors floating around. "Some of the lawyers think the ex-cop and his wife were scheduled for a divorce hearing and that she was with her boyfriend."

Mike shrugged. *Or maybe it had nothing to do with a wife, a boyfriend. Those poor people were so close to us.*

"And before I forget," Jane added, "Dave called. They learned that the ex-cop killed himself. Dave asked that you get a hold of him...needs to take a statement...no rush."

"Killed himself? Good. Crazy effing world, Jane. I'm goin' home. Ali's picking me up. Take off whenever you want."

After soaking his face with cold water, he threw some files into his briefcase knowing full well he would not so much as touch them. He gave a reassuring pat on his secretary's shoulder and went downstairs to meet Ali. As he got into the car he thought he saw that tall figure again across the street, head buried in a newspaper. *This is nuts. I need to get home.* Ali reached over, her hand on his shoulder. Then the tears…from each of them. They squeezed hands. The tall man looked up from the newspaper.

That's what's weird, Mike thought. *His eyes. Gray like a wolf. Who is he?*

"Handkerchief, please." Ali's tears were tears of relief.

After handing Ali a packet of Kleenex from the glove compartment, Mike turned and looked across the street. The figure was no more. *Christ, this is like Korea. I'm seein' shadows again. I remember shooting at shadows…night after night…half the damn time there was no one there.*

Ali proceeded up Court Street. Mike turned around. Nothing.

CHAPTER SEVEN
KATHERINE

As she had each Wednesday for the past five weeks, Sister Katherine Hennessey rang the bell at the suburban residence of Father Thomas Riley. The long hard winter that had lingered through much of May suddenly shifted to summerlike warmth. She loved the mix of lavender and dark purple lilac bushes that lined either side of the brick steps leading up the knoll to the priest's front door.

Just twenty-seven, Sister Katherine had decided during her solemn days in the monastery that serving as a sister must include another calling within her: the need to help children, particularly the underprivileged.

Upon completion of her School of Education studies at Chestnut Hill College, she was assigned a mentor to help prepare for the likely day-to-day classroom challenges she would face once she started teaching in the fall. Father Riley, an experienced faculty member at Chestnut Hill with degrees in philosophy, divinity, and education, was her mentor.

She paused before ringing the doorbell. Katherine took several deep breaths. Her fantasies were taking a toll. Ever since her first encounter with Father Riley, several years her senior, she felt something stir...something prohibitive. She found the priest alarmingly desirable. She had heard stories of sisters leaving the Order, resigning, seeking a life outside the church. She had been told of some who connected with priests, both leaving their service and entering a family life together. *Surely,* she thought, *I would never allow such temptation to sully my commitment to serve Him.*

She was surprised that it was Father Riley who greeted her at the door. Usually it was the housekeeper who took care of household items for Father Riley and one other priest who shared the multi-bedroom, elegant house.

"Good afternoon, Sister Katherine. It's always wonderful to see you. And, as always, right on time." Father Riley, six-feet tall, looked younger than his fifty years. With a full head of graying hair, the charismatic priest maintained and enjoyed his good looks and athletic body. If one needed to find Thomas, the search always began in the college gym.

Dressed in her habit, the trim sister followed Father Riley into his study located to the left of the entryway. She noticed an unusual sheaf of papers scattered on his desk.

"Oh my, Father, looks like you're in the midst of a major project. Student papers?"

"No, Sister Katherine. But at this point I would prefer working on student papers. I don't know whether or not you've heard, but the college is seeking to change its identity to a university. The president asked for my help. I'm working on a paper regarding the growth of our graduate programs to present to the Board of Trustees."

"Sounds interesting and exciting, Father."

"Actually, it is. The president is very much behind such a change. I'm trying to draft as persuasive a case as I can."

"Do you anticipate much opposition?" Katherine asked.

"Hard to judge. Catholics agreeing to change can be a challenge. But change may be for the better…in personal lives as well as institutions. Don't you agree?"

Katherine felt flustered. She shrugged her shoulders. Then, in an effort to regain her composure, said, "Oh, yes, change, I suppose, can be useful, even inevitable."

"Inevitable? Yes, you're quite right, Katherine. Inevitable. That's the correct word. It's often necessary."

The young sister crossed herself and nodded her head. "So complicated, Father. The whole matter of change, I suppose. What will happen? The outcome, I mean. Do you think the trustees will embrace transforming to a university?"

Father Riley sighed. "Well, perhaps we'll chat about it later. I would value your input. For now…"

Eye contact. Long pause.

Sister Katherine had grown increasingly more attracted to Father Riley with each session as well as more ill at ease. Her fantasies were troublesome. *He's just so alluring. I love those eyes. There's a gentleness. And such ruddy good looks. I love that square jaw. I've got to stop this. Does he see* **me**? *Or does he just see a mentee? Stop. Say something. Anything.*

"I know you played for Holy Cross, Father Riley. But I also know you've been very active with our football program here at CHC. What do you think about our new coach? How do you think they'll do this year?"

Father Riley laughed. "A football fan! We'll have to go to a game together this fall. I think Lou Turner's going to do an excellent job. He has my vote. He was a great running back at Dartmouth and then a fine assistant coach."

Katherine moved her head nervously at the thought of attending a game with the priest. *Just words or does he really mean it? I feel as though I'm back in high school. Was it inane for me to bring up football?*

She's uncomfortable. Maybe intimidated. The priest guessed that she found him attractive. Most women did. He was not a naïve man. He was often reminded of his good looks, athletic build, and charm. He enjoyed the fact that women were attracted to him. He felt that being a priest protected him but at the same time presented a mystery, something forbidden, that women found intriguing. He strayed on one occasion from his vows of celibacy. The Archbishop and college president were aware, but chose only to direct that Father Riley ask forgiveness in his daily prayers.

"How has this past week been for you, Sister Katherine?"

"Just wonderful, thank you, Father. In addition to working on lesson plans for the fall, I spent some time helping Monsignor McDermott at Catholic Charities."

"So I understand. Monsignor's a wonderful friend. So happy you're helping out. Please." Father Riley gestured toward the couch opposite his desk, on top of which was a cassette player.

Despite her fantasies and discomfort, Katherine enjoyed these sessions. She found them to be productive and meaningful. He was compassionate, direct and clear, explaining his theories and strategy in dealing with elementary school children. He recorded his teaching experiences with inner city kids from impoverished and broken homes. He had vast experience teaching at that level before going to graduate school and becoming a college professor.

"Sister, we're just about through with this phase of your education. Today, I'd like to review some of the hypothetical classroom situations we've been dealing with. But before we go into our final review, I do have one last scenario I've put on tape that I'd like you to consider."

Father Riley's method of instructing a neophyte teacher incorporated a series of cassette recordings he made describing difficult classroom experiences. His approach included having his mentee listen to the tape after he left the room so that she/he would not be distracted by his presence. They discussed the issues upon his return, usually a half hour later.

"As always," he said, "it's based on reality. A reminder that some of the scenarios we've discussed have been raw, both with respect to language and activity. And perhaps change." He paused, a slight smile. "I'll return in about a half hour."

Father Riley brushed a hand through his thick head of hair. He walked out of the study, leaving Sister Katherine, as was the custom, to listen to the tape alone. The Venetian blinds were closed. Artificial lighting, except for a lamp next to his reading chair, was dim. It was an atmosphere conducive to serious reading, deep thinking or…Sister Katherine stopped herself. *My imagination sometimes is absurd and if I'm not careful will be the curse of me.* She crossed herself.

A crucifix was neatly placed on the center of the wall overlooking the back of the priest's desk chair. Classical music played softly in the background. The knotty pine walls were lined with shelves filled with scholarly literature as well as texts authored by her mentor. Just as she had done during each of the past five weeks, Katherine turned on the cassette player.

The tape started: *Sister Katherine, I can't begin to tell you how much I have enjoyed working with you these past weeks. I know that you will be an extraordinary teacher. It saddens me to think of our sessions coming to an end…"*

She returned to the couch. She abandoned her customary upright position. *Somehow,* she thought, *today is different…and it's not just that it's the last session.* She slouched, kicked off her shoes. That was a first. *They pinch,* she rationalized. She leaned back. *I feel him…his arms are wrapped around me…he's so strong…moves close…we kiss…I can feel it…I know it's real…it's not my fantasy life…it's happening.*

The rich tones of Father Riley's voice on the tape seemed at a distance…*not even in this room,* she thought. Aware, unaware, she closed her eyes. She escaped…

Katherine's mind raced. She fought off thoughts of her biological father, always critical, insulting. She brought her mentor back into focus. She listened. Soothing. Stirring. His sound…so reassuring…so rife with sexuality.

Her thoughts were tangled. *Is this real?* Her imagination turned its dial to a forbidden place. *Are those his words? Is he actually saying this or…*Her feelings were a compound of shock, pleasure, fear, excitement. Katherine shook her head and jumped from the couch. She slammed the stop button. But she continued to hear the words. She covered her face. She could feel her wetness. *Is this true? Or is it…? I so want it to be real. But I can't…Were those* *his words I heard? Or was it...was it me? My imagination? I so want it to be him. But I must not...*

The tape had long since stopped. The room was silent, except for the soft music.

Did He just move? Her eyes locked onto the crucifix. Sister Katherine was paralyzed. Her legs felt useless. Her brain and heart confused. Her thought process was numb, her feelings without definition.

The door swung open.

CHAPTER EIGHT
KATHERINE

Father Riley stood in the doorway.

Katherine remained frozen on the couch.

Whose words did I hear? Was that him or was it me, once again in a morass of fantasy?

Katherine leaned back as if to retreat. She raised her hand, palm facing Father Riley.

"It's okay," he said softly. "Please. You look so upset. You are always safe here."

Katherine's mouth dropped open. She lowered her hand and moved forward to the edge of the couch. A part of her wanted to spring up and escape. But there was another force at play. She looked into his face and saw what she perceived as warmth and compassion. *There's no reason to be afraid. He said I'm safe.* Father Riley took a step forward.

"I can't help myself, Katherine. I can't deny my feelings. This is all so new. But it's real...the feelings I have for you."

He removed his collar and stepped closer to the couch. Katherine's neck craned upward. Excitement, fear, desire...she felt all of it. She was aware of her heavy breathing. She could smell him. Father Riley extended his arms toward her. As if on command, she accepted his gesture and reached up. He slowly and gently clasped her hands.

Is this really happening? She asked herself.

Katherine pulled her hands from his grasp and covered her mouth.

"Please, Father, you must not."

Despite her words, he felt her willingness.

Smiling, his blue eyes moist and electric, he stared into her face, which was flushed with excitement.

"You are a beautiful young woman, Sister."

The priest raised his hands and placed them softly on either side of Katherine's face. She loved the feeling. *It's okay. He told me I'm safe.* He lowered his head and kissed her gently on the lips. The tenderness of this moment was something she had never experienced. They stared, eyes fixed upon each other. A thousand questions…a thousand new feelings raced through her being.

Father Riley guided Katherine gently from the couch. He enveloped his arms about her, slipped a hand beneath her chin and lifted it toward his lowering face. They kissed, not forcefully, but with more intensity than a moment before. She felt the saliva run from the corner of her mouth. Her legs weakened. He brushed his hands lightly along the sides of her breasts. She felt herself shudder.

"We have every right to our feelings, Sister Katherine. This is not a sin. Giving unto each other is in the service of God," he said in a reassuring manner. Katherine raised herself on her toes and solemnly placed her lips on his mouth. As she started to withdraw Father Riley grasped her firmly and kissed her, his mouth open. Katherine pushed her hands against his chest. She thought she would be revolted by the wetness of his open mouth. But that was not so. She was frightened at the joy of this moment.

"This is so wrong, Father. This is not right."

"Katherine, my dear, these are not selfish needs. To love a mortal is to love Jesus. Trust me. You must always trust me."

With some effort Katherine pulled away, opened the study door and ran from the house. He turned to go after her, but the sister raced down the outside stairs. He watched as she fumbled with her car key. He knew better than to run to her. Neighbors had a way of keeping their eyes on him. Katherine slumped behind the steering wheel, caught her breath, then drove off.

* * *

That night the priest and sister, each in their separate homes, replayed the happening over and over again.

Did this really happen? I must not let it happen. Not ever again. I will erase this. It never occurred. Katherine tossed about in her bed. When she closed her eyes the frightening and judgmental face of her biological father appeared. Disapproving…always disapproving.

Katherine prayed. *Have mercy on me, O God, according to your steadfast love. Create in me a clean heart, O God, and put a new and right spirit within me. Do not cast me away from your presence, and do not take your holy spirit from me. Restore to me the joy of your salvation, and sustain me in a willing heart.* But the recitation of Psalm 51, seeking cleansing and pardon, did not annul her mortal feelings. She craved the presence, not of the priest, but of the man, Thomas Riley. His words reverberated: *Trust me. You must always trust me.*

* * *

In the morning, despite having had little sleep, Father Riley jogged to the college gym. He sat in the sauna contemplating his feelings. He did not venture into denial. He continued to admit his desire, his need for this *young beauty.* He spent much of the early afternoon shuffling papers, attempting to read, pushing aside most of his lunch. Around two thirty he drove to Catholic Charities knowing that Sister Katherine was scheduled to work that day until mid-afternoon. He parked his car on a street overlooking the building's parking lot. He recognized her Volvo. He was there for about an hour when he spotted Katherine emerge and head for her car. He heard some children call out to her. He was moved as he watched her bend to hug the youngsters. When they left, she looked about and waved at two nuns. He thought he heard her say "thank you." He mouthed those words but added "dear God" at the end. Father Riley was not repentant. He was grateful.

CHAPTER NINE
MIKE

Was I targeted today? Was the shooter targeting Danielle? Can't be. Were we next to the victims just by chance? Maybe the ex-cop just lost it...drugs maybe... and the victims were random. Mike felt the perspiration across his forehead.

* * *

Mike was anything but a "white shoe" lawyer from a privileged background. His Ivy League education came at the serious price of serving his country in combat. He was tough without the bravado. Competitive, quietly determined. Committed to his clients. He had little patience for criminal practice. He preferred the civil side of the law. And he loved the challenge of being among a handful of litigators who actually went head-to-head in the courtroom. Most large firm lawyers were making their money on mergers and acquisitions, estate planning, tax and corporate law. Few had ever seen the inside of a courtroom. Mike's upbringing was blue collar. He did his time as a combat Marine. And for the past several years he honed his skills as a trial lawyer, dealing with a variety of complex legal issues, ever-changing fact patterns, and emotional swings experienced by clients. Despite his makeup and background, the shooting in front of the courthouse, the killing of the nearby couple, shook him to his core.

"An awful way to celebrate your birthday," Ali said as she shifted the car into "park."

Mike went up to the bedroom and, despite sleeping much of the ride home, crashed within minutes. His dreams invaded his efforts to have a deep, easy sleep. The horror film revisited, luring him once again to Korea, his fight for life at the hell-like Chosin Reservoir. He would relive the terrors.

Communism was nothing more than a "bad name" to young Mike when he dropped out of college and joined the Marine Corps. The free world saw itself as living in the growing shadow of Communism in the wake of World War II. President Harry Truman became alarmed when the Chinese-backed communist regime of North Korea invaded the United Nations-supported South Korea on June 25, 1950. The President ordered American troops to South Korea to assist that nation in fighting back against the North Koreans. Korea was a desperately poor mountainous peninsula, its summer brutally hot, winter bitterly cold.

Mike was among the heroic survivors in December 1950 of the harrowing fight along the frozen terrain of the Chosin Reservoir. The indescribable conflict was referred to by many as "the Korean War's greatest battle." In his dreams Mike relived over and over the knifelike winds that exacerbated the twenty-five below zero temperatures. He felt the painful frostbite that plagued him and most every fighting man, but these Marines simply would not quit. Mike heard the nauseating crack of bullets over and over. The cruel "video" kept repeating the horror of hordes of Chinese troops coming at him and his buddies. He could never disconnect his mind from the burning smell of the machine gun and the frostbite which numbed his hands while he squeezed every round of ammunition being fed into the automatic weapon he took over when the prior machine gunner was killed. His nightmare replayed the numbness as he watched Chinese and North Korean fighters fall to their death. The horror of fellow Marines being eviscerated by enemy weaponry never left him alone…not in his dreams, not in his day-to-day life.

Around 10 p.m., while Alison was in the kitchen on the phone, she heard a thud from upstairs.

"Oh, my god. June, I've got to get off. Something's going on."

"Mom, Mom! Quick! Dad's on the floor." It was Hillary, oldest of their two daughters.

Alison raced upstairs. There was Mike on his hands and knees, his shorts and T-shirt soaking wet. She rushed to him and placed a hand on his back. Mike turned his head to one side.

"I'm okay. Just a bad dream. Hillary, sweetheart, you go back to bed. I'm fine. Give me a hand, Ali…please."

Alison assisted her husband as he got to his feet and then sat on the side of the bed.

"Wow. I'm soaking wet."

"I'll get you a towel, Dad," Michelle said.

"Kids, get a glass of water for Dad…please," said Alison.

Hillary and Michelle stared as Mike wolfed down the water and then motioned for more. "I'm fine, kids. How about some ice for your old dad?" The two of them darted downstairs to oblige.

"This was a big ordeal, Mike. The dreams, Mike? The same? The war?"

"Just a dream, Ali, I'll be fine. But I sure was given a new life today. I'm goddamned lucky, Ali. That couple, the ones who were killed, so close to me."

"It's no wonder the war came into your sleep. What happened today…so understandable that it would bring back your terrifying experience in Korea."

"How long have I been out?"

"Oh, Mike, it doesn't matter. You were wiped out by this ordeal. It's no wonder," said Alison.

His kids, deeply concerned about this strange scene, seeing their dad on the floor in his T-shirt and shorts, soaking wet, returned with the ice. One of them turned to Ali and moved her lips: "What happened?"

Ali responded: "Dad will be fine. Every now and then he, like so many other people who fought in wars, has bad dreams about some of the things that happened."

Mike took some ice in his hands and applied it to his forehead. As he had done so many times, he repressed the nightmare. He shifted and coated his being with the present.

His daughters stood in the doorway. "Are you okay, Dad?" one of them asked. "More water?"

"I'm fine, sweethearts. You guys go to bed. I'll go downstairs with Mom and have a snack. Just a bad dream."

"About the war, Daddy?"

"The two of you are the best. Now come over and give me a kiss and then you both need to get to bed. School tomorrow."

* * *

Mike and Alison went downstairs to the kitchen. He spotted the birthday cake sitting on the counter.

"Tomorrow night, Mike. We'll celebrate tomorrow night."

"That will be one meaningful celebration."

"How about some pasta salad? A little food will be good for you."

They sat and talked…about the shooting, about his case involving Danielle Webb, about their kids, about how lucky he was to have survived.

Danielle Webb. Was she the target? Was I a target as well? Is there something sinister going on?

* * *

Mike showered and climbed into bed and took a Valium. No doubt he would get a good sleep.

When morning came, well rested, Mike bounded out of bed. He rushed downstairs, where Alison was making coffee and the kids were downing some juice.

"Happy day-after-birthday, Dad," Hillary said. "Are you okay, Dad? You came home so early yesterday."

"And you went right to bed," Michelle added.

"Yup. Just some kind of crazy bug, but I'm totally fine now. And sometimes when I get sick I have some pretty crazy dreams.

That's why you heard me fall out of bed…a stupid dream. But I'm all set now…good as new. Hey, I've got an idea. Forget the bus today. I'll drive you guys to school."

"Hillary and Michelle, will you give Dad and me a few minutes. We need to talk."

Mike raised his eyebrows, tilting his head.

Husband and wife went upstairs and closed their bedroom door.

"Mike, it's already on the news. I heard it just a few minutes ago. Your name may be in today's papers…teachers may know…other kids may hear something from their parents. We've got to tell them."

"Oh, boy. That's really hard," Mike responded.

"Mike, they're not babies. And it would be just awful for them if they heard about it at school. Teachers, kids could easily say something. We can't let them hear about it that way. We've always been honest with them." Ali raised her eyebrows, shrugged her shoulders.

Mike sighed and then responded, "You're right, Ali. It's just my, our instinct to always try to protect them. Let's go downstairs and do it before I take them to school."

The four of them sat at the kitchen table. Mike explained just what took place, emphasizing that obviously he was fine…that the ordeal was over. The kids had some questions but seemed okay with the explanation, and actually happy that their parents had been open and honest with them.

"Tell you what. Since I'm your chauffeur this morning," said Mike, trying to lighten the atmosphere, "I'll drive you to school. And when the two of you get home today, we'll take a long walk together. The finishing line will be Brigham's…still the best damned ice cream in Massachusetts. Be sure to save some room for sundaes. And then cake tonight!" To say that he adored his daughters is an understatement.

"You're not going to work, Dad?"

"Nope. I'm playin' hooky. Celebrate my day-after birthday."

After he dropped Hillary and Michelle at school, he picked up *The Boston Globe* at the local drug store. Headline: TWO DIE IN COURTHOUSE SHOOTING. He scanned the article and, sure enough, his name and that of his client were among those described as "near victims requiring hospital care, but released." The article also included the fact that "the shooter was a retired police officer who took his own life in an alley-way off Cambridge Street."

"Oh, boy, the office phone's going to ring nonstop today. I'll call Jane and agree upon a consistent response. She can refer calls from the press directly here. I don't want to avoid the press and I don't want to put it on her to try to deal with them. Some reporters can be damned persistent," Mike said.

"You know what, Mike. I've got an even better idea. When calls come, I'll handle them. There's no way I'm leaving you. I'll call the school and let them know I'm not coming in. No big deal," Ali said.

* * *

Mike stayed away from his office and kept close watch over his family and home for the rest of the week. *Shooter's dead, but maybe some others are involved in whatever his intention was. Maybe I'm a little paranoid, but so be it.* Jane canceled his appointments and he would not be missing any hearings in the Suffolk Probate Court. The county closed the court until the following Monday. The powers that be felt they needed a few days to install some strengthened security. By week's end, his nervous gut and fear for his family lessened. Mike felt that he was ready to return to action. Jane called every day, making sure that her boss was on the mend and letting him know about phone calls and rescheduling of hearings. The Webb matter was on for Tuesday.

"Which judge? Did they say?"

"Mahoney," said Jane, knowing that Mike would not be pleased.

"Oh, no. That son-of-a-bitch hates women. He's a misogynist. What time are we on?"

"Two o'clock session. You're number three on the list."

"Call Mrs. Webb, please. I want her in the office for some Q and A's Monday afternoon."

"That's fine, but why do you need to run through questions and answers? Will the judge actually take testimony? I thought they relied pretty much on counsel when it's just a matter of temporary orders. Maybe you want to dictate an affidavit for her to sign?"

Jane was a pro. She knew the procedure. When couples split and one or both filed for divorce, the courts provided important but informal hearings for the purpose of issuing "temporary orders" regarding monetary support, custody and visitation, and living arrangements pending a trial, which probably wouldn't take place for another twelve to eighteen months. But this temporary hearing might be a little different. Mike was alleging physical abuse and was asking the court to remove the husband from the family home. Representations by both attorneys together with affidavits signed by the clients, and even submission of the photos by Mike, may or may not be sufficient. The court, particularly with Judge Mahoney presiding, may call for some limited sworn testimony.

"Tough to say. The photos should be enough. But with Mahoney I don't want to take any chances."

"Maybe he'll go easy on her. After all, the two of you were damn near shot. But I'll call and get Mrs. Webb in here Monday afternoon."

"Sympathy? Mahoney? Hardly. But who knows, maybe even that chauvinist will be moved once he learns Webb slugged his wife." Mike was encouraging himself. But it was true. There was plenty of precedence to order the ousting of a husband who battered his wife. And Judge Mahoney, despite his personal prejudices, knew the law; one punch should certainly be enough to pose a threat to the entire family.

"Thanks, Jane, see you Monday."

Mahoney's got the guts to throw this bastard out. The more I think about it, I'm probably better off with him than some of the others on that bench…some of the liberals who accept apologies and feel content with an order for anger management. Yup, Mahoney might not be the right guy if this goes to a full trial, but he just might be the right guy at this level. He won't be afraid to toss Webb. He won't ignore the power of the photos. And no financial strain on Webb. The bastard's got the bucks to buy a hotel, let alone camp out at the Ritz until he finds himself an apartment. And Mahoney doesn't have any love for those Beacon Hill blue bloods. They pissed all over the Irish. The more I think about it, the more I like it.

* * *

Mike sipped his coffee while sorting through the mail. It felt good to be back. *Normalcy works,* he thought.

"Hey, Jane, the phone. Jane?"

His secretary had gone to the restroom. Mike grabbed the receiver.

"This is Mike Lyons."

"Mike, Attorney Sofia Vasquez here."

"Ah. The Webb matter." Mike and his adversary had never met. Attorney Vasquez practiced with one of the largest Boston firms, better known for the banks and insurance conglomerates they represented rather than "riffraff divorce cases"…matters they usually farmed out. "What can I do for you?"

"You and Mrs. Webb had quite a close call last week. Fortunately, my client and I were already in the courthouse when that maniac started shooting."

Mike swallowed. "You're lucky you were inside, Attorney Vasquez. It was nasty. So what can I do for you?"

"I just need a little bit of a continuance. My calendar is all messed up with a pressing matter I've got in the federal court."

Why do those bastards always throw around "federal court?" They make it sound as though that's the major league club and our probate and family court is the farm team. Screw her.

"What does 'a little bit of a continuance' mean?" Mike asked. "If you need a day or two, that's fine. Any day this week will work for me as long as the court can accommodate us."

"Well, I could actually use a couple of weeks."

Cute. Son-of-a-bitch is looking for a cooling down period. Give her client a couple of weeks to play like a Boy Scout, beg forgiveness. And wait until the shiner he planted on Danielle's eye has healed.

"I'm willing to think about it," said Mike. "Provided your guy deposits ten grand with me tomorrow, which I'll escrow for Mrs. Webb. Make the check payable to her."

"Ten thousand dollars! I'm talking about two weeks, not two years," Attorney Vasquez replied.

"And provided that Mr. Webb packs his bags and vacates within twelve…well twenty-four hours. Your client, Attorney Vasquez…Sofia…is a dangerous man."

"Listen, counsel, that monetary demand is totally absurd and unreasonable. I'm simply asking for a lawyer-to-lawyer accommodation."

"You heard my terms. We're asking the court for an emergency order to have your Mr. Webb removed from the family home because he's dangerous. And we're also seeking temporary alimony and child support. Why don't you have a chat with your client. I'm sure you can persuade him of the advisability of doing all of this on a voluntary basis rather than having the court hit him with even more than we're asking. If I don't hear from you by the end of the day, I'll see you or one of your one hundred fifty lawyers in court tomorrow at two. Frankly, your client will score a lot of points with whoever may be sitting on this case if he voluntarily vacates. He punched his wife. They have two little kids. There's not a judge in America who won't toss him out. I think you've got one nasty client on your hands. He's too much of a threat to ask Mrs. Webb and her children to wait two weeks. No way would I agree nor would any of our judges grant such a continuance."

Mike was careful not to say anything about the photos. He wanted to spring them at the hearing. Like most trial lawyers, Mike had a taste for surprise and drama.

"I don't need your advice, counsel, thank you very much. I'll present my Motion for Continuance tomorrow afternoon. I'll courier a copy to you within the hour."

I love that "counsel" bullshit...old school sarcasm. This one's going to be a picnic. Mike heard the slam of the phone on the other end. He removed from his file the color photo of his client's bruised face.

CHAPTER TEN
DANIELLE

A cold breeze, the remnants of an undeterred winter, punctuated their silence as Mike and Danielle Webb approached the cobblestoned square in front of the gray limestone Suffolk County Courthouse where just days earlier they nearly lost their lives. The realization of just how close they came created an indelible connection.

Mike placed his hand on his client's back, ushering her toward the entryway. They were each deaf to the din of lawyers and clients shuffling about in the main lobby.

The two of them stepped off the crowded Art-deco style elevator into the marble columned hallway of the third floor.

"It's weird…" Danielle said.

Mike frowned.

"Being here. This place…where we damned near got killed…just a week ago," Danielle said.

"Very strange. We're lucky. It hit me as we were walking toward the entrance," Mike said. "Just awful about the couple who were killed. I understand they were lovely people, simply on their way to pass papers on a house they were buying. It was supposed to have been a happy day for them."

"I'm having constant nightmares. You? Are you able to sleep?" Danielle asked.

"Fitfully," Mike replied and then placed a hand on her shoulder, trying to be reassuring.

Danielle acknowledged the gesture. She turned to him for direction. He pointed to a corner at one end of a long corridor flanked by institutional beige walls in need of fresh paint, and wainscoting cracked and dulled by years of budgetary neglect. The dimly lit corridor was the place where lawyers and litigants congregated before their cases were called into the courtroom for hearings. A din of stories of personal misery and lawyers' advice repeated itself day after day.

"This spot is good," he said, lowering his briefcase near a corner. "We can talk here. Now remember, not a word in that courtroom until either the judge or I ask you to speak. I'll present the photos…

"I'm really nervous, Mike. Do you really think I'll have to talk in there?" she asked.

"Hopefully, not. The old adage: a picture is worth a thousand words. But if the judge does want to hear from you, you're all set. We went over everything that could come up. Just answer whatever questions may be asked truthfully and to the point. No need to embellish. And remember how concerned you are about the safety and wellbeing of your children. The judge needs to hear that."

Why is it I feel it's necessary to remind her that her children are what is most important? Doesn't any parent just get that without being coached by a lawyer? We can't take anything for granted…not even the obvious. I guess sometimes we over-coach out of abundant caution. But even then… Mike stopped himself.

Danielle nodded. Her eyes were moist.

"You're going to be fine. You did nothing wrong. Remember, *he* hit *you*, not the other way around. You have nothing to hide." Mike fixed his eyes directly upon hers. "Just tell the truth."

"You're so earnest, Mike…and so handsome." Her expression was both imploring and playful.

A minute ago she was tense. And now she's flirting. So damned sensual. Hold on, Mike. This is no time to be thinking of bedding down. You and Ali have a great thing going.

"Hey, we survived combat together last week," he chuckled. It drew a smile to her face.

"Compared to that," he said, "this'll be a piece of cake."

This business of being a trial jockey is all about coaching, instructing, reassuring, sending clients into the game prepared and confident.

He pulled the large envelope with the photos of his client's battered eye from his briefcase. "Now tell me a little bit more about Mrs. Jensen. How long has she been the full-time nanny?"

Before she could answer, Danielle clutched at his bicep, then pointed.

"That's him. There he is. My son-of-a-bitching excuse for a husband," she said, her voice breathless.

While Mike turned in the direction she pointed, he could sense her change. No longer covering her anxiety with flirtation, she was trembling. *I don't blame her. A gutless fucker...looks like a wimp...a nerd.*

"Good. I'm going to have a word with Mr. Brooks Webb's heavy ticket lawyer. Bad vibes on the phone. I want to see what she's like face-to-face. You stay here, please. I don't want any exchanges between the two of you...not until they're willing to talk settlement. I want him out of that condo. You deserve custody of those children and that's what we're going to get," Mike said.

He gave his client a reassuring look.

"Keep an eye on my briefcase, please. If they want to talk business, I'll let you know. In the meantime, stay put."

Attorney Lyons made his way through a cluster of lawyers, many of whom acknowledged last week's shooting. "Thank God you're okay, Big Mike." "Hey, Mike, it should have been your client on top of you," an inappropriate attempt at humor from one fellow trial lawyer. A couple of others openly referenced Mike's heroism in putting his body in harm's way to protect his client.

He knew that his adversary would attempt to hide her curiosity about the contents of the large envelope Mike was holding. It contained the photographs and the word "PHOTOS" was deliberately in large red letters on the face of the envelope. He wanted her to notice and be concerned. If a civilized negotiation was in the offing whereby Vasquez would agree to the terms Mike articulated during their phone call, then he would reveal the photos. If not, he'll spring them at the hearing. Mike noticed Webb's sallow complexion and that his brown hair was askew. He wore thick glasses, looked as though he hadn't slept well. His charcoal gray suit was rumpled, in need of a good pressing. Webb's thin-lipped mouth was taut.

"Sofia Vasquez? Mike Lyons." Mike extended a hand, clutching the envelope with the other. She barely offered hers.

Snooty and pretentious, Mike thought to himself.

"Yes. Good to meet you, Lyons." Vasquez's eyes fixed on the envelope.

"It's Mike. I'm an informal kind of guy. Good that you're here and not in the federal court." *Check out that supercilious smirk.*

"So, Ms. Vasquez, are you actually going forward with your Motion to Continue? I mean, why bother asking for a continuance? We're here. So why not simply go forward on our Request to Vacate and for Temporary Custody?"

"Well, counsel, we'll just have to wait and see, won't we. The kind of matter you raise could take some time, and as I told you on the phone I've got some other pressing matters. The court has a heavy load today. I rather suspect Judge Mahoney will welcome the opportunity to put this off for a bit."

Smug. All wrapped up in her navy blue pinstripe suit. Real know-it-all. She has zero idea as to what Mahoney would welcome. I think I'm going to have a picnic today.

"You know I'm going to have to oppose any effort to delay. You can make short shrift of this whole thing and save our clients a lot of legal fees if you and Mr. Webb can agree to the reasonable offer I put to you yesterday." Mike raised his voice. He wanted to be certain that Webb heard "the reasonable offer" part, wondering whether or not Vasquez had even conveyed his proposition to her client.

"See you in the courtroom, counsel." And with that Vasquez turned her back to Mike and faced her client.

Nasty. Probably wants to milk this Webb for all she can get. This thing's not going to get settled. She's going to want a full-fledged trial...self-serving State Street mentality: rack up the billable hours. And those self-righteous corporate bastards point their fancy fingers at us, the "low-life" divorce lawyers. "Taking advantage of the vulnerable." the phrase Archibald Adams, President of the Boston Bar Association, had the unmitigated gall to use during that recent Conference on Fees. Not a word about their hourly rates.

Unwilling to heed her counsel's advice and feeling left out and paranoid that a deal might be struck without her presence, Mrs. Webb made her way over, carrying Mike's briefcase.

"Hi, Brooks," she offered cheerily as though the four of them were best of friends and headed to Symphony Hall.

Her husband did not acknowledge her. He remained tight-lipped, head turning away from her, vacant expression on his face.

Just as Mike placed his hand on the small of Danielle's back to guide her away, Joe Ginsburg, the court officer, stepped into the hallway and announced: "All parties in the Webb matter."

"That's us. Let's go." Mike gestured to his client to move forward into the courtroom.

"Hey, Mikey," the affable court officer squeezed Mike's hand. "Jeez, you okay? Wow! I called your office. Jane gave me the word...said you were gonna take the week off. Smart. I was concerned about you, pal."

"Thanks, Joe. You're one of the good ones. I'm doing just fine. Joe, this is my client, Mrs. Webb, and these folks are Attorney Sofia Vasquez and Mr. Webb." *Disarm the enemy with courtesy.*

"Nice to meet you. The judge will be back on the bench in five minutes. He's looking over your papers in chambers. Please take your seats."

* * *

The high-ceiling courtroom was flanked by dreary beige walls, exhibiting portraits of yesteryear's dour looking judges…all old…all male…all white. A grand carved oak bench for the judge was raised well above the level of the people having business before the court.

The Honorable Wilfred P. Mahoney emerged. He was a large man with a powerful voice, which he used freely to intimidate lawyers and litigants whenever he was displeased with the quality of questions or witnesses' evasive answers. His face would redden when displeased, and when he lifted his six foot, two hundred twenty-five-pound frame from his high-backed chair, even those inexperienced with his ways got the message. "Don't dance with me," he would bark. "Ask a simple question and don't lead that witness." "Sir, I want a straight, direct, crisp answer to that question. Do you understand?"

Mike rarely enjoyed appearing before Mahoney, not because there was a bad rapport between them, but Mike simply didn't care for the judge's lack of sensitivity toward the public, who already felt marginalized just being in the circumstance of having to air so much about their personal lives and wrecked marriages. But he also felt he would be at a distinct advantage. Mahoney was tough and not the type to countenance any son-of-a-bitch, particularly a fancy Brahmin, who slapped his wife around.

"Webb matter," the clerk announced. Mike beckoned to his client to follow him. Brooks Webb and Attorney Vasquez approached the bench as well. The lawyers centered themselves, guiding their clients to either side of them and slightly to the rear as if to protect them from the judge.

"Attorney Lyons, I'm happy to see you and happy to know that you came out of last week's horrendous incident unscathed. Terrible thing." The judge shook his head, his face grim.

Mike acknowledged the judge's kindness with a nod and a soft "thank you." *First gracious words I ever heard from this guy.*

"Attorney Vasquez, I don't think I've seen you here before, but you are most welcome in my court. I understand that fortunately you were not outside in the square when the shooting took place."

Mike thought: *Will this guy ever stop calling it MY court? This place belongs to the people, or has he forgotten? Put the robes on some of these political...stop it, Mike. After all, Wilfred was gracious enough to acknowledge that I damn near got shot last week.*

Vasquez managed a condescending smile and said something about her and her client having been safely inside the courthouse when the shooting occurred. She did not utter a word about Mike and Danielle surviving the tragedy.

The judge picked up Vasquez's Motion to Continue and waved it dramatically, then peered over his glasses and directed himself to her. "Counsel," he started, "since you and Mr. Webb..."

Sofia Vasquez's arrogance got the better of what she had been advised against by a colleague familiar with this judge: *One thing you never want to do is interrupt God.*

"If Your Honor please..."

The judge leaned forward, removing his glasses. His expression announced his chagrin at having been interrupted.

"...my client and I are prepared to waive our Motion and proceed with Attorney Lyons' request for Temporary Support, Temporary Custody and his groundless plea to have Mr. Webb vacate the family home...to which, I might add, we are adamantly opposed."

"Good idea, Attorney Vasquez," the judge barked with a curl of sarcasm. "You're here. I'm not about to grant a continuance.

But Attorney Vasquez, in my courtroom you do not interrupt the judge. All right, let's proceed. I'll hear from you Attorney Lyons."

"If Your Honor please, let me cut to the chase. Should Mrs. Webb be called upon to testify she will tell the court that on the date in question her husband, Brooks Webb, frustrated by something that happened at the lab where he works as a chemist, left early, arrived home at about 3 p.m., and decided that his angst gave him license to smash his wife's face in the area of her left eye. Closed fist, I might add, Your Honor." Mike got right to the heart of the matter. He knew he had to grab the judge's attention and ire as quickly as possible. Then, he skillfully used a dramatic pause. He took a measure of Judge Mahoney's reddening countenance and glaring eyes.

Mike shook his head from side to side, a pained expression on his face. He broke the effective silence. "Your Honor, I offer these photos as Exhibit One." After handing the evidence to the judge, he provided Vasquez with copies.

Mike noted that his adversary merely glanced at the photos and did not seem the least bit perturbed. She offered no objection, not that such an effort would have the least chance of being sustained.

She's playing like Cool Hand Luke, Mike thought to himself.

Judge Mahoney examined the pictures, stood up from his chair and slapped them onto the bench.

Score .All net. Mike maintained a serious "I-feel-my-client's-pain" expression.

The judge turned to his clerk. "Mr. Noonan, swear in the witnesses. And I'll hear from Mrs. Webb first."

In his typical unorthodox style, Judge Mahoney did not beckon Mike to proceed with questioning his client. The judge bulldozed and took over himself.

"Do you adopt what your lawyer has just said?" he asked, his tone carrying all the way to Manhattan.

"I do, Your Honor." Danielle's voice was soft, demure, her face on the verge of tears.

"What was the essence of the conversation or activity that precipitated this assault?"

Maintaining a mellow tone, reaching for a tissue, she answered: "Brooks, my husband, has a temper. He gets…well…upset I guess is the best way of putting it when things don't go his way. Sometimes it's like having another child. It seems that someone at the lab expressed an opinion that an experiment that Brooks had been working on was too costly. My husband yelled at me, saying 'this woman'…the woman at the lab, Your Honor, 'doesn't know what she's talking about.' It was as though I was the one who had criticized his work. I tried to be supportive, but he just kept ranting."

"You say you tried to be supportive? Just what did you say?" the judge asked. Mike's client sobbed. "Mr. Court Officer, some water for Mrs. Webb," the uncharacteristically sympathetic judge directed.

She thanked the judge and sipped from the cup. She flashed a knowing glance at Mike.

She's enjoying this! Good for her. He nailed her at home; she'll nail him here. I love justice…or is it vengeance I'm thinking about?

"You all right, madam?"

"I'm fine, thank you, Your Honor."

"Please proceed."

"I begged Brooks to calm down and try to understand their point of view. I said that after the weekend goes by he can go in Monday and have a cool and rational discussion about the value of his experiment."

"And then what happened?"

"He screamed at me. He said I was always taking sides against him. He swore at me…called me a dumb…I can't use the 'c' word, Your Honor. And then, without any warning, he hit me…in my eye." She gestured to the area where there was still some muted yellow and black.

"I'm so afraid of him, Your Honor…afraid for my children."

Mike thought: *Perfect add-on. But is she performing? Is she over the top? Or am I just being cynical…too many exaggerated stories over the years?*

The judge glared at her husband. Then turned to the witness.

"Where were the children?" the judge asked.

"They were out with Mrs. Jensen, our nanny. She was going to take them for an overnight. Their things were already in her car. They love going there." Danielle paused and then blurted out: "Your Honor, I'm afraid of him. I'm afraid he'll hit me again and I'm afraid for my children."

The kids staying with the nanny overnight? I don't remember her telling me that…not at all. She said something about making lunch for them. I'm sure of it.

Mrs. Danielle Webb lost control, tears flowing freely and her body trembling. The judge pointed his chin toward Mike and said: "That's enough testimony, Mrs. Webb. You may step down."

After a ten-minute break, Judge Mahoney took his place at the bench.

"Counsel," he started, "I remind you that this is an informal hearing. We are dealing only with the issuance of temporary orders. I'm going to dispense with cross-examination. Everyone will have the opportunity to conduct thorough direct and cross-examinations should this matter go to trial. Everyone in agreement? Ms. Vasquez? Mr. Lyons?"

Mike surprised his adversary by articulating his opposition to waiving cross-examination. He felt that his client could handle cross-examination; that all cross would do is buttress and strengthen their case. And he wanted to be able to take a crack at Mr. Webb. Vasquez spoke up. "If I may be heard, Your Honor."

Still seething after Mrs. Webb's testimony, Judge Mahoney leaned forward. "I'll hear you, counsel. But be brief."

"Your Honor, I think that your suggestion is excellent. I'm certainly willing to waive cross at this time but reserve the right to do so at trial."

Prissy. Currying favor, Mike thought.

"Reservation and waiver noted. Attorney Lyons?"

"Sorry, Your Honor, I respectfully disagree. I think the witnesses should be subject to cross-examination at this time. After all, we're dealing with assault and battery…and we've got young children involved. I think as much thorough testimony as possible is in order despite the fact this is a temporary order hearing," Mike argued.

Mike felt he had banged home his point to the seasoned judge that his client was simply telling the truth and could withstand any type of cross Vasquez might attempt to throw at her. He also suspected that Vasquez was not the least bit prepared to conduct a cross-examination.

"I'm issuing my evidentiary order. No cross-examination for either side. Cross will waste too much time; not necessary at this preliminary stage," the judge bellowed.

"But, Your Honor, this level may well set precedence for the entire case," Mike pleaded.

"Nonsense. We'll proceed without cross-examination."

Too bad, Mike thought, *not a chance that Vasquez would lay a glove on Danielle.*

"Kindly note my exception, Your Honor."

"Noted." The judge cleared his throat with what sounded like a large volume of phlegm. A habit with which the divorce lawyers appearing before him on a regular basis were familiar. Many thought it often occurred when "Wilfred knows he just blew an evidentiary ruling."

At least I've got my objection on the record, Mike thought.

Some attorneys, still green with respect to handling matrimonial cases, tend to minimize temporary order hearings. Mike knew better. *Judges are human. The first impression is*

*formed at these hearings and they are not easily erased. Screw up
at this level, and you could bury your client's chances at the full
trial.*

"Let's proceed. I'll hear from you sir, Mr. Webb. Raise your
right hand and Mr. Noonan will swear you in."

Brooks Webb took the stand. Mike noted the perspiration on
Webb's pale forehead and that his hands shook as they clutched at
the front railing of the witness box.

Attorney Vasquez started to ask a question, but the judge
waived her off and asked: "You've heard your wife's testimony?"

"Yes, sir." Catching a glimpse from his lawyer, Webb
quickly amended "sir" to "Your Honor."

Brooks Webb stood erect and stoic.

"Did you inflict this injury to Mrs. Webb's eye and face?"
Judge Mahoney asked, while raising one of the photos toward the
witness.

"I did."

*This is great. He admits to the battery. We're home. Round
one to us. The judge knows Webb is loaded. Judge's going to toss
him today. We're getting those kids.*

Mrs. Webb, standing to the side and rear of Attorney Lyons,
scuffled nervously as the judge then asked: "You hit her with a
closed fist?"

"I'm not sure, Your Honor." Webb swallowed nervously. "It
may have been with the side of my hand."

Judge Mahoney turned to Vasquez. "If you have any
questions, go ahead. Remember, we're talking about temporary
orders here. I don't want a cascade of irrelevant questions."

*Hell, he never gave me the chance to ask my client questions,
but that's the way Mahoney operates…kind of like a sheriff in the
"wild west." And I think this is his signal that he's got all the
evidence he needs.*

Mike's adversary stood, hands grasping her lapels as though she was a barrister at Old Bailey. Her mouth displayed a confident smirk.

Makes me want to wretch. But what's she so confident about? Or maybe she's thinking about the fat fee she's going to generate.

"Tell the court exactly what took place when you arrived home on the Friday in question," she directed.

"When I walked into the apartment, I called out but no one answered. I guessed that everyone was out. It was a beautiful day. As I headed down the hallway toward our bedroom, I heard some noises."

"Before you proceed, Mr. Webb, had you come home early because of some sort of a disagreement at the lab?" Vasquez asked.

"NO! I came home early to see my children...to get an early start on the weekend. It was a beautiful day and I thought I'd surprise everyone."

"And did you surprise someone?" Vasquez asked, a curl to her cadence.

"What *kind* of noises did you hear?" the judge interrupted, his pace slow and deliberate. His curiosity had morphed into suspicion.

Oh no! Don't tell me. Did we just toss the ball into the other team's hands? Mike had tried too many cases not to see the storm clouds. He struggled to maintain a poker face, but his innards were in turmoil as Webb, at first stammering, answered.

"I...I...I heard my wife and the voice of a man coming from our bedroom."

Mahoney flashed a sharp knife-like look at Mrs. Webb, and then cast a knowing glance toward Mike.

"What happened next?" Sofia Vasquez asked.

The entire courtroom was still. Litigants and lawyers were enjoying the salacious drama unfolding before them.

"As I was opening the bedroom door my wife was pushing it back against me. She told me something like 'everything is all right; just go to the kitchen' and that she would be right with me. I wasn't having any of it. I pushed open the door and she backpedaled. I saw a man struggling with his trousers. He ran by me. I was shocked. My wife. My own home."

"And then?" Vasquez asked.

"I remember that my wife was wearing a robe. I pulled it open. She had nothing on underneath. I grabbed her arm."

Mike turned in the direction of Danielle Webb. She shook her head and mouthed the words *he's lying...not true.* It was difficult to say whose face was more crimson: the judge who had long since emerged from his chair, or Attorney Lyons' client.

Either he's making this whole thing up or my client is a first-class liar, Mike thought. *And how does the stud manage to run out if he's struggling to put on his trousers? I've got to have a shot at cross on Webb.*

"Is that it? You just grabbed her arm?" The judge asked.

"No, Your Honor. I spun her around as she tried to get away from me and I...I struck her."

"Near or at her eye?" The judge held up the photo.

"Yes, sir...Your Honor. I was beside myself."

"*Lessons One, Two and Three,*" said Professor Sean Murray back at law school. "*Never, ever believe your client...at least not until you have cross-examined the hell out of him or her, and even then, be careful. Divorce clients, understandably not at their best, can be treacherous people,*" he warned.

Judge Wilfred Mahoney had heard enough. "You may step down, sir."

Mike may have been on the verge of fouling out, but he was still in the game.

"Your Honor, this line of testimony absolutely calls for cross-examination. May I..."

The judge interrupted. "No, you may not cross-examine. I've already ruled quite clearly. This hearing is limited to emergency...temporary orders. You'll have your chance at the trial. In the meantime, I'm issuing my order. You, Mrs. Webb..."

Mike turned and gestured that Danielle stand. "Your Honor," she burst out. "Brooks' story is a lie."

"Madam, that's for this court to decide. You'll have your chance to demonstrate at the trial that your husband is, as you say...not telling the truth." The judge continued:

"Hear me and hear me clearly. I am ordering you, Mrs. Webb, not your husband, to remove yourself from the marital home within the next seventy-two hours. I grant temporary custody to Mr. Webb, provided that the nanny remains in his employ. My written order will contain terms for visitation and temporary alimony based upon my review of the financial statements which counsel will submit no later than noontime tomorrow together with a copy of the most recent joint tax return. SO ORDERED," he barked. And with that the judge, already standing, turned, and charged into his lobby. He slammed the door, making certain that the packed courtroom had no doubt about his wrath.

As they left the courthouse, Danielle insisted that her husband made up the entire story. Mike's head was spinning.

"Why didn't I get a chance to tell my own...What are you going to do about this?" she asked.

Standing in the center of the square in front of the courthouse, Mike turned to his client. *What unbelievable nerve. She has the temerity to ask, "what am I going to do about it?"* Mike glared at Danielle. He was never happy with himself when he lost his composure or chastised a client...or anyone, for that matter. Consequently, he controlled his demeanor. "I'll let you know," Mike responded to his client's question. "I'm going to let this settle in. We'll meet in a couple of days. Mrs. Webb, bear something in mind. You want me on this case? Then you be straight with me."

"I am straight with you. I'm telling you the truth." Tears. "Can't we appeal?"

"The appeal, madam, will be the full trial on the merits. We...you and I...have a lot to talk about. Call Jane about an appointment. In the meantime, Danielle, you need to make living arrangements for yourself."

"Oh, that'll be easy. We have a vacation condo in Newport. Judge didn't say I couldn't use that, did he?"

Mike shrugged. "No, he did not." His facial expression said *you're a cool one...got it all figured out.*

With that, Mike Lyons, his thoughts scrambled, made his way to his office, where he had an unproductive day musing about the shocking turn of events in his case. And beating up on himself for not having suspected that his client's story may well be a fabrication. *I should've thought about something like this. I let myself get blindsided. I took her word. I should have gone after her in a prep cross-examination more thoroughly than I did. But there's something about that husband of hers...maybe after all is said and done, he's the liar.*

* * *

"Ali", Mike said to his wife that evening, "today was my swan song. I'm getting out of this trial business. I'm gonna sell shoes for Thom McAn. That way, my only headache will be whether or not I've got enough sizes."

"Mike," Ali replied, "you're not going to be a shoe salesman. I've heard that line before. But, Mike, get out of this one while you can. It sounds to me as though Mr. Webb may be telling the truth. And the way you've described Danielle Webb...she sounds like trouble, Mike."

"I hear you, Ali. You're probably right..."

"But, I know...I've heard it before...you and your tough trial lawyers love a challenge. What is it you say? Oh, I remember: you, the real good ones, when the going gets tough, mount a full court press."

CHAPTER ELEVEN
FATHER RILEY

Father Riley waited until Sister Katherine drove her Volvo out of the Catholic Charities parking lot. He followed, keeping a safe distance behind. He would be mortified if she became aware that he was *stalking her*. Just as he started to turn into a gas station to make a U-turn and head back to Newton, he watched as Katherine pulled into an A & P parking lot. He was tempted to follow her into the supermarket.

I'll let her be, he thought. *But sooner or later, I must have her. She's so beautiful, so young, so tempting.*

The Jesuit drove back to his home. Concentration was difficult. His mind kept darting to the image of Katherine, the softness of her eyes, fullness of her lips. *There's such an innocence about her...a sweetness...a kindness...my vows...I cannot. I have committed myself to a life of service to the Church...a life of chastity. I am a priest, a servant of the Lord Jesus.*

Nausea set in followed by a migraine headache. It was as though someone had implanted a jagged rock inside his temple. He removed a vial of Fiorinal with codeine from a desk drawer. He walked into the kitchen, poured a glass of orange juice, added a Compazine and downed the combination of pain and nausea killers. He sat on a kitchen chair, tucked his hands between his knees, and bowed his head toward his lap.

What have I done? Have I wounded you, my dear Katherine? Am I the fool of all fools? I mean no harm. Who am I? What have I become? I must go to you. Must ask your forgiveness.

Within moments the tortured priest was on his knees in front of the toilet. He wretched until there was nothing left but air. He staggered into his den, thrust himself on the couch, and pulled his knees to a fetal position. Soon the pounding in his head began to ease. Sleep finally came. His dreams were of a young boy, begging for someone to come and save him from temptation.

Only the Lord can save me, but I must do everything I can to help the Lord save me.

Father Riley woke up and rubbed his hands through his hair, and then began to massage his forehead. He walked upstairs, grateful that his housemate and housekeeper were not around. He took a long hot shower. When he stepped out, he reached for a towel and stood looking in the mirror. He leaned over the sink and made eye contact with his image. He stared in silence.

Who are you? Do I know you? What is happening to Thomas Riley?

It was nine o'clock in the evening. Father Anthony de Blasio, Director of Public Relations for the Archdiocese and long time friend of Father Riley, picked up the phone.

"Anthony here."

"Anthony, it's Thomas. I'm afraid I'm in a bit of a fix."

"Well now, that's nothing new for you, my friend," replied Father de Blasio lightheartedly. "And what is it you want from me?"

"Come on, Anthony. Don't play with me. This is serious." His voice dropped to a whisper. "I think I'm falling apart."

"Oh, good Jesus, no. Don't tell me. Is it what I'm afraid of, Thomas? You? I can't bear to handle another one of those nightmares. Please, please tell me it isn't."

"Anthony, I may be a damned fool, but nothing that evil. No, nothing like that."

"Whew. Then it'll be easy, whatever it is. Our fallen priests with young boys…I can't stomach dealing with them anymore. Do you want to come over here or would you like me to come to your place?"

"Neither. Meet me at St. Ignatius…half hour?"

"Oh, this *is* serious. See you shortly."

* * *

Father de Blasio, the first to arrive, sat in the nave waiting for his friend. He luxuriated in the scent of incense lingering from a late day funeral mass. The burning smell was always a source of pleasure for the priest, uplifting his own spirit. He reminisced to himself about his glory days with Tom Riley when they were teammates on the Holy Cross football team. *There I was, an offensive lineman always throwing blocks and paving the way for Tommy. He was so quick and fast coming out of our backfield.*

"You look terrible," he bayed as Father Riley entered the church. "Just like a priest in need. I knew you couldn't be one of *them,* but for a moment you gave me a fright."

"I'm sorry, Anthony. I'm so wrapped up in my own self, I completely put aside the burden you're dealing with these days."

The Archbishop, concerned that recent complaints from parishioners about children being sexually abused by priests, had turned to his trusted confidant, Father de Blasio, for help. The Archbishop asked Anthony "to take care of things. Get the mechanisms in place, Father de Blasio, and by all means, keep everything as discreet as possible. These men are an aberration. Arrange for therapy and transfers. And we'll get some of these cases settled."

Father de Blasio had earned the respect of many priests as well as the press because of his even-handed and diplomatic manner. He was concerned that they were just touching the surface of a deep festering problem.

"Your Excellency, these men must be investigated thoroughly and with openness. Their work must be suspended. You must consider defrocking. To do otherwise is an injustice to the victims and the integrity of our faith."

"I'm not ready for the openness you're talking about...not yet, Anthony. Investigations? Certainly. And I've managed to pay compensation to dispose of some of the claims. But not open to the public. We're not ready for that. I suspect some of the accusations are exaggerated. And I'm certain that mental fatigue, overwork must have played into this aberrant behavior."

Father de Blasio acquiesced. He was unreservedly loyal to his Archbishop. This was known by all who knew Anthony.

He was relieved to know that pedophilia was not what tortured his longtime friend and colleague, Tom Riley. After graduation from college Thomas followed Anthony to the seminary. Their friendship was solid.

"Confession box or, as has been my habit of late, my office? Your choice." Father de Blasio gestured to his friend.

Father Riley shook his head. His expression was grim.

"I take it that means 'no' to the box?" Father de Blasio asked.

Father Riley nodded.

'You're slow to speak tonight, Thomas. Come. Come to my den of stories where there just might be a wee bit of libation tucked away for two old pals." He smiled and put his arm around the shoulders of his fellow Jesuit. Thomas appreciated his friend's warmth. He returned the kindness with a smile, albeit forced.

The big man pulled open a desk drawer, removed a bottle of Chivas Regal, held it toward his counterpart with an expression that asked if he could do with a pinch. Thomas Riley, still silent, held up a hand and indicated a small space between his thumb and index finger. They clicked glasses. "To good friends...and to the Lord, Jesus Christ." That brought a chuckle and a question from the sullen Riley. "Do you think He...?"

"Without a doubt," Anthony interrupted. "He couldn't have carried it all off without one of His blessings to His mere mortals...fine whiskey."

The two shared a healthy laugh, looked at each other, and enjoyed that wonderful burn of the first taste.

"Now, Father Thomas Christian Riley, tell old friend Anthony what's going on." With that, Father de Blasio's lower lip protruded, his eyebrows raised. His warm eyes and understanding expression relieved some of Father Riley's tension. He opened up. He spoke in detail of his feelings for Katherine...of the kisses...of Katherine running from the house...his stalking her today. Anthony sucked in a deep breath and exhaled a long anguished sigh.

"Is this your confession? Are you asking Him for forgiveness, absolution?" There was a hue of sarcasm in Anthony's tone.

"Anthony, come on, you've known me for so many years..."

"Oh, I see, we're not priests tonight. Maybe not even Catholics? Just good ole buddies?"

Thomas looked at his friend pleadingly. His expression screamed *Help Me.* He was desperate for understanding and thought he was rightfully clamoring for forgiveness and, to an even greater extent, guidance from Anthony.

"Maybe what you're looking for is approval. You just want your buddy Anthony to say, 'Oh, it's okay. Go right ahead. Believe that you're in love with this sister and do whatever it is you will.' I suspect, Tom, that's what you're after."

Irritated with what he felt was condescension and confrontation, Father Riley exploded: "I thought you, you of all people, might understand."

The room grew still, deflated of all its air. Neither man said a word. Father de Blasio was shaken. *Betrayal. We have both betrayed,* he thought. He stood, turned his back to the confessor.

Father Riley realized too late what he had done. He had delivered a message he wished he could retrieve. He stained the friendship by inadvertently opening an old wound. Was it inadvertent? Was it on some level exactly what he wanted to say? His defensiveness overrode the bond of understanding between these two men. He felt the shame of deception and betrayal.

Father de Blasio turned and faced him, a peaceful look on his face. Anthony's head bobbed up and down as though in agreement with the blow delivered by Thomas. He broke the silence, raising his large open hand.

"You're quite right," Anthony said. "I'm a hypocrite and I'm afraid…afraid of what I've done in the past. We could launch into the Scriptures, couldn't we? Pretend that we are finding all kinds of comfort in admitting our sins."

"Anthony, please, I had no right…"

"No, no, Tommy, my boy. You're perfectly correct. Who am I to judge? I have cavorted with the devil. I pray for His forgiveness every day. And I lashed out at you with sarcasm. You had every right to defend yourself, to remind me that I am a mortal."

He poured another drink, looked at Father Riley, tilted his head offering to pour for his friend as well. Father Riley, wounded by his indiscretion, while at the same time knowing that it was the truth, declined.

This isn't about being right or wrong. I violated Anthony's trust in me.

Feeling like Judas, and desperate to soften his betrayal, Thomas offered what he hoped would be solace.

"But this is different, Anthony. This is…"

Father de Blasio, his expression grim, interrupted: "Uh, uh. Different, you say, because we fornicated with women rather than destroy little boys? That's how I've always rationalized it to myself when I listen to these disgusting priests. And I have the audacity to console myself with their misery…each of them drenched in denial." He added sarcastically, "I only destroyed the life of a vulnerable recently widowed woman, not the life of a child."

"It *is* different, Anthony. Oh, Anthony, I'm so deeply sorry I implied…"

"Implied? No implication. You said what you had a right to say. I'm only grateful that I didn't go further and insult you with some self-righteous sermonizing."

Father de Blasio repressed tears. "You know, Tom, one of the only differences between me and them?"

Tom raised his eyebrows expectantly.

"I ask forgiveness every day for Lillian; that she forgive herself; that she know in her heart that she was a victim…my victim. These pedophiles, these sordid men who have damaged children irreparably…and I'm telling you, Tom, one day this will all come out. These priests are twisted, Tom. Not one of them speaks of the need to help those whom they have violated. Most deny the complaints and the parishioners are afraid to put their children's word against *men of God*. The pedophiles…fellow priests, Tom…should be consumed with shame and deceit. But are they really any worse than someone like me? Am I nothing but a hypocrite? Have I not deceived Our Lord Jesus Christ?"

"Anthony, you're such a good and caring man."

"I once thought so. But, Tom, haven't you and I exploited our victims just as they did? I am party to keeping all of this pedophilia criminality hidden. And we're just seeing the tip of the iceberg. And in a different time I overwhelmed a lovely woman who put her trust and faith in me as a priest."

"Just as I did, Anthony, not too many years ago. And here I am again, wanting so badly to have Katherine."

"Thomas, I took total advantage of my power. But I did believe I loved her. Just as you did when you lost your way, and as you are now. The emptiness of loving someone we can't have. You, my friend, must accept the reality of our vows."

"Anthony, you do understand, don't you, that I haven't…"

"Made love to her? Had intercourse? In your soul you have…a thousand times. You've kissed this innocent one. And I fear you're on your way to knowing her sexually."

Father Riley responded with a closed mouth smile of admission and acknowledgment.

"Anthony, you always paved the way for me. Protected me when we were buddies on the gridiron. That's why I've come to you."

"I know what's coming next, Tom," Anthony said. "I've been there. And I know that you want to know about me and Lillian. What was it like? Was I in love? I'll give you answers." He removed his collar. He felt less a sinner without the collar.

"Were you, Anthony? Were you really in love with her?"

"Who's to know? I know that I love the Lord Jesus Christ. I thought I loved Lillian. But in retrospect, my good friend, it was all about the thrill of carnal knowledge, power and control." He paused. "She was bereft. Her husband of twelve years gone. She was desperate for comfort. I took advantage. I allowed it all to happen. I lied to myself. The excitement of the ease with which it all unfurled was thrilling. Her body, her beautiful needy being was mine." His voice dropped. Silence.

Finally, Anthony spoke again. "Don't do it, Thomas. Dig deep. Don't replicate your prior sin. Stay away from her. Trust me. If you don't abstain, you will suffer. Resist excuses to see her. If you allow yourself to be intoxicated by your power over her you will wind up destroying her and yourself. Don't betray Jesus Christ as I did. If you don't heed my counsel, I promise that you will be, as I am, filled with shame and hypocrisy. You will invite a life of unbearable suffering." His words, his tone, were compelling.

Father Riley clutched his crucifix. "I hear you, Anthony. Every day we must repent. We must be grateful for our service to Him. I know that in my heart He has forgiven you. I shall always seek His forgiveness. Thank you, good friend, for reminding me who I am and what I am meant to be. I am ashamed."

"Thank you, Thomas. Don't ever allow yourself to suffer once again the pain of betrayal. Betrayal and deceitfulness and shame."

The two Jesuits stood and grasped one another's hands. They walked out into the night. They parted.

He's my friend, my dear friend, but what about my obligation, my devotion to His Excellency? Father di Blasio thought.

How fortunate I am to have such a dear and caring friend, Thomas Riley mused as he made his way home. He swallowed the cool summer night air. *Can I do this? Do I have the strength?*

When he entered, his phone rang. It was eleven forty-five.

He lifted the receiver. "Father Riley, this is Katherine."

CHAPTER TWELVE
KATHERINE

"Father Riley, this is Katherine."

The priest smiled. *She needs me.* The power was exhilarating. But he knew that he had an obligation to resist. He had promised Father de Blasio. Hadn't he? But hearing her voice stirred an intoxicating desire.

"Father Riley? Are you there? This is you, isn't it?"

"Yes," he finally answered. "How can I help you?" And then added with a superior note, as if to drive away his craving: "This is a very late hour. I take it this must be a matter of urgency."

The priest leaned back. *I'm playing with her head. Is this not a greater sin? And I know that I must exercise restraint...I must heed Anthony's advice. I must not encourage her. But how I crave her, her youth, her innocence.*

"I'm so sorry. I'm so sorry," she repeated. "Forgive me." And with that, Sister Katherine hung up.

He was stunned. But what else could she do? The dial tone lingered. He stared at the handset. In the recesses of his being, he felt that repetitive, gnawing sense of abandonment.

"Oh, no! Don't hang up. Don't leave me," he said aloud.

"Thomas, are you okay?" It was Father Walsh with whom he shared the house. He was upstairs.

"Yes, yes, Pete, I'm...I'm quite all right. Thank you for your concern."

Father Walsh, tying a sash around his crimson robe, scurried down the circular stairway in the elegant Commonwealth Avenue home purchased by the Church and leased to Chestnut Hill College.

"You look pale, Thomas. Are you certain..."

"You're so kind, Pete. My sister. You know how she has a habit of calling late at night after her kids and husband are all tucked in. I'm supposed to be going to her place on the Cape. But…but something's apparently going on with the family."

"Oh, my. I could hear you, Thomas. Your voice sounded stressed."

Thomas reached over to the decanter of Scotch sitting on a silver tray on the nearby bookshelf. *My opiate.*

"Ah, now, that's the calling of the moment," said Pete as Thomas poured two healthy tumblers. "I'll run into the kitchen and get us some ice."

"Perfect," said Thomas. As his friend disappeared, Father Riley held the glass to his nose. For a moment, the peaty aroma served as a distraction. But only for a moment.

"Here we are," said his returning housemate. "Do you really believe our habit of using ice with this fine Scotch detracts from the real taste?"

"Absolutely not. To you, Pete, and your upcoming vacation. Newfoundland? Is that where you told me you're headed, Father Pete, to St. Peter's Church?" He cloaked his inner angst with a chuckle.

They clicked glasses.

"I am…"

The phone rang.

"Excuse me, my friend, it's my sister again. I think she needs some good old brotherly counsel." Thomas winked the thought *I know you understand.*

He lifted the phone from the receiver. Father Pete took a sip of his drink. He stood, staring blankly at Thomas, a soft, gentle, closed-mouth smile.

"I think I'm going to need some privacy with this one." Father Riley then mouthed the words: "Sister…baggage…family."

"Oh, of course." Pete nodded and promptly exited.

"If I don't see you in the morning, have a wonderful time," Thomas called out as he heard his fellow Jesuit's footsteps on the stairway.

He knows better. He's too smart. Well, maybe not. Good ole Pete can be very naïve.

He felt a surge of power. "Yes," he voiced into the phone.

"Father, forgive me," Katherine started.

You're asking me to forgive you? To forgive you for what? For my indiscretion? For your being so beautiful? For coming into my life?

"What is it, Katherine? What do you want of me?"

Confused, hurt, she stammered: "I cannot sleep, Father. I haven't slept for days. I thought maybe…" Her voice dropped. He could hear the sobbing.

It's not my mother…it's not my mother. The images of his liquor-saturated father, swinging his only hand, large and scarred, across his mother's face, and then storming out of the tiny Brooklyn apartment, his mother slumped in the chair, sobbing quietly into the hands covering her worn face. The young boy couldn't bear her torment. He struggled with what he saw as his responsibility, and would always go to comfort her. He wasn't aware then, but as the scene repeated itself in various permutations over the years, he resented his duty to his mother. He loathed his father, but in some pathological way, admired the man's power over his wife. But his mother, *Mommy,* needy as she might be, was the only constant in his life. His anchor. And then, weeks after his father's last exit, she jumped from the platform as a Manhattan-bound train was arriving. He was alone. Abandoned. Then the Church stepped into his life.

Thomas slumped into the oversized leather chair next to the phone table. He felt his hand, manipulated by some other force, slip below the waist of his trousers. There was only one thing that mattered now. He must have her.

He shut his eyes in an attempt to avoid the bronze crucifix hanging on the opposite wall.

"Oh, Sister, I feel terrible for you." He cast aside his earlier businesslike tone, his voice now intentionally seductive.

Katherine was relieved at what she felt was compassion. *He does care.*

"Thank you, Father. I can't tell you…"

"You are a special person, Sister. I'm afraid I did a terrible injustice. Would you like to come here? Talking will do us both a world of good."

"Thank you, Father. I…I would like to come over…just as I used to. Your counsel is always so helpful."

"Then it's settled. Come for lunch tomorrow. Does one o'clock suit you?"

"I look forward to it," she said.

"Now, perhaps, we can both sleep. Goodnight, Sister Katherine." He placed the phone on its receiver.

CHAPTER THIRTEEN
KATHERINE

It was the beginning of a new era for nuns and sisters. Since the late fifties many of these women acted upon their growing impatience with the lives of seclusion that the Catholic Church had imposed upon them. They were leaving their religious communities and opting for lives in the lay world.

Bishops of multiple archdioceses concurred with the new spirit of the Second Vatican Council. Nuns and sisters had to be released from the rigidity that had been imposed upon them. Failure to recognize this would result in thousands more abandoning their service to the Church.

And so Sister Katherine, along with her peers, were permitted to live in their own homes, choose whether or not to wear a habit or secular clothing, and drive their own cars.

* * *

Katherine stared into the mirror, nervously adjusting her blouse. *Leave the top button open? To say that I'm frightened is a vast understatement. I'm torn. I can taste him. Jesus, dear Jesus, protect me from my weakness. Oh, dear God, save me from myself. Do not let me cheapen my love for you…my commitment to all that is good. Allow me to summon my strength so that my loyalty remains with all that you have taught me…with all that is good.*

* * *

Father Riley busied himself in the kitchen, preparing sandwiches. He carefully selected a bottle of wine.

Ah, yes. This Sauvignon Blanc will be perfect. Simple, crisp.

Do you know what you're doing, Thomas? he asked himself. *I want her. She's so charming, sweet…young…and very beautiful.*

But it's wrong. I've promised...Him...myself...my good friend, Anthony. We'll just talk...yes, just exchange thoughts about her upcoming school year. Yes, that's what it will be...just normal conversation.

The priest went into the dining room and, as though he had done it multiple times in the past, set the table, including purple and blue hydrangeas he clipped from the back of the house.

Music? Yes. Dvořák, Symphony *No. 9. It's appropriate,* he tried to convince himself. *Nothing wrong about having some lovely music. It will enrich the afternoon. I so long to kiss her...just once. That's dishonest...just once. Face it, Thomas, you want to make love...to own her. Stop. Now. Stop.*

He kept glancing out the front windows. It was pouring. Then he saw her car pull to the curb at the foot of the stairs that climbed the knoll toward the front door. He waited. The car door had not yet opened. He peered but it was difficult to see through the moisture that had formed on the car windows.

Katherine leaned forward against the steering wheel. *This is fine. A student in search of wisdom from her mentor. Am I deceiving myself? I know that I need and want to see him. I know he'll be able to refrain, to keep his distance. I trust him.*

The car door swung open, and Father Riley watched as Sister Katherine opened an umbrella and scurried up the stairs.

"There you are," he said as she reached the landing outside the front door. "Come in...please."

He extended his arms to help remove her wet jacket. She watched as he opened the coat closet, brushed some coats aside and slipped her jacket onto a hanger. She stared at the shock of black and graying hair that fell into a looping curl over his forehead. Father Riley paused, looking into Katherine's eyes, then extended his hand to take her umbrella.

"You're very brave to come out in such weather," he said.

She watched as he shook the wet from her umbrella, opened it and set it in the foyer.

He's a beautiful man. So regal and...caring. Yes, he's a caring man. I have such faith in him. He has taught me so much. That lovely mouth. Did those lips take mine? Was it real? His words...were they real? Katherine, stop this...now. This is blasphemous. I'm a contradiction.

She needed to say something. "It's lovely not being in our clerical clothing." *I sound like a schoolgirl.*

"Summertime," he responded. "Holiday time. A good time to be casual. To relax." He closed the vestibule door. "Your umbrella will be dry by the time you leave."

Why does that frighten me, his closing that door? I should leave. I had the courage and good sense to run out of here last week...that shocking day. Why am I standing here? I must go, right now. There is seduction in the air. I have the power to stop it.

Katherine leaned slightly toward the closet door.

"Father Riley," she started, "I think..." *What I want to say is I'm broken and that I must get to that door...now. But I say nothing else. He knows. I see it in his eyes. Just my quick glance captures his knowing look. It's a look of seduction and love and invitation. It's a look of frightening power, yet there is also softness, a kindness that I see. Or am I deceiving myself? Is there really love...love for me...in that beautiful face? Am I a fool ready to succumb? Will I destroy all that is good that Jesus has taught me?*

Silence, except for the sound of the driving summer downpour against the side of the house.

"You started to say something, good sister." His voice was calm and authoritative as he turned on the music.

"I, I...I'd forgotten what a lovely place this is. So conducive to the work you do, Father Riley." *I imagine myself running down the front steps just as I did before. I had the courage and good sense to do it then. Why not now?*

The priest stood just a few feet in front of her, his six-foot frame a mountain of temptation. He deliberately did not block the path between Katherine and the front door.

She wondered: *A calculated gesture? He's positioned himself in such a manner that there would be nothing to prevent me from leaving.*

As though he read her mind, Father Riley gestured slightly, but resolutely, toward the closet, miming that he would oblige and get her jacket so that she could leave.

Is he playing with my head? He knows. He knows that the Church has empowered him, but more importantly that I, at this very moment, have empowered him. Do I want him to make it impossible for me to escape? Escape? Is that what I'm doing to myself? Making myself his prisoner? He's clever... so compelling.

"Come, come in, Sister Katherine." The priest gestured toward the dining room. "I've made us a wonderful picnic lunch." He laughed. His smile brought crinkles around his eyes and mouth. *Such an endearing and charming part of his too good looks,* she thought.

Katherine had never been in this room before. Her previous mentoring visits always were limited to his study. She admired the mahogany wainscoting. There were two large arched windows extending from the ceiling to a few feet above the parquet floor. Eight high-back chairs surrounded the mahogany dining table. The bronze crucifix hung by itself upon one of the end walls. She instinctively knelt: *"May Christ's words be on my mind, on my lips, and in my heart. Protect me from betrayal."*

"Please, Sister Katherine, sit." She watched as he started toward her chair. He stopped short of pulling it out from the table.

"I'll just duck into the kitchen and get our sandwiches," he said.

"Does your housekeeper have the weekend off?" Katherine asked.

"Yes, indeed. She has left me to fend for myself. Father Walsh has gone off as well."

She was excited and nervous and numb about the fact that they were alone.

In a minute, he brought in a platter of sandwiches cut into quarters.

"Compliments of Father Thomas Riley. And a lovely bottle of wine. May I pour?" His voice was unusually rich, its tone friendly and warm...and ominous. He sat to her right at the head of the table.

The conversation was mundane, pretense about Katherine's upcoming school year. They even spoke of the weather, and then some gossip about faculty members retiring from the college.

A second glass of wine. And then a third. Katherine felt herself crossing over, leaving behind all that she valued.

"Sister," he broke an awkward still. "I'm so pleased that you called. May I...may I be brutally candid or must we pretend?" Katherine could feel her face blush.

"Sister Katherine," he leaned forward, extending his hand toward her. "I beg your forgiveness." His eyes welled. So did Katherine's. Relief. *It* was out there. They moved from the banal.

"I'm a fool," he said. "And a hypocrite. I had no right."

She felt the need for him...and for Him to save her from that need.

"Oh, no, Father..." She stopped. She was about to apologize. The habit of her gender, of her subordinate position in the Church. She wanted to assure him that it was not she who should forgive; that it is the Lord our God from whom he must seek forgiveness. But instead she remained silent, shaking her head from side to side, placing her hand reassuringly on his. Touching.

Words of self-pity flowed from his mouth. She didn't remember exactly what they were until "...but I confess to you, Katherine, that when I said I love you..."

Loving her. To be loved by this man. *So worldly, knowledgeable and sophisticated,* she thought. Much then became an exquisite blur. Tender, yet provocative. Her head was spinning. She felt an excitement she had never before allowed herself to feel. He spoke of love. They each stood. He pulled her toward him and took her into his arms. She thrilled at his touch and felt compelled to give of herself, recklessly abandoning her vows and all that had been so precious to her. His being was something she could not resist.

"We will leave the Church," he said. "We will have a life together."

Father Riley took Sister Katherine's hand, nodded reassuringly and led her up the stairway and into his bedroom.

"Father Riley...I'm frightened, but I so trust you."

"I adore you, my Katherine. Since the very moment weeks ago when you first walked into this house."

They embraced and then Father Riley eased Katherine onto the bed.

"Father Riley..."

He pressed a forefinger against her lips. "It's Thomas, dear Katherine. I pledge my love to you. I shall resign...we shall resign. I want you more than anything in the world. I cherish your goodness. I shall forever take care of you. We shall have a life of our own, the two of us...together. It's okay. We have each served faithfully. It's our time now."

Katherine was enraptured and yet terrified. *Leave the Church? Resign? A life together? Is that what he said? Did I really hear that? He loves me. Oh, I so want to be loved...by Thomas.*

"No fear, dear Katherine. You...we...have every right."

As Katherine started to lift herself from the bed, Father Riley gently turned her face toward his. He cupped her chin in his hand, leaned forward and stopped short of kissing her.

"I understand," he said. "Perhaps this is too soon."

She shook her head slowly from side to side. "I so want to be with you, Thomas. A life together…"

"Yes, dear Katherine. A beautiful life together."

"But Father, we cannot sin and remain faithful followers of the Lord. I cannot do this. I must leave. Forgive me."

Father Riley was possessed by the need to possess.

"My dear Katherine, recall the Apostle John: 'If we confess our sins, He is faithful and just to forgive us our sins and to cleanse us from all unrighteousness.'"

As he removed her clothing, he leaned over and kissed her.

"This moment, my Katherine, shall be my covenant of trust." Feeling ecstatic, intoxicated by his words, she succumbed.

CHAPTER FOURTEEN
MIKE

"Hey, Mike." It was Bobby Shapiro, a young lawyer breaking into the litigation business. They were standing in the Golden Dome Coffee Shop situated between the State House and rear of the building that housed the Suffolk County Probate and Family Court. The aroma of freshly made cinnamon buns transformed this hangout for statehouse politicians and trial lawyers into a coffee break oasis. The old cliché: *if walls could talk,* best sellers would be hatched in this colorful enclave of wheeling, dealing, and gossip. Mike brushed a napkin across his mouth, lowered his coffee mug to the counter.

"How're you doing, Bobby?"

"I'm getting there. Still cutting my teeth, I guess."

Mike chuckled. "You'll be fine. Just watch out for the snakes."

"So, Mike, this sounds a little dumb, but are you okay? That shooting and all…"

"I'm doing just fine. Thanks for asking, Bobby."

"I heard that the shooter was some ex-cop?"

"Yup. Killed two innocent people. Then sometime after running from the courthouse a couple of people from that den of iniquity on Cambridge Street recognized him. Ducked into an alley and shot himself. I don't know much more than that," Mike said. He did not verbalize the terror he felt about the possibility that he and his client may well have been the targets.

Mike raised his cup to his lips, looked at the woman on the other side of the counter. "You know, Fran, you make the best damned coffee in the city, but you need to do something with those cinnamon buns."

"Now Attorney Lyons, you wouldn't be knocking Fran's buns, would you now?"

Mike nearly choked. "Fran, the Lord would ship me directly to hell if she knew what I was thinking about your buns."

"Dirty man," she said, wiping a cloth across the counter. "And I didn't miss that…makin' the Lord a dame just to curry favor with Fran." She shrugged a shoulder, tossed her head of long red hair. "What'd you think about that Kuscsik lady from up in New York State winnin' the women's division in that Marathon yesterday?"

"Now that was big. First time the ladies were finally officially acknowledged."

"I'll check out back and see if I've got some of those cinnamon *coffee cakes*." They exchanged winks.

"Speaking of snakes, Mike, what can you tell me about Judge Murphy?" young Shapiro asked.

"Colleen? Never, ever a snake. You got a case before her? She's the best. Knows her stuff. A real mensch. She'll call whatever you got as she sees it, fair and square. One of the best appointments the Governor has made," Mike replied.

"Thanks, Mike. That's encouraging. Nice to hear." Bobby picked up his briefcase as if to leave and then set it down. He leaned in toward Mike.

"I just took in a real heavy personal injury case. Seventeen-year-old kid. A gymnastics catastrophe. He's now a quad. Probably over my head. Any interest in collaborating?"

"Quad as in quadriplegic?" Mike asked.

The young lawyer nodded. "Really bad. His life's destroyed. Whole family's in a state of shock."

"Absolutely, I'm interested. Thanks for your confidence, Bobby. Clients are smart to have hired you. Give me a call and we'll set something up. You're doing the right thing to collaborate with someone. Catastrophic cases like this require mountains of work and sizable funds to finance it. I have a substantial line of credit and if we need to tap into it, that's what we'll do. Experts alone can cost a bloody fortune."

It's the way it happens…cases…timing. A major case that would involve a ton of work, large responsibility to the youngster and his family, considerable outlay of money, and potentially a substantial fee at the end of the case. It's a credit to a young lawyer who recognizes that such a matter requires an experienced litigator.

"Great," said Bobby. He retrieved his briefcase and headed outside.

"Bobby," Mike shouted.

The young lawyer turned around.

"Be direct. Don't waste words. Look Judge Murphy in the eye. Tell your client to dress down. Nothing fancy. A plain suit, fresh shirt and tie or blouse. You have the guy or the wife?"

"The wife." Bobby appreciated the advice he was getting.

"No upscale jewelry. Modest earrings. Who's on the other side?"

Bobby answered as he walked back toward Mike: "Some guy by the name of Albright. Mitch Albright."

"Albright! If you shake hands, count your fingers." Mike shook his head.

The young lawyer's color paled.

"A snake? I thought it was the judges I had to worry about," Bobby said.

A couple of nearby veteran courtroom lawyers glanced over. "Clue the rookie in," one of them chuckled.

"Bobby, in this business, you gotta worry about everything, everyone. But not this judge. Just let Albright mouth off. He likes to put on a show for his clients…thinks it justifies his outrageous fees. He can get real dramatic, particularly if your lady has had some extracurricular activity. Has she?"

"No. Not this lady."

"Don't be so certain. The best of us can get fooled very easily. In any event just let Albright spew his venom. He usually winds up choking on it. Colleen tangled with him more than once when she was practicing. Don't get down in the gutter with him. Play it cool. The judge will let him rattle for a few minutes, then she'll shut him up, remind him where he is. You just stand tall and look like a priest. Get me?"

"Will a rabbi do?" Shapiro laughed nervously. "Thank you, sir. I owe you."

"Forget that 'sir' business. It's always Mike. Your quad case is major. Call me around five. I'd like to arrange to meet your clients with you as soon as possible. Tonight if it's doable with them. Gotta move quickly."

"Will do. I'll set something up. Thanks again, Mike."

* * *

Mike looked into the mirror behind the counter. He smiled, remembering some of the cases he'd had with Colleen Murphy. She was one of the ablest matrimonial lawyers with whom he had ever dealt. Smart, lots of *joie de vivre*. They had locked horns but never a harsh word between them. In fact, when Colleen's hubby decided to play house with a court officer twenty years his junior, and Colleen wanted, as she put it, "to kick his ass out of my bed forever," it was Mike to whom she turned for representation. As a fellow lawyer he refused to charge her. Not long after she was divorced Colleen was appointed to the bench. Mike's was the first invitation for the swearing-in ceremony.

With Colleen on the brain, Mike walked back to his Court Street office. It was three thirty and an unusually warm April afternoon. He fantasized about the affair with Colleen that had never happened.

Jane greeted him with some pink message slips. He stopped cold when he looked at the first. He raised his eyebrows, stared down at his longtime secretary friend.

"I was just thinking about her," Mike said waving the message slip.

"Mike," she said. "It's important. She's off the bench and would like you to call her pronto." Jane shrugged, then offered: "Something to do with the Webb matter?"

"Webb? Judge Murphy has nothing to do with that case." Mike cocked his head to the side. The Webb case was months away from its November trial date. *Does Jane know something?* "What makes you think it's got anything to do with that bag of worms?"

"You," she replied. "A couple of weeks ago you said, 'They're all talking about it.' I asked 'about what?' You said, 'The f---ing Webb matter.' You said 'all the judges are crowing about how you got hammered by that bitch...meaning either our client or the woman representing the husband, or both.' You said that. Those are your words. So all I'm saying..."

"I get it, but you know sometimes I exaggerate when I get uptight." Mike waved his hand in his long trusted friend's face and headed into his office.

"You want me to get her on the phone?" Jane asked.

"No need. I haven't forgotten how to dial a phone."

"Tony! Hi. Mike here. I got a message your boss called. She keeping you busy these days?"

"Torture, Mike, pure torture. Our infamous jurist is anxious to talk with you. Maybe something to do with that Webb doozy...I don't know. Here comes her whip now. Ouch! She actually kicked me. Hold on." Colleen Murphy took her judicial responsibilities seriously, but she had a playful side.

"Mike, How are you?"

"Just fine, Your Honor. And you. Enjoying beating up on everyone?"

"Am I ever."

"So, to what do I owe the honor of being called by Her Honor?" Mike continued the friendly jousting.

"I'll make it brief. I apologize for such short notice, but is there any way you could stop by my apartment this evening, possibly around seven? Andrea Schwartz and Cindy Jones will be there. I want to discuss an article I'm doing for the Bar Journal. An hour is about all I'll need."

"Flattered to be asked to help. I'll swing by at seven. It'll be nice to see you and get caught up with Andrea and Cindy. Is Cindy still running around with that Manchester jerk? Any particular issue you're struggling with?"

"No gossip, Counsel. I want to get your thoughts about the proposed revisions regarding guardian ad litem reports and testimony. I'm including a section about those changes."

"I hope it includes the right to cross-examine the GAL."

"Absolutely. They need to be accountable and subject to truth-probing. I know that's near and dear to your heart. Thanks for your help, Mike. Is Scotch still the drink of the day?"

"Nothing fancy, Your Honor. A cold beer would be perfect. See you at seven. I hope I can be of help."

* * *

Mike stepped into his office reception area. "Nothing to do with Webb, smartass," he said playfully. "She wants to discuss an article she's writing. Needs some sage advice."

Jane smiled, a knowing look on her face. "You haven't a clue, have you?"

"What are you talking about?" Mike responded with the grin of one waiting to be flattered.

"You know damn well she had it big for you when you were handling her divorce."

"Jane, she was a vulnerable, wounded pussycat. Her son-of-a-bitching husband betrayed her. She was looking for approval, warmth, comfort wherever it might come from. Nothing more than pure friendship between us."

"Keep it that way," Jane responded, turning her attention back to her IBM Selectric.

"What do you mean, 'keep it that way?' For your information, Ms. Know-It-All, there'll be two other lawyers there *and* there just happens to be a woman named Ali to whom I have pledged my loyalty."

"I certainly hope so. But you love to flirt," Jane responded.

"Enough!"

She crouched over her typewriter, adjusting the roller.

* * *

After making telephone arrangements with Attorney Shapiro to meet with the family of the young quadriplegic, Mike wound his way onto Mount Vernon Street, a stretch of Beacon Hill he enjoyed. Henry James called it "the most proper street in Boston." Mike always admired the former stables that had long since been converted into homes, and the magnificent mansions on the opposite side, one of which was used as a location in the Steve McQueen, Faye Dunaway thriller, *The Thomas Crown Affair*, just four years ago in 1968. Louisburg Square was Mike's favorite detour. And he was mindful that the Webb home was among the exclusive townhouses there. Sometimes he found himself tipping his head to the statue of Columbus presiding over Boston's only private park, surrounded by a wrought-iron fence. He admired the Federal style row houses lining both sides of the historic and pricey cobblestoned square. Mike thought about the many famous Americans who once lived here, including Louisa May Alcott and the architect, Charles Bullfinch. *I've got to take the kids for a tour here one of these days. It'll be a great Sunday activity. Let them learn something about this city.*

His eye caught an odd sight. Leaning against the wrought-iron fence was a bedraggled looking woman peering at the statue of Columbus. Her faded fuchsia pants were baggy and stained. Her head was covered in part with a knit ski cap. She had a black braided ponytail and was wearing an oversized Boston Celtics jacket that had seen better days. He noticed that she held a cigarette and a container of Dunkin' Donuts coffee. And curiously, she had a camera draped around her neck. Mike tried not to stare but was nevertheless transfixed as he watched her shift feet, crush the cigarette beneath one of her sneakers, then aim her camera toward Columbus.

Wouldn't expect a camera in the hands of a woman like this. Is she shooting just the statue or is she really after the mansion in the background?

Within moments, two strapping men wearing blue suits and ties descended upon the woman. Mike did not see them come out of any of the homes. They just suddenly appeared like Navy SEALS surfacing from the cover of a nighttime body of water.

Mike moved closer as the men quickly approached the unkempt woman.

"Madam," one said. "Loitering is not permitted in this area."

"Neither is smoking," the other added.

Their tones were officious.

Mike observed one of the men reaching for the woman's arm and, he thought, the camera. She pulled away and clutched her camera. In the process she spilled some of her coffee on the shoes of one of them.

Mike saw her face for the first time as she looked up apologetically at the man whose shiny black shoes were now doused with coffee. *I feel so badly for her…being bullied…probably in her late forties…tough to say exactly. She's been through the "wars." Life's not been kind to this woman.*

"I'm sorry," she said, her low and hoarse voice barely audible. "I din't know I was doin'…what was that word you said? Somethin' like 'lawyering?'"

"Loitering, madam. Want me to spell it for you?"

Sarcastic prick. Look at them. Getting it off on a vulnerable lady. Or is she all that vulnerable? Something about her…

"Time to leave, sweetheart. We don't want any trouble, do we now?"

"I ain't your sweetheart," she hollered.

They each grabbed an arm. As Mike felt the heat rise within him he noticed a man checking out the scene from behind a partially opened curtain on an upper floor of the row house toward which the woman's camera had been directed. *He's the one who probably called these animals to chase this woman. Wait a minute, that's number fourteen...the Webb address. Is that him...Brooks Webb? Was she taking photos of him...of the front of their building? Of Webb? I wonder what that's all about?*

The woman tried to pull away from their grip. She was frightened. "I din't do nothin'. I'm just lookin' at Columbus here. I thought this was a free country."

Mike noticed her protecting her camera. And he could see that, surprisingly, it was not an inexpensive model.

"You're quite right. It is a free country," Mike barked, making his way toward the three of them. "You guys police officers?" Mike knew damned well they were nothing more than private security. "If you are, I want to see your IDs. If not, take your hands off her before I have the two of you booked for assault and you find your asses on the wrong end of a civil rights violation complaint, to say nothing of a civil suit which I personally will file tomorrow morning in the United States Federal Court." *Did I just say all of that? Mikey, boy, here you go again. Leave this thing alone. Leave it alone? It's a blatant violation of that woman's rights. Goddammit, what'd I become a lawyer for?*

Amazingly, the men did as instructed, their mouths open with the surprise of it all.

"Whoever you are, mister, this is a private park," one of them said threateningly.

"Brilliant," Mike responded. "But tell me, Mr. Security Man, just what part of what code gives you the right to manhandle this citizen? You telling me there's a code that says when there's a private park and a citizen is looking at a statue in that private park, that private security men have the right to invade *her* privacy? Touch, let alone grab, a citizen, or even a non-citizen, while she gazes harmlessly upon a replica of the man who discovered this country and takes a photo? Give me a fucking break. I'll tell you what code. None." The two suits glared.

"And who the hell are you? Some jerk-off lawyer?" One of them barked.

"Easy with that tone." Mike lowered his briefcase and pointed a finger at the one who spoke. "Trust me, it'll get your rear-end fired. You think these blue bloods want a front page lawsuit?" He made a sweeping gesture toward the houses. "You think they're going to rush to your defense? They'll toss you and the outfit you work for and hire another quicker than you can say 'but please…' Yup, that's what I am…one smart lawyer. I'm *her* lawyer." He handed each of them his card.

"Her lawyer? Since when?" the taller of the two challenged.

"Since right now. Any other questions?" Mike asked.

The woman had comfortably distanced herself and was headed toward Mount Vernon Street.

"Nice work, big boys. You scared the crap out of this woman." Mike gestured in her direction. He raised his voice so that she could hear him. "I can't wait to see your smirking faces before a judge." He stared at their name badges, giving the impression that he was memorizing them. He called after the woman. The men disappeared just as mysteriously as they had come on the scene.

"I'm leavin', I'm leavin'," the woman hollered.

"You don't have to leave, ma'am," Mike shouted as he jogged toward her. "I'm your lawyer. I'm going to help you."

"I don't need no lawyer. But you sure as hell done a good job scarin' 'em off. That is Columbus, ain't it?"

"Yes, it is." Mike extended a hand. "Mike Lyons."

The woman glanced at him suspiciously, then took his hand.

"And you are?" Mike asked.

"Pocahontas."

Mike joined her in laughter.

"Really? Is that what they call you...Pocahontas?"

Her expression changed. Her eyes filled with moisture, the bags beneath them prominent, her thin-lipped mouth curled downward. She saw him notice the tracks on her arm.

"I'll see ya, Mr. L...What'd you say your name was?"

"Mike. Mike Lyons. If you ever need a lawyer, I'm there for you. No fee."

He handed her a card.

"Got five bucks for a photographer?" She bent her head, looked straight down at the cobblestones.

"I'll raise the ante to ten if I get a real name," said Mike, trying unsuccessfully to get a clear look at her face which was now mostly covered by her thick black hair. At some point she had undone her ponytail.

"Hoda."

"Hoda, nice to meet you," Mike said as he pulled his wallet from his jacket pocket. He removed two ten dollar bills.

"Hoda," he said, extending the money toward her.

She raised her head and peered into Mike's eyes. She swung aside the hair that had been covering her face. Her eyes were bright and there was something that struck Mike as though this woman knew him. She put out a hand. Mike placed the bills into it.

"I'll be seein' ya," she said.

He felt a lump rise in his throat. "Take care, Miss Hoda. I hope I do see you again sometime. And remember, if you ever need a lawyer..."

She stopped, turned around and said: "Maybe it's me you'll be needin'. Never know, do we?"

"You were photographing more than our boy Columbus, weren't you?"

She raised an arm, offered a single wave, and then scurried down Mount Vernon Street.

As Mike made his way toward Colleen Murphy's apartment, the disheveled looking woman's last words resonated: *Maybe it's me you'll be needing.* And that led him to thoughts about his dad, who often spoke about the need to help the less fortunate and who, more than once, recited James Garfield: *I never met a ragged boy in the street that I may owe him a salute, for I know not what possibilities may be buttoned up under his coat.*

CHAPTER FIFTEEN
MIKE

Mike paused before ascending the steps leading up to Nineteen West Cedar Street. It had been awhile since he and Ali uncorked a bottle of champagne with Colleen Murphy to celebrate her new Beacon Hill apartment. Colleen had invited Mike and Ali for dinner, not only to see her new apartment, but also to express her appreciation to Mike for having represented her so well in connection with her divorce. The governor appointed Colleen as Justice to the Probate and Family Court bench just a few months after that get-together.

Mike's thoughts took him back to that night after he and Ali got home. Their marriage had been so strong then. Not anymore. Something evaporated. Mike wanted it back. He remembered their playfulness as they got ready for bed that night.

"She has a thing for you, you know," Ali said.

Mike smiled. Ali just might be a little jealous. "You're crazy," he replied as he stepped out of the bathroom, toothbrush in hand. Flattered, he added, "You think?"

"Come on, big boy," Ali said, "you can act out all your fantasies right in this very comfy bed."

He loved the playfulness. But not long after, somehow, things changed. Mystifyingly, the magic of their strong connection started slipping away. *Something has changed,* he thought to himself. *Ali…she's grown so distant.*

Mike's thoughts floated to the normal home front evening routine. Bungling his way while trying to help the kids with math homework. He thought more about the routine, same most every night. After the kids, he does dinner cleanup while Ali catches up with *The New York Times* and paperwork for her next day. *We don't talk about it. I just feel it slipping away.*

* * *

"Attorney Michael Lyons, you sir, are late for court." It was the Honorable Colleen Murphy swinging open her blue colonial front door. A handsome woman in her mid-forties, she maintained a trim and shapely figure.

"Well, how do you like it?" She stood with her hands on her hips, her perfect posture emphasizing an enviable bust line. Dark jeans and a short-sleeved V-neck white cotton T-shirt added to her alluring persona.

"Great. You look great," Mike said. He was still standing on the first step.

"Not *me*, counselor…my *door*…my new blue door. Colonial blue. You like?"

"Oh, of course. It's fabulous."

"And check out that knocker. I bought it from Jake Handy's uncle. Authentic circa 1890."

Oh, good lord, tell me she didn't say "knocker." Lyons, grow the hell up.

"Jake Handy!" Mike exploded. "That three-dollar bill! What a sad excuse for a lawyer. The bar examiners were asleep at the switch when they admitted that fraud. *He* belongs in the antiques business. Such a phony. Fancy Newbury Street address. Closed Wednesdays? What a bullshitter."

"You're such a jerk, Lyons. You're jealous because he's better looking than you." With that, she reached out and cupped her hand on Mike's cheek. "And I didn't buy this knocker from *him*. I bought it from his uncle, a perfectly 'legit' guy. Anyone on the Hill will tell you that. The man is a sweetheart. Told me how lucky I was. He had just purchased it from the estate of some old-line Revolutionary War family."

Mike shook his head. "The Governor's Council should require all nominees for the bench to take a naivete test. You are unbelievable…'just purchased it from some Revolutionary War family.' And I suppose he told you that he had ten other people begging to buy it."

"You're such a cynic. You've never even met the man. Enough." She beckoned him up the front steps. "Come on in. The others are already here."

"Remind me to tell you about this homeless woman I met on my way. I think she was bringing some authentic Beacon Hill trash trinkets to your antiques guru."

"You made that up. And I will remind you." The judge planted a playful elbow into Mike's side as she ushered him into the dining room.

Greetings were exchanged. Mike apologized for being late and briefly referenced his experience with this "interesting down and out woman with a pretty fancy camera." Andrea offered a cheek and Mike dutifully planted a soft kiss. Cindy, who never really cottoned to Mike for reasons unknown to him, extended a hand. Judge Murphy took the lead.

"I'm so grateful that the three of you are here. You're generous in giving your time and expertise to help me with my article for the Bar Journal. When it came back from the editor I was distressed about some of her changes. That's why I did a rewrite, which I sent to each of you. So why don't we go around the table. I'll get some cold beers."

Rewrite? Did I get a copy? Shit, I have no idea what I might have done with it. Probably buried in the pile of articles on my desk. I'll say not a word. The shooting just a few months ago did have residuals, one of which was Mike's lagging behind in keeping up with legal publications. Concentration when reading had become an issue.

The discussion was affable, efficient, and productive. If any of them started to digress, the judge was quick to bring them back on point. After a little more than an hour, three lawyers and a judge actually were in harmony about the modifications.

As they were gathering their things to leave, the judge asked if Mike could stay on "for just a moment."

"Again, thank you both so much," she said, turning to Attorneys Schwartz and Jones. "The article will include recognition of your contributions. You've been so helpful." The lawyers stepped outside.

"Our pleasure," said Attorney Schwartz as she reached the sidewalk. "Acknowledgment is hardly necessary, Your Honor."

"You're very gracious…both of you. But I insist. See you soon." The judge paused to admire the spectacular pinks and blues in the early evening sky. Her momentary pleasure quickly gave way to something that was troubling her. *Friendship or ethics?* she asked herself. *Is it unethical to pass on information to a practicing lawyer regarding his case that's in the hands of another judge? What about the ethics of that judge? Is it unethical not to inform a lawyer of a potential conflict of interest on the part of another judge? And what about friendship and an ethical…no, a moral duty that one friend owes another? Listen to your gut,* Colleen said to herself.

"Well," Colleen said to Mike, her back pushing the front door shut. "That went quite well, don't you agree?"

"That's got to be a record. Three lawyers and a judge in one room usually take ten hours to agree upon each other's names. Shows us what can be done when billable hours aren't in play," Mike said.

"What's with you and Cindy?" Colleen asked. She busied herself, straightening the frame of a photo on a side table.

"I haven't a clue. We never locked horns in any matter of any consequence. At least, I can't remember anything. Just bad vibes, I guess. Was that what you wanted to talk about?"

I'm scuffling, Colleen thought to herself. *Get to the point. It's unfair to Mike.*

"Well, she is a cold customer," Colleen said. "But one hell of a good writer. I heard that Hale & Dorr is interested in bringing her over for their appellate work."

Mike couldn't have cared less. He simply nodded.

"No, Mike, that's not at all what I wanted to discuss."

"I'm all ears, Your Honor."

"Sit down, Mike." She hesitated, looking at her watch. "Oh, would you like to call Ali? It's after eight."

"Whoa! Thanks for the reminder. But I'm going to use the little boys room first."

He splashed cold water on his face, stared into the mirror. *Oh, man, I'm all messed up. Even Colleen sees it. What do you mean "even Colleen?" She's as intuitive as they come. Ali's been so cold. Why? Maybe it's my imagination. I really have been wiped out...burning the hours lately. The goddamned Webb case is getting under my skin. And I start trial soon on the Hennessey travesty. Maybe I'm the one who's been remote. That's it. Ali is just reacting to my being "out there." Crap, there's a wall between us. She doesn't open up. She doesn't talk, just the mundane stuff. And what about you, Lyons? Do you talk? Really talk? Has it occurred to you in your self-involved misery to ask her what's going on? All you talk about is your bullshit cases. Are you afraid? I am. Of what? That she'll tell me the truth.* He stopped himself, tossed more cold water on his face.

* * *

Mike stepped into the kitchen and called his wife. He immediately felt the chill in Ali's voice. It raised his anxiety level.

* * *

"Is everything okay?" Colleen asked.

"Everything's fine," he stammered, his voice rising an octave.

The judge cocked her head to the side, her eyes wide, her right hand extended toward her friend.

"You're amazing," he said. "You wrote the book on intuition."

"Just comes with the territory. We women were born with many special attributes. Intuition is one of them. Anyway, angst is written all over your face." She smiled and put a hand on Mike's shoulder. "Anytime you need a good listener you know I'm here for you."

"You're a sweetheart. Thanks Col…judge."

"Mike, we're friends," she said, shaking her head from side to side. "I'm always Colleen to you. You know that. I'll never forget how wonderful and gracious you were in handling my divorce. My brain was numb during those awful months. You were always there for me." She moved a couple of steps away, paused, raised her eyebrows, then jocularly added, "But I'll never forgive you for the you-know-what you gave me in that Freedman case."

"Are you kidding me? Hey, that was six years ago. You and your greedy client got one hell of a deal…took my guy to the cleaner."

They laughed. Then stopped. Silence.

Everything in the room changed. The air, the scent of the lilies, the light, the texture of the walls, the feeling of the space. They stood and looked at each other. The kind of look that said so much: *We're good friends. That's all. Just good friends. There's a connection, but whatever exists now between the two will have to suffice. It happens between friends, casual acquaintances, lovers: "The look." It's always important. Sometimes it's acted upon. Rare? For the most part people simply get on with their lives. Some forget the look. Others suppress it. While others cling to it and wonder.*

"So," Judge Murphy broke the silence. "My unsolicited advice regarding you and Ali?" She paused, waiting for Mike's reaction.

"Go ahead. Let me hear it," he said.

"You've become a workaholic, Michael Lyons. All wrapped up in the stuff of your clients. And you know I know what I'm talking about. For all I know, that's what drove my ex to bed down with a kid. Not a child-child, but she was barely twenty-one." She took a breath. "I know that the trial of your case against the priest and Archdiocese starts soon and that you've got a tough one with the Webb matter. But you've gotta stop. Take some breaths, count to ten. Mike, my friend, you had such a close call with that horrific shooting. Learn from it. Family, Mike. Don't neglect your wonderful wife and kids. They're more important than any damned case."

"You're an angel, Colleen. I hear you. You're absolutely right on." But the reality was that Mike wouldn't deal with the chasm between him and Ali until late fall.

"Let's go into the living room and sit. I've got something I want to share with you," said Colleen.

Mike thought: *Transitions. Life is filled with them. One chapter ends, another begins.*

"Lead the way, Your Honor."

* * *

Mike plunked himself onto a Herman Miller chair, his feet up on its ottoman. He feigned relaxation.

"That was my husband's favorite."

"I remember all too well. I fought like a bastard for you to keep it. And I knew you didn't give a damn about it. You just wanted to stick it to him."

"Yup. And he had it coming," she said.

"I'm all ears," said Mike.

The judge gestured that she was heading to the kitchen. She returned shortly with two beers.

"Well," she started, and then took a taste of beer. "Mike, when you represented me against that miserable son-of-a-bitch excuse for a husband," she swallowed hard, "you went more than the extra mile."

Mike enjoyed the compliment, but put his hands up as if to say, *I was simply doing my job.*

"No, no," Colleen insisted, "I owe you. You saved me. How many times I was ready to fold, to sign anything just to get rid of that cancer and get the divorce over with. But you wouldn't let me. You insisted I hang in until we got the right kind of resolution. You were great. And let's not kid each other. Having a lawyer for a client, and particularly someone like me, is hardly a day at the beach."

"Colleen, you're embarrassing me. I was just doing my job."

"And don't forget, Counselor, you were more than generous." She shook her head, her facial expression earnest and wide-eyed. "As I said, I owe you."

"Your only debt, Your Honor, is our everlasting friendship."

The judge's eyes filled. She took another sip of beer.

Mike spread out his arms. "What's the mystery?"

The judge took a deep breath. "The Webb matter."

I'll be damned. Jane was right.

"And, by the way, Counsel, since we both know that what I'm about to discuss is totally out-of-bounds, this conversation remains between us." She raised her eyebrows, tipping her head, embarrassed that she might be insulting her friend by mentioning the need for confidentiality.

"Other than the smut column in the *Herald*, not a soul," Mike kidded.

"I know that I can count on you to sell me down the Charles. Seriously, your Webb case is already notorious among the probate judges. Swedish bombshell sinks her tentacles into one of the wealthiest families in America. You know that you're up the creek without a paddle as far as Judge Mahoney is concerned. I understand that Mr. Webb testified at the informal hearing that he caught his sweet wife in the sack with a Ritz bar pickup and that's why he tattooed her eye. Mahoney's made up his mind. I appeared enough times before him, Mike, to know that once that stubborn

Irishman makes up his mind there's no changing his thinking," Colleen said.

"Nothing like rushing to judgment. Mahoney didn't even give me a proper chance to cross-examine. I know what you're talking about, Colleen. I'm worried that he's gonna kill me on this case." Mike said.

The judge looked perplexed.

"Do you know anything about my adversary?" he asked Colleen.

Colleen continued. "I understand Sofia Vasquez used to be with the AG's office, handling white collar crimes. She left. Went to BU Law for a Master's in taxation, then joined that white shoe firm, Weeks, Ward & Bigelow. She's been handling some transactional work and, are you ready for this, she's the number one tax advisor for the wills and estate planning section."

Mike shrugged. "Did she do any trial work while she was at the AG's?"

"I'm told she prosecuted a couple of big ones. Didn't make any friends in the AG's office and wasn't particularly liked by the defense bar. Word is she was self-righteous, but very capable in the courtroom. Attorney General liked her work but couldn't stand her personally. Told me the people at the office referred to her as "Ms. One-Way.""

"I feel vindicated," said Mike. "I've had something gnawing at my gut that Mahoney took a quick liking to her. He grabbed onto her client's story within seconds. And, as I said, precluded any cross-examination. Threw my gal out of the family condo pending trial. All my leverage to try to negotiate something went down the toilet. And Colleen, you should have seen that smug look on Vasquez's face."

"Are you ready for the bomb?" the judge asked.

Mike's mouth dropped open. "What've you got?" he asked.

"Just where do you think the Honorable Wilfred Mahoney had his will and estate plan done? You have all of one guess."

Mike jumped up from his chair.

"At Weeks, Ward? At Vasquez's firm?" Mike exploded. "And neither one of them said a word!"

Attorney Lyons' brain cells exploded. *A classic case of conflict of interest. It just takes the appearance of conflict for a judge to be obliged to recuse himself/herself.*

"What a fool that Mahoney is," said Mike. "And that Vasquez...not a word."

Colleen nodded as if to warn that Mike be careful in dealing with such a lawyer. "So now you have something to get Mahoney out of the case," Colleen added.

Mike sat with his mouth open, nodding his head in thanks.

"I'll call Ali," Colleen said, "and let her know that I kept you and that you're on the way."

"Thanks, Colleen. I'll be nice with Wilfred. I'll get him off the case without nailing him. As for that Vasquez..."

"You never heard it from me. Now get home. Leave your briefcase in the office. And let that lawyer stuff go for a couple of days. Enjoy some family time," Colleen said as Mike made his exit.

CHAPTER SIXTEEN
MIKE

Mike felt wary about the Webb matter but nevertheless, when he entered his office reception area, his concerns didn't keep him from admiring the vase of fresh lilies perched on each of two small teakwood end tables. He enjoyed the abundant amount of light pouring in through the large windows behind his secretary's workspace.

"Whoa," said Jane Donnell, "if you don't mind my being blunt, Mike, you look like…"

"I know, I know…I look like shit. Couldn't sleep a goddamn minute last night." Mike lowered his briefcase.

"It's that Webb case, isn't it? Getting under your skin."

"And then some. Do me a favor…"

"Large black coffee?" asked Jane.

"Yes, ma'am…iced. And please don't forget one of those coffee buns."

Jane peered into the petty cash box. Mike picked up his briefcase and headed into his office.

"Oops," she said. "Surprise. The coffers are dry. I don't suppose…never mind, I've got some cash."

"Great," Mike said. "And be sure to get yourself something."

"My, how generous we are today," she playfully responded making her way out.

Mike dialed his phone. "Sean? Is that you? Your voice has gone to hell."

"My man, Mike. Good to hear from you. What time is it? And as for my voice, nothing that some tea and honey won't cure. Not like Scotch, but it's a little early. So, the time, please, and what can I do for you?"

No, Professor. It's really what can I do for you? If only there were some magical way to ease your pain. I know that work is helpful and I'm grateful for our collaboration. And you're doing the bar reviews is also useful in cushioning your daily grief. You're just so unique in being able to take the most intricate and boring principles of law, bring them to life and explain the complexities and exceptions to case decisions so that even sixth grade students would be capable of presenting the matter with an air of expertise before the highest court of the land. You're that good, Sean Murray. But you need to stay sober and show up for those bar review lectures.

Ever since the murder of his wife and sons, Sean medicated himself with alcohol and an occasional loveless one-night stand. In a valiant effort to try to restore some feeling within his damaged soul, Sean impulsively went to a dog rescue center and came home with a mixed breed. Mike felt it was an encouraging sign when Sean playfully named the dog "Bark." The dog was a constant companion during the night hours when the professor labored over the writing of legal briefs. "That dog," he said more than one time, "knows more law than some of our judges."

Sean Murray, superb lecturer and legal scholar, suffered a loss in a manner no other human could possibly comprehend. Yet through it all…his crisp legal thinking remained intact, despite the nightmares, hangovers, and dalliances. "His thorough research, clear writing, and brilliance never wavered," Mike would often say.

"Jesus, Sean, you sound like I look. Do me a big fat favor. Meet me at Patten's at noon. Lunch is on me. I gotta run something by you. And drink some goddamn coffee…NOW!"

"Hey, hey…easy, young man, I'm the professor, you're the student…"

Mike responded, "Coffee…not a cold beer…and that, Private Murray, is a direct order…remember, I wore the stripes, not you."

Patten's Restaurant was located on Court Street, in the heart of Boston's legal district. Established in 1928, it was the local watering hole for the city's trial lawyers. The bar filled by five thirty every weekday afternoon, and war stories bounced off the walls, each yarn of bravado more embroidered than the last. It was an understatement to say that the egos of the courtroom warriors raced out of control, particularly after being fortified by whiskey or a mug or two of cold beer. Noontime lunches were much more sedate than the late afternoon brag sessions.

Mike, at a table, watched as one of his favorite men in the world entered the restaurant.

"I'm on the bright," said Sean, adjusting his customary polka dot bow tie. He patted his paunchy gut. "Haven't had a taste since last night." His ruddy, still handsome face offered an impish smile.

"Sean Murray, you always were a great teacher, and a rare combination of totally nuts and brilliant at the same time. You're one great big cliché. I know you remember the flick, *Anatomy of a Murder*. I swear the actor Arthur O'Connell must have stalked you and modeled his character after you."

"Can't be. His character liked fishing. I loathe it," Sean said. Mike was reminded of how Sean's Irish grin lit up lecture halls.

"So, Counselor, you got something going up to the U.S. Supreme Court? I hope it's interesting." Sean brushed his hands along the sides of his still thick head of hair.

"Nope...not yet, at least," said Mike.

Sean beckoned as if to say: *so tell me what this is all about.*

"You know my Webb case, the one where my client..."

"Got nailed by the Honorable Wilfred Mahoney during the hearing on temps," Sean finished Mike's sentence while glancing at the menu. "But that's about all I remember. Oh yeah, she was shacking up with some other guy or something salacious like that?"

Mike replied, "Most people would say 'juicy,' but not my erudite professor. He has to ring poetic with 'salacious.' And she wasn't exactly shacking up. And her rich-ass husband may well be lying about the whole thing. And if she was messin' around, it was a one-time screw-up."

"Apt use of the expression, I would say," said Sean.

The bantering stopped. Mike, in a bracingly factual manner, delivered the details of what had transpired before Judge Mahoney a couple of weeks ago. He spoke of Danielle Webb's eye being seriously bruised. He told Sean that he filed the necessary documents to go forward seeking an order from the court to remove the husband from the marital home and to award temporary custody of their children to his client.

"And then came the bombshell," said Mike. "Her mega-wealthy husband admitted he whacked her. Then peered up at Mahoney with the goofiest look and whined that it was because he found his wife in bed messing around with another guy…in *their* condo bedroom. The fucking spectators, my loyal colleagues of the bar included, loved it."

Sean said, "And Mahoney, who has a deplorable record when it comes to finding for women, ordered your harlot, not the pugilist husband, out of the home."

"Tossed the woman out without even giving me a chance to conduct any cross-examination or putting her back on the stand so that she could refute his bullshit story," replied Mike, his eyes wide open and arms extended incredulously.

"For Pete's sake, Mikey, what on earth did you think you were going to accomplish on cross of the husband? He'd just keep insisting that he was telling the truth and Mahoney would lap it up. And didn't your angel client tell you about this? And if you did put her back in the witness box, your opponent would have chewed her up."

Mike replied, "I've got the *right* to cross, damn it. She's got the right to deny and refute."

Sean raised his eyebrows and put up his hands. "You're talking like a schoolboy, not the damned fine trial lawyer I know you to be. What'd I preach back at school when you're knocked down onto the mat? Trial lawyers need to rise and get right back to it, but *sensibly.*"

"Professor, I would have been able to make my point during cross-examination that the law doesn't permit a husband to clock his wife...not even when he finds her in bed fucking her brains out, which wasn't even the truth. If there was a guy there, hubby-boy should have whacked *him*, not her. No excuse to hammer her. Tell her he wants her out, call her whatever names he wants, but no slugging. The asshole husband lets the fucker put on his pants and hightail it out of there, and then he whacks his wife." Mike swallowed some water.

Sean motioned with his hand for more.

"Had she told me about this, you ask? No way. As a matter of fact, she denies it...says he's an unmitigated liar. And I believe her...I think," said Mike.

Again, Sean spoke without words. His doubting expression messaged the cliché: *and I've got a bridge to sell you.*

Mike responded. "I know, I know, you taught me a long time ago...careful with your clients, they're not always forthcoming. I looked over at her after that richer than God bastard spun his yarn. She had her face in her hands, sobbing and shaking her head from side to side and mumbling 'no, no.'"

The professor, entertained by Mike's passion, spoke: "Second of all, I'm not in agreement that you have an absolute right to cross-examine during a hearing for temporary orders."

Ignoring Sean's different take on the law, Mike went on, his face reddening, "And you should have seen the puss on Webb's lawyer. She's a pompous one. She should've told me about this before we went into the courtroom. And she didn't because she wanted to ambush me. Cheap shot. And maybe, just maybe she concocted the whole episode."

Sean roared, then gestured for Mike to calm down. He admonished his former student for not having probed and tested his client's story more aggressively before they stepped into the courthouse.

"Basic stuff, Mike. I thought I pounded this into you guys (there were only two women in Mike's class) at school. But deaf ears, I guess. Who knows? Maybe Mr. Brooks Webb wasn't lying at all. Maybe Attorney Michael Lyons is blinded by one good-looking sexy client."

Mike raised his eyebrows and tipped his head to the side.

"I've gotten the full scoop from Jane about Mrs. Danielle Webb," Sean said.

Mike lifted his hands up in surrender mode "You're telling me I've been bushwhacked by my own client?"

"Maybe, maybe not. What I'm saying is when you prep her for trial, probe…go after her about the possibility that she might have been playing house…that her husband's story is what actually happened. That's what I'm sayin'."

Mike nodded that he got the message.

They talked about what a tough custody battle Mike has on his hands, what a lousy track record this justice has when it comes to women's rights, and that under the circumstances in this case and by Judge Mahoney's standards, Mike is in a hole.

The trial lawyer caught his breath.

"Sean, she may be a tramp, but I've got a job to do. My 'harlot,' as you describe her, may be a perfectly good mother. She may be a far better parent than he is or ever could be. You should see this guy. He and his lawyer, Sofia Vasquez, make a great couple. They're the living definition of the word 'smug.'"

Mike discussed the extraordinary wealth of the Webb family and that Attorney Vasquez would more than likely do everything she could to prolong the custody battle and all other aspects of the case.

"She's one of those self-righteous holier-than-thou types, Sean. Under the guise of respectability bullshit, she wants to run up the clock on this one. I can just imagine what the hourly rate is that she and her firm are charging this guy." He paused, then said, "I know it's a tough situation. I just want a level playing field. I want Mahoney off the case. He's blinded by what he's already determined is her infidelity and will never listen to any expert testimony about her parenting skills. I know I can come up with an honest well-qualified shrink who will see that my lady, with all her blemishes, is still a good and deserving mother. And that's despite her playing with this other guy that one time...if what her husband says is true. I just might have a shot."

"One time? How sure are you?" asked Sean.

"I think she's leveling with me. I had her into the office the next day and told her how pissed I was that she lied to me, telling me that her hubby came home all upset about something at work and took it out on her physically. I told her I was thinking of withdrawing and that she should think of getting someone else to represent her. I gave her your lecture about the need to be straight and forthcoming with her lawyer."

Sean said, "And she begged you to stay on the case," a sarcastic smirk on his face.

"Cried. They were real tears, insisting that his story was all fabrication."

"Careful, Mikey boy. I detect something going on here that ain't gonna serve you well," admonished the professor.

"Give me a break. She's sexy all right," Mike broke out with a locker room grin. "But I'm not stupid."

He held up his hand toward the professor's face. "Trust me, my friend, there's no way I'd ever mess around. Besides, I've got problems at home and I'm not about to make matters worse. A client like this..."

"Ali's a great wife and a great mother. Whatever's going on at home, fix it. You're a lucky guy, Mike."

The moment was somber. Mike nodded. He put up his hands, reassuring his friend and himself that he was not about to stray and certainly not with this client.

The two of them agreed that as far as the law is concerned, Mr. Webb had zero right to hit her. They agreed that if Brooks Webb was telling the truth her infidelity was inexcusable, but not a justification for physicality. In response to Attorney Murray's question, Mike explained, "They have a full-time nanny and she had taken the kids to a park for the afternoon."

Mike went on. "If his story is true, then go after the damn stud, not his wife…words, sure…but not hands. I wanted to establish on cross that Webb is a wimp and that he was afraid of the stud, lets him leave, and instead nailed Mrs. Webb."

"You're a good lawyer, Mike. And there was that case, *Simpson vs. Simpson*, where the mother was a hooker. The Supreme Judicial Court upheld the trial court's decision that despite her not so noble profession, the children's best interests were better served if she had physical custody rather than the father. Granted, there were a lot of extenuating circumstances, but the mere fact that she was *a lady of the night* did not disqualify her from being the custodial parent."

"But I fear Mahoney will dismiss the rationale of that case out of hand," said Mike. "And my client's not even a hooker. Mahoney buys the infidelity story and…" Mike slammed a fist into his other open hand… "he's already condemned my lady. She'll never get a fair trial with him," said Mike.

"Hey," said Sean. "He may be tough and a misogynist but he likes you. You've always made out pretty well before him." Sean paused, looked at Mike quizzically. "Do I sense that you've got something in mind?"

Mike then told Sean that he learned that the judge had had his will and estate plan recently prepared by Vasquez's firm.

"You're playing with me!" Sean was baffled. "And your source is reliable?"

"Absolutely…one hundred percent…without question," Mike responded.

"I'm guessing from your face, Mike, your source is anonymous?"

Mike nodded, gesturing with both hands, palms toward his friend.

"And you're thinking about the ethics rule that if there is even the *appearance* of a conflict of interest, a judge must recuse himself/herself."

"Precisely. The judge's mandated impartiality is tarnished. The blindfold of Lady Justice has been removed. And I'm incredulous that Mahoney didn't recuse himself right off the bat. And that snake Vasquez never said a word! I didn't learn about the estate planning stuff until after the hearing."

"Did he pay a fee for those services?" Sean asked.

"Whoa! I didn't even think about that," said Mike. "He wouldn't be that greedy, would he?"

"One never knows," said Sean. "They put on those robes, rule, not just preside, in what they think are *their* courtrooms rather than the courtrooms of the people. We both know that some of them get drunk with power. Not all of them but some have been sitting on their judicial perch too long. Even the best of them loses good judgment at times. Let me poke around and see what I can find out about whether or not the Honorable or not so Honorable Wilfred Mahoney accepted the services without a fee. That would add frosting. Either way, you've got more than enough to get Wilfred removed. And I'm talking more than just the case. Can we order? I'm aching for some clam chowder."

"Sounds good. Of course." Mike beckoned to the waitress.

* * *

Two nights later the phone rang at the Lyons home.

"Sean Murray! How nice. Mike told me about your lunch the other day. You've got to come over for dinner. Bring the dog. I'll call in a couple of days and we'll set something up for next weekend. Hold on, I'll get Mike."

Mike took the phone. "Hey. That was quick. Come up with anything?"

"First of all, it's the law and research and brief writing that are my preferred brands of Scotch. But I must admit, a little taste of sleuth work was fun. I cashed in some chits with a friend who's with one of the white shoe firms, Adams, Finch & Tobias. He's got a good buddy over at Vasquez's place. The will and estate plan was done six months ago. To date the firm hasn't sent a bill. And hold onto your seat…your friend, Vasquez, is a tax adviser to the estate planning department. Ole Wilfred should damn well have recused himself. I've got a suggestion as to how best to handle this."

"That, Professor, is why I have you on my team. I think I'm loving this. Let's have coffee tomorrow morning. I don't want the judge's neck, but I sure want to rattle that Vasquez. Never said a word to me. She's devious, Sean. Some of those old-line firms are above it all."

* * *

The next morning, the professor and Mike laid out their options. They agreed to take the high road. Mike would be appearing before Judge Mahoney many times in the future. He wanted his respect, and did not want to embarrass him. Of even greater importance, Mike's future clients would be treated very well in that court. When word gets passed around among the other justices of the Probate and Family Court, they will appreciate the fact that Mike didn't blast this conflict of interest out in the open; would reflect upon the entire court. Although Mike had every right to file a motion to be heard in open court, he instead opted to pursue diplomatic channels as the best highway to justice regarding this situation. Get the word to the judge via closed channels. Let the messenger be someone who the judge trusts and won't cause him to fly off the handle, get into a defensive rage, and invite an ugly fight that could even end with the judge's suspension.

"The judge is tough. He's going to be embarrassed that he didn't do the right thing and decline this case on his own," said Sean. "We need just the right guy...or gal."

"Joe Ginsburg," Mike burst out.

"Perfect. The judge's court officer, or should I say personal valet?"

"Joe's got a solid relationship with Mahoney," said Mike. "He's street savvy...knows how to pick his spots. And besides, he loves those tickets to Fenway I put in his hands each year."

Sean raised his eyebrows.

Mike responded, "I know I'm breaking the rules, but these guys can't afford the crazy prices at Fenway Park. Ever since the Impossible Dream Season in '67, that place is sold out...tickets at a premium."

Sean Murray leaned back and roared. "You know, Mike, this is fun. I can't wait to see how all this unfolds. My bet? Mahoney bows out of this one before the week is over."

"More fun than they ever taught at law school. We should design a course...give it together. *Justice: Behind the Scenes.*"

Sean chuckled.

Mike went on, "Yup. No desire to embarrass Wilfred. No hand grenades. Strictly the diplomatic route. The stage for the next scene in this drama is this evening, some basketball court in the South End. Opening game of the Lawyers Spring League. Joe's playing for the Court Officers."

"Perfect setting, Mike," said Sean. "But what about Vasquez and her failure to inform you that her firm did this work for Wilfred?"

Mike shook his head.

"Clearly unethical, but my guess is that you aren't going after her?" Sean said.

"I'm a lot of things but I'm not a hypocrite. I'm obviously not a purist, Professor. After all, it's an inside source that tipped me off."

"So be it," agreed Sean. "You'll get Wilfred out and let the chips fall where they may."

* * *

That evening, after the game, Mike and Joe Ginsburg drifted off to a local pub. Another lawyer who participated in the game wandered in, flashed a knowing look their way as if to accuse Mike of *fraternizing*. Ginsburg, not one to take anything from anybody, responded. "What? We can't have a brew and talk about the game? Come join us," knowing full well that the somebody would get the message and decline.

"One of those tight-ass prigs. Thinks a trial lawyer having a beer with a friend who happens to be a court officer is off limits. Jerk," said Mike.

Mike laid it all out to the court officer, precisely and clearly. He emphasized that he did not want to embarrass the judge.

"I'm doing your judge a favor, Joe. It's called saving face."

"It's also called smart," Joe replied. "Keep this from getting out…keep it in-house. I get you, Mike. And I appreciate how you want to handle it. You could be a prick and file a motion and bring out all this crap in open session. Even if my man then saw the light, the document would be on file and the conflict issue would be all over the courthouse network."

"To say nothing of the Judicial Conduct Commission," said Mike.

"I hear you," said Joe.

"This way, Joseph, we keep it clean. No one gets hurt. My lady gets a chance. And there's scores of other cases for your boss. All he has to do is tell the Chief that he's overloaded, that this Webb case may well be a lengthy trial and that the rest of his docket will suffer," Mike suggested.

Joe raised his bottle of beer and said, "Absolutely. And this way we'll keep it from leaking. Sometimes His Honor doesn't think and then springs a leak. I'll talk to him. He'll listen."

"A just plumber's wrench," Mike said. They exchanged smiles, downed another beer, and shook hands.

"You're a good man, Mike. Lousy set shots tonight, but a good man."

"I saved my best shot for you...right here. Thanks, Joe."

"Your client? She's hot." Court Officer Ginsburg flicked his hand.

"As they say, Joe, too hot to handle. Stay the course, Joseph. Like me, you've got a good thing going at home. Your job and your Angelina are too precious."

They left the pub, shook hands again.

I'd love to be a fly on the wall for this one, Mike thought to himself. *I can see Mahoney's face get redder and redder, then he'll think, and then...well, who knows, his stubborn nature may get the better of him. But my betting is he's too smart to let his pride dominate and keep him from doing the smart thing...the right thing. In time, he'll thank me...I'll be okay with future matters before him. He'll respect me for keeping this quiet.*

CHAPTER SEVENTEEN
DANIELLE

"Hell," the judge barked at his court officer. "Lyons knows I'm a straight shooter. Just because I had my will done by Vasquez's law firm..." He sat, stood, then paced.

"I'll be damned if I'm going to be told what case I can handle and what I can't," the judge said.

"But Your Honor," Court Officer Ginsburg offered, "what do you need this nonsense for? As I said, Mike wants to keep this off the record. He's a good guy and would never want to do anything that might embarrass you, but he's got to do whatever he must on behalf of his client." Joe paused as if to remind the judge of an attorney's ethical duty to represent his client zealously and that would include taking steps to have a judge remove himself/herself from a case if there's just the appearance of a conflict.

"Bullshit, bullshit!" The judge cleared his throat and looked for a place to spit. He turned, jaw protruded, face fire engine red. He paced the floor of his lobby, paused. Looked out of his window. Joe, the judge's trusted friend for many years, stood in silence. He knew Wilfred well. *Let him be...he'll make the right decision.*

"Joe, it was just a hearing for temporary orders. It's not like it's a full trial. There's nothing wrong..." He paused to clear his throat again and then expectorate. He looked at his court officer with an expression of surrender.

The veteran court officer knew that the judge was too savvy to let ego prevail; that it might take a few more minutes, but he knew "his" judge would make the right decision. "I don't need all that crap," the judge said. "Listening to self-righteous arguments about the *appearance* of a conflict." The judge considered the publicity of such a hearing. His failure to say anything in open court to all parties about the fact that the law firm of one of the involved lawyers had recently done some work for him coupled with the fact that he inadvisably did not insist upon paying a fee, however modest. He knew it could prove to be, if nothing else, embarrassing. Lawyers whom he had tormented in his courtroom would be euphoric to see the judge put in such a position. His fellow jurists would pretend to sympathize, but actually might enjoy seeing all knowing Wilfred sweat a bit. Although he realized that he had blundered, and that a door was open to him to escape allegations of impropriety in open court, his ego didn't want anyone dictating to him.

"Christ, Joe, maybe I did make a mistake. But I don't want anyone strong-arming me out of this case or any case. The hell with it. I'll send a check to the firm," his expression asking whether or not that gesture would cure the problem.

"A good idea, Judge. But Mike Lyons may still feel obliged to file a motion asking that you withdraw. Sending a check helps. I get that, Your Honor. But I think Mike's still going to feel that he has to move to ask you to recuse yourself. Why risk a hearing in open court? You've got one hell of a caseload as it is. If there is a hearing the newspaper guys could get a hold of it and we'd have…"

Wilfred Mahoney interrupted. "I know. You're right. They'll have a feeding frenzy with our friggin' Supreme Court's bullshit about *even the appearance of a conflict may be sufficient to require a justice to recuse himself…or herself.* And I suppose I wasn't too smart not to have insisted upon paying a fee. It just slipped my mind." He squinted his eyes, tilted his head a tad to the side, sending the message that he recognized that he used bad judgment.

"We judges are held to an awfully high standard, Joseph."

His confidant nodded, pleased that the judge arrived at the right decision.

The judge went on: "Lyons is really giving me a chance to get out gracefully. I've got to hand it to him. He's one of the good ones, Joe. But I've been damned good to him over the years."

The court officer nodded as if to say, *you're making the right decision.*

"Screw it, Joe," the judge went on, "we don't need this aggravation. That self-righteous Judicial Conduct Commission loves this kind of bullshit. I'll tell the Chief how overloaded my docket is."

He paused, looked at the stack of case papers on his desk. "And goddamn it, it is. She can assign somebody else to this case. Too bad, this could have been interesting...and juicy, to say the least."

* * *

Brigham's vs. Bailey's. Two competitive Boston institutions, each boasting that it served the best ice cream and hot fudge sundaes in the city. Devotees of each knew the exact locations of their ice cream parlors throughout Boston as well as the suburbs. When Joe Ginsburg called Mike, they agreed to meet at Brigham's in historic Faneuil Hall.

"I'm relieved, Joe. You did a great job. In the worst way I didn't want to present a Motion to Recuse in open court. No point in embarrassing the judge," Mike said as he spooned some hot fudge dripping down the sides of his ice cream dish. "Best part," he grinned.

The court officer chuckled and did the same. "Mike, the judge appreciates how you handled this thing. He's already spoken with the Chief, explained that his docket's full...that it's keeping him up nights. She acknowledged everything he does for the system and said she would remove him from the case forthwith and reassign it within a day or two."

They dug into their sundaes like a couple of eight-year-olds. A kind of celebration.

* * *

Mike filed a motion for a speedy trial. He had to. His client's husband had been awarded temporary custody of their two young children, albeit with the condition that Mrs. Jensen, the full-time nanny, remain in her role of caring for the children. Mrs. Danielle Webb was humiliated by the limited visitation she was permitted to have with the children, and livid that her husband won round one. *She*, not *he*, was the one ordered out of the house.

Most litigants battling custody often felt animosity. Vitriol, bitterness, accusations laced with exaggeration, sour stomachs, and monster headaches are the norm. With many it has little to do with the law's standard: *what's in the best interest of the child.* Sadly, all too often, parents are at their worst during custody litigation. Their egos and pride overwhelm the need to focus on their children's needs. For too many parents, it's all about *winning, revenge, and humiliating the other spouse.* The kids become pawns in a very rough and expensive battle.

Mike was an experienced trial lawyer and usually quick to get a good read on people. But Danielle Webb, attractive, smart, alluring, and challenging, had his head spinning. He wrestled with the question: Is she fundamentally honest or is she a pathological liar? He deflected sexual fantasies about this woman. He was determined to keep the proverbial desk between them.

* * *

Mike shared the news with Sean that Judge Mahoney opted out of the Webb case.

"But Sean, this lady is driving me nuts. I can't get her out of my head. Was she actually in the sack in her own home screwing some pickup? She insists that's all crap. Says that her husband lied about the entire scene."

"Mike, my boy, turn me loose. Let me play Sherlock Holmes, click on my detective brain, snoop around and see what I come up with," said Sean.

"Not yet, Professor. I don't want to risk shattering her confidence in me, which is what would happen should she find out I've been prying behind her back. Let's see how things go. I'll have a trial date before long. I don't want to risk anything while I try to prep her. But I do want you to meet with Dr. Leonard and find out his assessment of her."

"I didn't know Doc Leonard was on board," said Sean. "What about Larry Armont? Isn't he the shrink for the ex-nun? I thought you and Larry had a strong rapport."

"We do. I think he's one of the best. But I don't want to run the risk on cross-examination by Vasquez of her establishing that my psychiatric expert is already working with me on another case. That might give her an opening to try to attack his integrity, create an inference that he'll say anything to help the cause, whoever my client might be. I gave Danielle three names, excluding Larry."

"Did she resist the idea of going to a psychiatrist?" asked Sean.

"Not after I explained the necessity of having a professional and expert opinion about her parenting skills and relationship with her children."

"Good thinking, Mike. You must have had some fine trial instruction back at BC Law."

"Yup. One of them was *the* very best." Mike extended an arm toward Sean's shoulder.

Mike said: "And I told Arnie Leonard that I don't want a written report. Nothing that I might be obliged to turn over to Vasquez. So I'll rely upon your interview with him. I have a release from Danielle enabling Doc Leonard to share all with me or anyone I designate."

"When are you starting your prep with Webb?" Sean asked.

"Tomorrow. Jesus, Sean, I'm so wrapped up in this thing, I'm letting some of my other cases slip. Would you mind handling a couple of motions for continuance? I'll fill you in later with the details."

"Never a problem, you know that. But Mike, can you handle a piece of personal advice from your old worn out law prof? I'm concerned about you and this Webb woman. Keep it in your pants. You've got a great marriage, great kids, five-star family life. Don't mess it up."

"Miss Jane Donnell filling your head, no doubt. But not to worry," Mike said.

After a pause Sean said, "Tell me something, Mikey, and I might be reaching where I ought not go, but I care about you, so I'm going to stick my neck out. Is everything okay at home?"

"That obvious? To answer your question…in a word: nope."

"Whatever's going on, Mikey, get at it. One hell of a lot more important than any of the cases."

"Thanks, Sean. Have a good night."

As he walked to the garage, Mike thought: *How hollow: Have a good night. There's no such thing for my friend. He'll medicate himself with booze. And why not?*

* * *

The next day Mrs. Webb arrived at Mike's office. After some small talk, Attorney Lyons launched into a reminder about the importance of Danielle being forthright throughout her testimony. Her persona was demure and with a coquettish smile she acknowledged her lawyer's stern advice.

"Let's get started with some questions and answers," said Mike. "And I want to lead off with the day you say Brooks punched you. Then we can back up and get to a lot of the marital history. Okay, we're in court. You're on the witness stand."

Danielle straightened her posture, put on a serious face.

"So, Mrs. Webb, you're telling this court under oath that your husband made up a bogus story of finding you in bed with…?"

"Yes," she responded emphatically.

Mike came back with a stare that could cut diamonds. He wanted to put his client to the test.

"I'm telling you, Mike, he comes over like a Boy Scout. He's a freakin' liar. He and that pompous lawyer cooked up the whole thing." With that she leaned back, pulled at her soft pink cashmere sweater and let the tears flow.

"I know, I know," she said. "I can't talk like this on the stand." She reached for the box of Kleenex on Mike's credenza.

"I understand," said Mike.

"Do you mind if I smoke?" she asked.

He gestured as if to say *not a problem* even though it was. It turned out to be a bigger *problem*, at least a surprise. Danielle Webb pulled a packet of Cigarillos from her handbag, not cigarettes. She lit up, quickly recovered from the tears and grinned.

"Shocking, isn't it?" she said.

The lawyer pretended not to be surprised. *I'm not going to let her throw me off track. But she is a piece of work.* He wiped his hand across his mouth, erasing a smile that was about to emerge.

He challenged his client. "So, you want me to believe, more importantly, the judge to believe that your husband concocted that entire story?" Mike held out his hand. He got up from behind his desk, came around to his client and peered down at her. That penetrating stare of his sending the message: *This isn't a game, lady. Your stakes are high.*

She shifted in her chair, shrugged, put her head down.

She said: "You don't believe me, do you? You and that judge who you said was too quick to buy that crazy story, who you said should have let you conduct cross-examination, now you agree with him." She crushed her Cigarillo and then looked at Mike imploringly.

He tried to be steely, squinting his eyes. She shifted in her chair, pulled at her pleated skirt in such a manner as to reveal much of her thighs while recrossing her legs.

There's no question that Attorney Michael Lyons' testosterone level was rising. He heard his professor's voice admonishing him: *Too many divorce lawyers have put their licenses on the line for an easy liaison. These women are vulnerable, some desperate to know that they're still sexually attractive.*

Then Mike conjured up Ali's admonition: *Mike, this woman's a pathological liar. She's a harlot. Get out of this case. She's poison...lost her moral compass. Forget the tempting fee. You've got plenty of other work. Let her find another lawyer. We're paying our bills. We don't need her money. She's trouble.*

Mike thought to himself: *But what if she's telling the truth? Just maybe. Her husband with or without that tight-assed snob of a lawyer just may have made this whole thing up. And there was not a word said by Brooks Webb why he didn't stop this guy from running out...why he didn't take him on. He just let this mystery man slip out of their home? And punches his wife instead? There's something creepy about Mr. Husband. At trial, I could have a picnic with him.*

He looked at Danielle. She read the message in his eyes. No messing around...just the case and the truth.

She responded. "Mr. Lyons, I am telling you. He was pissy-eyed about being taken for granted at that stupid lab where he does his excuse for work. God knows we don't need the money. The Webb fortune. Trusts throwing off serious money."

"So, what exactly is it you say happened?"

"It was a Friday. I told him I was happy that he came home early. He was in a foul mood, complaining about something at work. I suggested that we could go to the club, play some tennis, grab a drink. Next thing I know he just hauled off and clobbered me. He was in a rage and plain and simple took it out on me because I was advising him to cool down."

"So, the guy in bed with you? A fiction?" Mike asked.

Mike noted that her usual creamy complexion reddened and that she spoke about going to the club rather than spending time with the kids.

"Do I have to tell you this whole thing again?" she asked.

Wanting to challenge her, Mike fired back: "And do I think your husband, a well educated man, member of a prominent old-line Boston family, and his lawyer, who may be pompous but covets her position with a powerful Brahmin law firm, are dumb enough to make up and present such an alibi in court? Under oath?"

"He's not dumb," she agreed, "but devious is his middle name." She stopped abruptly and lit up another smoke.

Mike wrinkled his nose in disapproval. "By the way, those things stink." He waved his hand and then continued: "His lawyer may be devious as well, but she's not dumb. She wouldn't counsel your husband to perjure himself."

"My not so bright husband may never have told her that he was making this whole thing up," said Danielle.

"Do you honestly think your husband ignored the ramifications of perjury and went ahead and outright lied to the judge?"

She became defensive: "So, Mike, are you saying that I ignored the whatever about perjury and had the audacity to bullshit you and the judge?"

She leaned back and pointed a gotcha finger toward her lawyer.

"Okay," said Mike, "your point is made. I needed to be sure." *I sure as hell hope she's giving it to me straight,* he thought. "Okay, let's get back to a Q and A format…just as it will be when you're on that witness stand. Under oath, I might add."

With that the lawyer and his client went to work. Mike went over scores of questions that he would ask and that his adversary would likely ask on cross-examination. He emphasized the activities and relationship between Danielle and her children, impressing upon her the need for a judge to understand the detailed manner in which she carried out her parenting responsibilities.

"You've got a full-time nanny, Danielle, so a judge is going to be suspect that it is she, not you, who does most of the childcare."

"But that's not so," she said.

"Okay, we're back in court. Please tell the judge just how a typical day in your household begins."

"I wake the kids every day, help pick out their clothes, and then make breakfast," Danielle answered.

"Well, what about Mrs. Jensen, the nanny?"

"Most of the time, she doesn't sleep in our apartment. Her day usually begins around ten, after I've taken the children to school and preschool. She cleans up the kitchen, makes the beds and usually has a project or two until I pick up the children from school, which I do most days."

"And when you don't pick them up?"

"She takes a taxi and gets them."

They spent the next two hours fine-tuning the testimony about the details of her daily routine with the children as well as her husband's lack of involvement. Mike was impressed that his client was an attentive mother.

"I'm beat," Danielle said.

"Understandable. We'll call it a day. Come in tomorrow around noon."

They each stood.

"Thank you, Mike. I think I'm going to be the best prepared client you ever had."

Mike smiled in appreciation. "See you tomorrow. Think about some of the highlights of your interaction with teachers at their schools and doctors as well."

"Will do." She stunned Mike as she placed a hand on his back and gazed seductively at his face. He felt himself stir.

He dipped a shoulder, stepped to the side, turned and made eye contact. *I would like so to yield…to have her…right here...right now,* he thought to himself. He knew better. He put up a hand, palm outward.

"You're a beautiful woman, Ms. Danielle Webb. But we have a serious case on our hands. Comprende?"

His client responded with a knowing smile of rejection.

"Tomorrow then. And we're all business."

She nodded and said, "Someday, Mr. Serious Lawyer."

Mike could feel the heat of flattery, embarrassment, and trouble rise within him.

"You, madam, are incorrigible."

With that, Danielle stepped into the reception area, said goodbye to Jane and waved at Mike with a wink.

"Your wife's a lucky woman," she said as she exited.

Mike avoided his secretary, walked back into his office and went to the window.

Am I crazy? How can I continue to represent this woman? Hasn't she crossed the line? Whatever that line is. Is she more than a playful flirt? Wraps her arm around me? That's all I need. Play around with a client and I'll be chopped liver. Lose Ali, my kids, my ticket to practice. Ali's right. Jane's right. Women know. Maybe I should just quit, get out of this Webb mess. Web? Whoa. Never thought of that...Mike Lyons caught in a web.

He stepped into the reception area.

Jane looked up at her boss. Her expression said it all.

Mike threw his arms in the air and said, "I know, Jane. But she's our client."

"Just be careful, Mike, that's all I'm saying. I still don't trust her."

The phone rang.

"Michael Lyons office," Jane said. "Oh, yes, Attorney Vasquez, let me see if Attorney Lyons is available."

Jane held a hand over the receiver. "It's the enemy camp," she mouthed.

"I'll take it," said Mike.

"Hello, Sofia. How are you?" Mike started, his voice strong and affable. He knew why she was calling.

"Attorney Lyons," she started…

Mike thought to himself: *Attorney. What a condescending twit.*

"Attorney Lyons, I got the copy of your Motion for a Speedy Trial. I'll let you know whether or not I'll assent. But did you hear that Judge Mahoney has removed himself from our Webb case?"

"I'll be damned. Any word as to why?" Mike enjoyed playing with his adversary. For the moment he'll save the day when he'll confront her about not letting him know her firm had prepared Wilfred's will and estate plan.

"Not a clue," she said.

Bullshit, lady. You know goddamned well why he opted out. And won't you be thrilled if I remove myself from representing Danielle. Jane and Ali are both probably right. But I'm not a quitter.

CHAPTER EIGHTEEN
DANIELLE

When Danielle arrived at Mike's office, he greeted her with a cold glare and gestured to a chair.

"Sit."

"It sounds like you're giving a command to a dog," she quipped.

"Mrs. Webb, I'm serious."

"*Mrs. Webb*," she mimicked. "This must be serious."

"I'm going to get right to the point. And I know that you know what I'm talking about," Mike started. "I thought a lot about this last night. Maybe it's not such a good idea for me to continue to represent you. You may be better served by another lawyer. I can give you names of the best."

"Oh, no. You *are* serious. Mike, please forgive me. I didn't mean anything. It was just my wild side being a flirt that got out of control. I promise I'll behave."

"Danielle, let's not bullshit each other. We're both adults. You were coming on to me, plain and simple."

"I'm sorry if it seemed that way. I was just trying to be…friendly."

Mike looked at her as if to say *I just said let's not bullshit each other.*

Danielle suddenly got up and went to the reception area. She faced Jane.

"Ms. Donnell, would you kindly tell your boss," she pivoted toward Mike, who was now standing in the threshold of his office, "that I'm an honest woman. I admit I get out of hand every now and then but I'm honest. And besides, I'm well aware that at this stage in the case he can't just walk out. Not unless I agree. That's the law. And I'm not agreeing." She thrust out her chin as she pointed toward Mike.

She remained looking at Mike. "You're the best. I'm not letting you withdraw. No sir. And as I said, I will behave."

Mike was taken aback by his client's familiarity with a matrimonial court rule determining the circumstances under which a lawyer may withdraw from representing a client when the case has progressed through much of the pretrial stages, as this case had done. If the client refuses to permit her lawyer to withdraw then the lawyer must seek the court's permission. On another level, he was flattered that she wanted him to continue to represent her.

She's persuasive. I'll give her that. And she's got me right by the jewels. If I go before the court asking to get out I could compromise her entire case. No matter how I couch it I'd be damaging her chances.

I can hear the judge: "In other words, Counsel, what you're saying is that your client is immoral."

"Well, Your Honor, what I'm trying to say is that I can no longer represent my client zealously as required by the Rules of Conduct."

"And why is that, Counsel?"

"She tried to come on to me, Your Honor." That'd sure as hell wake everybody up. No way could I be that blunt, but any judge, just looking at her, would certainly have his suspicions.

"So, Counsel," I imagine the judge saying, "we have a woman fighting for custody of her children and you are telling the court she has a character problem?"

Well, Mike thought, *maybe not those exact words, but the message would be clear no matter how discreetly I couch an argument to withdraw. Her case would be damaged even if I were to pussyfoot around with something like "the necessary attorney-client relationship has broken down, Your Honor." Judges are not fools, particularly the Honorable Kelvin Henry, who's been designated as our trial judge. Her case would be irreparably harmed.*

I'm not going to abandon ship. And it's got nothing to do with her sexy body and flirtatious manner. I'm a lawyer, goddammit. We can't pick and choose. We go with the best of what we have. Take the cards as they're dealt. We lawyers take an oath to do our best, whatever the evidence, whatever the circumstances, to represent our clients zealously. We don't quit just because there are a few potholes along the way. This isn't estate planning. There's never anything clean and neat about a custody battle. No client is perfect. And no lawyer is either.

I've never run from a fight. She may be whatever she is, but she's entitled to have me give it my all. Her husband is blah, ineffectual. After all is said and done I'm certain she'd be the better parent for those kids. He's a liar, a coward, or both. If there was a guy screwin' his wife in his bed, why didn't he whack him? Instead, like a wimp, he lets the guy run and smacks her. Why did he let the guy run? I'm gonna do my job. And there's our kids' college fund. This client can afford to pay. I do my share of pro bono cases.

* * *

Mike snapped out of his reverie. "Mrs. Webb, I'm not the least bit doubtful that a judge would let me withdraw, but that process could hurt your case. I don't want to do that. If you want my services and we have a clear understanding, then I'll stay on board."

"There's no question, Mike. I so want you in my corner. I know I can get a little crazy, but it's just the pressure and the rotten decision Mahoney made. I'd be thrilled if you would continue to be my lawyer," Danielle responded. She looked at him as though two lovers had just resolved a quarrel.

* * *

During a session when Danielle was being prepared for cross-examination, Mike's questions were intense. He was probing to determine her vulnerable spots.

"Whose side are you on?" she yelled in frustration.

"Danielle, you want custody of your children? We're not at your tennis club," said Mike with deliberate sarcasm. He wanted to nail his point that Danielle was going to have to be ready to withstand what could be a withering cross-examination. *Prep her for the worst.*

Mike continued, "Your husband's lawyer is going to go after every piece of you that she thinks will help their case. She wants to press your buttons, exploit your weaknesses, coax you into losing your cool. Don't fight with her. Don't get cute, no matter how smart you are. And make no mistake, you're one smart woman. But on that stand you have to be even smarter. Answer each question briefly, only what is asked without adding any bullshit. And always, always stick to the truth. Embellish, try to evade answering, try to color the truth, then you're a sitting duck. You'll be playing into their hands."

She leaned back in her chair and rolled her neck as if it were stiff.

Mike added, "And I know you can do it. Kill them with your forthrightness and integrity."

She nodded.

"All right, here we go. We're back in court. I'm role-playing Vasquez." Mike raised his eyebrows as if to ask, "Are you ready?"

"Now tell the court, Mrs. Webb, were you an hour late on three different occasions this past month when you were to pick up your children from preschool and you failed to call the school to let them know you'd be late?"

"There was terrible traffic. My car phone wasn't working," Danielle answered.

"NO, GODDAMMIT! Start with the simple direct answer, 'Yes.' That's the truth. If you jump into your explanation without first giving the forthright response, you'll look defensive. Just answer the question. Don't get defensive. Don't let the judge question your honesty. And he will if you evade and don't give a direct answer. The truthful, straightforward response is simply 'yes.' If I feel any answer you give needs an explanation, then we'll take care of that on re-direct examination. And then you can talk about traffic conditions and your broken car phone in response to my questions. Okay, let's try it again. I've just repeated the question, which is what Sofia Vasquez will happily do over and over until she gets a direct answer to her question and only that question. That's the way it works."

"YES," Danielle shouted. "I was fucking late."

She grinned.

She's playin' with me. But I'm stayin' out of her game.

Mike glared at her.

Danielle got the message. "I mean, yes ma'am, unfortunately, I was late three times."

"Perfect. A nice clear, crisp, honest answer. The judge will respect you for being forthright, particularly because the substance of the answer is not in your best interest. All you can do is win with that kind of simple honest response. As I said a moment ago, you and I will get to the explanation when I conduct re-direct examination. In fact, better than that. We'll bring this out during my direct examination of you before she gets to do her cross." said Mike.

"Okay, I think we've done enough for today. We have lots of time before the trial gets started in November," Mike said.

He checked his appointment book. "How about next Wednesday at two? We'll do another 'Q and A'."

Danielle nodded. "Thank you, Mike. See you next week."

* * *

A week before the start of the Webb trial, Mike and Professor Sean Murray got together over coffee and hashed and rehashed what the order of witnesses should be.

"Mike," said Sean, "I'm thrilled that Judge Kelvin Henry will be presiding. He's smart and he's fair."

"And streetwise," Mike added.

"And it doesn't hurt that the two of you served in Korea," said Sean.

"Gotta get your wars straight, Professor. I was Korea. Kelvin was in the 'big one,' World War II." Mike grinned. "So, let's tackle what the order of our witnesses should be."

Sean nodded and started: "Let's hold Danielle until the end. Let the judge get a good solid portrait of her via the testimony of the supporting witnesses before she takes the stand and is subjected to Sofia Vasquez's cross-examination. If you lead off with Danielle and Vasquez successfully nails her during cross at that early stage in our trial, we're cooked. Kelvin, I'm afraid, will be ninety percent on his way to making up his mind," counseled Sean, "and not in our favor."

"And our supporting cast would be meaningless at that point. But that's assuming Danielle loses it during cross," Mike added.

"Yup. All of the testimony by our other witnesses about what a wonderful human being she is and what a good mommy she is could be lost in the wind if she has already fouled out of the game early during cross," said Sean.

"But you're assuming that she won't hold up when Vasquez goes after her. I've prepped her to the nth degree. She may handle it very well," said Mike.

"That's great, Mike. Let's hope so. And if she does, we end our case on a high note. I vote we save her for last."

Mike nodded and mumbled, "I hear you."

Sean said, "And with Danielle going last, Vasquez will then have to start her case as soon as she finishes her cross." Sean added some milk to his cup of coffee.

"And we know that she'll have her parade of similar people. It never fails. And they'll all testify adamantly what a great dad that stiff Webb is," Mike said. "And then the battle of experts: our

Dr. Leonard, and their psychiatrist, Dr. Martinez, each opining about which parent best serves the interests of the children. Martinez's got an honest reputation, but just doesn't have nearly as much to go with as Doc Leonard does because it's clear that Danielle spends much more quality time with those kids than their excuse for a father."

"I can hear Dr. Martinez now, trying to buttress Brooks Webb's parenting skills…what a prize-winning dad he is." Mike added sarcastically, "Can you believe it? Webb even took the kids to cartoons at the Coolidge Corner Theatre one Saturday. With the emphasis on *one.* I know I'll score points when I cross examine Martinez. She simply won't be able to dodge the hard reality that Danielle is much more involved with the kids' lives than Brooks Webb. And I can't wait to get at Webb on cross," Mike said.

"You'll have a party with him, Mike. I know that," said Sean.

"It's going to come down to the testimony of the parents and how they come over to the judge. I know I can dismantle that creep of a husband of hers and give the judge enough to realize Webb's been anything but a real caring attentive dad. I can sense it. There's something weird going on with this guy."

"Sometimes, Mike, it all seems like a charade," said Sean.

"Kelvin's going to take a good hard look at them…decide who's giving it to him straight and then ultimately who the kids should live with and how to divide the loot. Hell, if this were a sane system, which it isn't, we'd all agree to waive the trappings and just let a good old-fashioned wise judge like Kelvin interview Mom, Dad, and the guardian ad litem and then make a decision. Save a lot of time and money."

Sean responded, "But Mike, my friend, they're not all as sound and reasonable as Kelvin. We need the, as you put it, 'trappings,' to keep the others in check. You quite reasonably asked Judge Mahoney to appoint a guardian ad litem to interview all of the witnesses, write a report, and submit it to the court. He unwisely turned down that sound and timesaving suggestion. No way Kelvin can reverse Mahoney's decision on this. Judges don't like to do that to each other. So we've got to go full steam ahead with a trial."

"Okay, Sean. We'll lead with the others. Save Danielle for last."

"Give me a shout if there's anything you need," said Sean while the two of them shook hands.

* * *

"ALL RISE. Hear ye, hear ye, hear ye. All persons having business before this Honorable court, draw near and give your attention and you shall be heard. The Honorable Kelvin Henry presiding. God save the Commonwealth."

The court officer, proud of the way he bellowed the opening, inappropriately flashed a good luck smile at Mike. He felt camaraderie with Mike. "After all," he would say, "it was Mike who stood tall before the state legislature trying to get a pay raise for the state's court officers."

The judge, the first African American appointed to the Probate and Family Court in Massachusetts, who fought his way from the streets of Brooklyn to serving as a combat pilot with the Tuskegee Airmen in WWII and then onto a fine legal career, signaled everybody to take their seats.

Judge Henry was a no-nonsense man well ahead of his time. Aware that the portraits hanging on the walls of his courtroom depicted only white judges of yesteryear, he took action and together with his Black court officer removed all of them. "Let's remove any implicit bias in this courtroom. It's for ALL the people. Let's get some of the more modern day jurists, including women and Blacks. Until then let the walls be bare of racism."

Judge Henry addressed the litigants and their lawyers: "Ladies and gentlemen, I address these brief remarks to the clients and all others interested in this case. As I understand it based upon my reading of the pretrial memoranda submitted by counsel, this matter is largely about the custody of two minor children, ages

four and five. And with respect to that issue, I will listen to the
evidence in light of the broad legal test: *what is in the best interest
of the children.* And I will entertain all evidence properly
presented regarding financial issues and the allegations of adultery
and cruel and abusive treatment."

Judge Henry then nodded toward Mike, signaling that he
should proceed with his case on behalf of Danielle Webb.

"May it please the Court," Mike proceeded with a crisp,
forceful tone and resonant voice.

Throughout the first two weeks of trial, teachers, neighbors,
the children's pediatrician, a child psychiatrist, the nanny, and Dr.
Arnold Leonard, the psychiatrist engaged by Mike to meet with
Danielle and assess her emotional health and stability and offer his
opinion as to her parenting skills, were among the cascade of
witnesses Mike produced. Mike demonstrated that he was a master
at establishing an effective cadence during his questioning. The
essence of the testimony of the various witnesses he put on the
stand on behalf of Danielle was that she impressed them as an
attentive, loving, caring, and capable mother. The pediatrician
spoke of "the strong mental health" of the children as a direct
result of "Mrs. Webb's mothering." And Dr. Leonard was sure to
include "Mrs. Webb's positive influence upon the children. There
is no question in my mind that the children's interests would be
best served with their mother as custodial parent," a conclusion
based upon six sessions with her and a session with each child,
plus one with Mr. Webb (each side had been granted the right to
have their expert psychiatrist meet with the other spouse).

During cross-examination of Dr. Leonard, Attorney Vasquez
referred to the incident when Mr. Webb found his wife in a
"compromising state in their own bedroom…a liaison with another
man. Isn't that a clear indication of her morality and poor model
for the children?" Attorney Vasquez asked.

Dr. Leonard responded: "Assuming your premise in your
question is correct, that happening tells us something about the

marriage and that she was unfaithful. But such an indiscretion does not necessarily have any connection with her parenting skills, love for her children, and the manner in which she nurtures them. And she does nurture them…superbly, in my opinion."

"Arnie was really strong," Mike whispered to Sean as Dr. Leonard completed his answers to Sofia Vasquez's cross-examination.

"I agree," said Sean. "Just have him repeat his opinion that she's the better parent for the kids."

"Any re-direct, Mr. Lyons?" the judge asked.

"Just one question," Mike responded.

Mike adopted Sean's suggestion and asked that Dr. Leonard repeat his final opinion regarding which parent would best serve the children's interests as custodial parent. The doctor did so.

"We've already heard his opinion," Sofia Vasquez blurted out.

"I take it that's an objection, Counsel?" the judge asked.

"Sorry, Your Honor. Yes, I object on the basis that the question has been asked and answered."

"Your objection is a tad late, Ms. Vasquez. It should have been raised immediately after the question was asked and before the witness answered. In any event, I'm going to allow the question and answer to stand. You'll have the same rights when your expert testifies, Ms. Vasquez."

Mike cupped a hand over his mouth and whispered to Sean, "She has a look on her face as though somebody peed in her morning oatmeal."

* * *

It was Monday afternoon, November 20, 1972. The cold air from Boston Harbor as well as the choppy Charles River signaled the possibility of an early winter. Nevertheless, spirits were generally high among the populace as the Thanksgiving holiday break was just a few days ahead. The entire country was ready for some relief from the anxiety of the ongoing Watergate scandal,

which would ultimately result in the resignation of President
Nixon.

Mike addressed the court. "Your Honor, I have just one more
witness, Mrs. Danielle Webb. May I suggest that in light of the
fact that it's 3:30, the court consider adjourning for the day?"

"Excellent suggestion, Counsel," Judge Henry said.
"Attorney Vasquez, are you in accord?"

Sofia Vasquez had little choice but to nod her approval,
although agreeing with any suggestion by Mike felt as though she
had made a monumental concession.

"There being full accord we shall adjourn. But bear in mind
that we will not reconvene until the Monday following
Thanksgiving. That would be a week from today, November 27. I
have other matters with which to deal tomorrow and the courts will
close at noon on Wednesday."

Judge Henry stood and then stepped to the side of the bench.
He unbuttoned and brushed the front of his judicial robes to the
sides as if to signal a different tone.

"As I think about the holiday, I'm mindful about the
testimony of Mrs. Jensen, an obviously capable nanny for the
children. I recall quite specifically when she spoke of the fact that
both Mr. and Mrs. Webb left the family home after an early
afternoon Thanksgiving meal last year, leaving the children for the
rest of the day and evening with Mrs. Jensen. I am disturbed that,
absent any extenuating circumstances about which I have heard
nothing to date, these parents would not have insisted upon being
with their own daughter and son throughout the *entire* holiday."

Judge Henry took a sip of water. He gestured to Mr. and Mrs.
Webb to come forward and stand in the well of the courtroom.
Danielle's face was scarlet. Her husband's countenance was ashen.

"I trust that each of you knows better. And I want to think
that you will have the good sense and pleasure on this
Thanksgiving of spending the *entire* day and evening with your

children." The judge cast a look as if to say, *"with this case going on I can't imagine you wouldn't do as I suggest."*

The judge's face bore a closed mouth smile. He wrinkled his brow. "Are we in accord?"

"Yes, Your Honor," said Mr. Webb.

"Oh, absolutely," Danielle said.

Mike glared at her. She picked up the clue. "Yes, *Your Honor*," she dutifully added with just enough of a seductive blink of her eyes for all to be aware and to make her lawyer want to strangle her.

She's got a death wish. Clients can fuck up hours of work with just one stupid gesture. Nice going, smartass, Mike thought to himself.

"Noted," said the judge. "I know I don't have to insult you by issuing an Order." He raised his eyebrows and flashed a knowing glance at Mike that said it all: *Counsel, you've got your hands full with this one.* "This court is adjourned until 10 a.m. Monday, November 27. A happy holiday to all." And with that Judge Henry left the bench.

Sofia Vasquez and her client faked an attempt to hide their smug grins. The blinking was not lost on them.

Danielle came over to Mike as the courtroom started to empty. She read his face.

"What?" She asked. "What'd I do that was so wrong?"

"I think you have a death wish," he said as he shoved papers into his briefcase. "My office tomorrow at two," he said sharply.

"Yes, sir." She saluted and spun into a military about-face.

Attorney Lyons shook his head. *My client is certifiable,* he thought. Sean glanced knowingly and joined Mike in gathering their papers. Something pulled Mike's attention. He turned. He saw a tall man enter the rear of the courtroom.

I've seen him before. The hospital. After the shooting. And he shadowed me later that day. I'm sure of it.

Mike watched as the tall man brushed by Danielle while she exited the courtroom. Mike then observed what appeared to be a heated exchange between Brooks Webb and the tall man.

Curious, anxious, Mike rushed toward the exit doors.

"Counsel," barked his adversary.

Mike turned.

"A happy holiday to you and your family," said Sofia Vasquez, who had lingered behind him.

I doubt that you really mean that. You're all gloat because my damned fool client inbounded the basketball right into your sleazy arms. Score one for you, Sofia Vasquez, but I play all four quarters.

Mike returned the ostensible good wishes and then darted into the hallway.

The tall man was nowhere to be seen.

CHAPTER NINETEEN
ALI

JULY 1972

"Ali, I'm so happy to see you."

"Sorry I'm late," Ali said.

"No worries. He's still speaking, although I think he'll be finishing up pretty soon."

June Prescott, a Sudbury neighbor of Ali and Mike, was hosting a gathering for 5th Congressional District candidate, Tim Sullivan. Despite it being vacation time for many suburban families, the living room was packed. Ali accepted iced tea from her friend and then quietly took a place leaning against the entryway to the living room.

One of the attendees raised his hand. Although Tim was in the process of making a point about his plan to improve the economy in the Northeast, he graciously acknowledged the attendee.

"Are you okay with a question?"

"Absolutely. As I said earlier, I love questions—anytime."

Tim smiled and gestured toward the questioner while asking for his name.

Ali thought, *there's a charm and grace about the way he handles himself. Attractive.*

"There are several candidates in the Democratic primary. Ten, I think. Who do you consider your toughest competitor?"

"I'm frequently asked that question. John Kerry is our toughest competition. At the moment the polling shows that he has a lead but we're closing in rapidly. I have the highest regard for combat veterans."

"Didn't Kerry just recently move into the District?"

"You're absolutely correct. And I take issue with his political shopping. John and his wife bought a house earlier this year in Worcester so that he could run in the 4th District. They never moved in. Then he rented an apartment in Lowell just so he could run in our 5th district. Maybe that qualifies him as a carpetbagger…I don't know." The candidate paused, extended his arms as if to say *he loathed cheap politics.* "What I do know is that I've lived and worked in this district my entire life. I know our local needs and opportunities better than any of the others seeking this office."

"So, you see him as an elitist?" another asked.

"I don't like that word nor do I like labeling anybody…except myself." With that he broke out in a winning smile, and added, "as long as the label is accurate: honest, effective, and determined." The mock self-aggrandizing expression on his face prompted good-natured laughter.

"Charming guy, don't you think?" June whispered to Ali.

"And handsome," Ali said.

"Like a movie star," June said.

"Is that his wife?"

"The sexy blonde seated to his right?"

"Yes."

"No," June whispered. "Somebody said she doesn't like campaigning. This gal's name is Linda. She's his campaign manager."

"Oh?"

"And this Linda's super smart. And, my friend, he's much too savvy and straight to be fooling around," said June.

"I didn't say a word," Ali protested, continuing to keep her voice at a whisper while covering her mouth.

"But I know what you're thinking—just like most every woman here today." June paused and then added, "I guess there are some rumors."

Ali raised her eyebrows. She watched as Tim Sullivan paused and sipped from a cup. As he looked up, their eyes made contact and locked for one very long second.

"Before I conclude my remarks, I'd like to address what's on everybody's mind these days. The Watergate burglary. I'm absolutely convinced that the two young reporters with *The Washington Post*, Woodward and Bernstein, will not refrain until they get to the bottom of this. I'm already on record as saying that I think we'll learn that President Nixon was totally aware of what was going on and although it will take time, this will all come out in the wash. Not only as a Democrat but like each of you as an American patriot, I'm appalled at this deliberate attempt to sabotage the Democratic National Committee Headquarters."

"Do you think the Attorney General might also be involved?" a woman asked.

"I don't know. I certainly hope not. John Mitchell isn't the president's lawyer. He's *our* lawyer...the *people's* lawyer. And I like to think he's smart enough to know he doesn't have any right to meddle in the campaign."

I like this man, Ali thought. *He's clear, sexy. And those gorgeous blue eyes...startling!*

"Tim," another woman spoke up, "we hear some refer to you as a 'socialist.' Any comment—I mean is there anything to that?"

"Thank you for that question. So important. Again, we get into labeling. The conservative press loves pinning that label on anyone whose leanings are liberal. If 'socialism' means I'm in favor of compassionate government, of watching public funds so that a reasonable portion is used to help the needy and unfortunate among us. If 'socialism' means I favor a wider share in national prosperity...that I, like Senator Ted Kennedy and other reasonable legislators, would fight for affordable health care for all Americans, then socialism means patriotism."

With that, all rose and burst into applause, including Ali Lyons.

"And let me add, please, the conservatives get it all wrong when they preach the line that *affordable* health care—and I mean *affordable* for the *country* as well as the individual American—would deplete our treasury. They use the fear tactic—and you and I know they're just plain wrong and out of touch. Ladies and gentlemen, thank you so much. And once again, I express my heartfelt gratitude to June and Stanley Prescott for being so generous to open their home and give me an opportunity to meet and speak with all of you."

Ali turned to her friend.

"June, is he for real? I'll gladly write a check. He's smart...and a hunk."

"Ali Lyons, welcome to the club. He's not only got 'it,' but he's the real thing...not just another blowhard opportunist. And he certainly isn't doing it for the money. Why don't you volunteer to do some work for him?"

"Now that's a first-rate idea."

"And Ali, my dear...well, I agree, he's a handsome one."

"And charming."

Ali opened her handbag to search for her checkbook.

"Hello." It was Tim Sullivan.

Ali was caught off guard and dropped her handbag.

As he bent to pick it up, Tim said, "I just wanted to introduce myself and thank you for coming today. I noticed you leaning against the entry area."

"I'm so sorry. Very clumsy of me. Thank you so much," Ali said, flustered, as Tim recovered her pocketbook.

"All part of a candidate's pleasure," he said good-naturedly.

"Tim, I'm very happy that I got to hear at least some of your remarks. I would like to be of some help..."

"This is Linda Abrams, my campaign manager. We can use all the help we can get. Linda will fill you in with what's going on and talk about our needs. I really thank you." He smiled. Ali, observant by nature, was aware of his bright and well cared for teeth with a slight upper protrusion, which she found attractive. She was also aware that he extended his hand and lightly touched her shoulder. She was not offended. To the contrary, she was flattered.

As the candidate turned to say goodbye to others, Linda Abrams gave Ali one of their brochures.

"We'd more than welcome your help, Ms. Lyons. I suggest that you come to the Wayland headquarters at your convenience. If I'm not there, there'll be lots of folks around, including a staffer by the name of Toby Barnes. She'll help orient you and get you started—door-to-door canvassing, telephone calls. And if I'm not mistaken, I understand you're a school psychologist?" said Linda.

"Now I am impressed," said Ali. "How do you know that?"

"Oh, nothing clever. Your friends, June and Stanley, just mentioned that's what you do and that you're a good writer."

"They're very kind," said Ali.

"We may be able to put your writing talents to use in addition to the mundane tasks that I mentioned."

"I'm excited to be of help in any way I can. I've never worked for a politician before."

"Any idea as to when you might be able to drop by our headquarters?" Linda asked.

"Hopefully, within the next couple of days."

"Perfect." Linda extended her hand

As Linda and Tim Sullivan departed, he turned and waved.

Ali, who had joined a handful of people on the front lawn, returned the candidate's gesture.

"Oops, I forgot to write a check. I guess I'll bring it to headquarters...tomorrow.

For the first time in months, Ali Lyons felt inspired...excited.

CHAPTER TWENTY
ALI

Hillary and Michelle were enjoying their first week at an unusual summer camp in Upstate New York. In addition to crafts, music, and some sports, societal issues and political discussions were woven into the fabric of each day.

Mike bounded into the house after an uneventful summer day at work. "Ali," he called. No response. There was a note on the kitchen table: *Salad in fridge. Went to Sullivan HQ. Should be home by 10. Ali.*

Wounded by her absence, not only of the moment, Mike reached into the refrigerator for a bottle of Heineken. After a couple of swallows, he took Macbeth, the family's black standard poodle, for a jaunt.

"Macbeth, my pal, me thinketh our Ali has a thing for the candidate. Any advice?" Mike was convinced the family pet understood exactly what he was talking about. "I've got to confront this situation, Macbeth, but I'm chicken. What if her answer is 'yes, there is something going on'? Then what?"

The poodle wagged his tail vigorously, paused by a lamppost and raised a leg.

Ali believed that Mike was no longer faithful. As far as her intuitive judgment was concerned, Mike's obsession with Danielle Webb went beyond that of being her lawyer. *Every other word from him these past several weeks has been Webb this, Webb that; "Oh Ali, what a challenging case." And the phone calls from this witch—nothing can wait until Monday. She always manages to call on weekends. My husband is literally caught in Madam Webb's web.*

Lovemaking between Ali and Mike had dwindled and on those rare occasions when they were intimate, Ali no longer climaxed.

Ali was more than frustrated. She felt isolated and angry.

* * *

"Mrs. Lyons, welcome." It was Linda Abrams.

Ali extended her hand.

"Come, let me introduce you to some of our staff. And then I'm off. Tim is speaking in Wayland this evening. After that he and I are going to have a powwow about tomorrow's session in Lowell. We want so badly to connect with the folks in that area. That city's really in turmoil and, Cronin, the likely Republican candidate is local. We need to deliver a meaningful message."

"A whole different cut from the affluence out here. But Tim strikes me as an empathic man…one who can relate to people who are having a tough time."

"Well, we try. Ali…may I?"

"Of course. I'd be insulted if you kept calling me Mrs. Lyons. I like to think I'm not *that* old."

Linda introduced Ali to staff and the volunteers on hand. Ali felt a buzz of excitement and anticipation.

"I'm off. Take care, Ali. And thanks again for helping out."

The person in charge of volunteers was all of twenty-seven, sharp and deeply committed to the candidacy of Tim Sullivan.

"So tell me, Mrs. Lyons, what your availability might be like. I see on the information sheet that you're a school psychologist and that you do some writing."

"Well, the writing's primarily reporting about students' progress, needs, recommendations, advocacy statements. I've also written a couple of papers for the Office for Children. That sort of thing. As for my availability, I'm pretty flexible. I have the summer off, so I can get started whenever you can use the help. But we'll be going to the Cape in August."

"That's terrific. Where on the Cape?"

"Wellfleet. We've rented at a place called Surf Side for years."

"Tim and his wife have a beautiful summer home in Chatham. They usually spend much of August there. So we're going to use that house as makeshift summer headquarters."

"Fabulous. I'm sure I'll be able to help there as well while we're on the Cape," Ali said.

* * *

Ali settled in with daily trips to the Wayland headquarters. For the first couple of weeks she spent hours on the phone and did some door-to-door canvassing. Her contact with Tim Sullivan was limited. He popped into the office occasionally, offering his appreciation and lifting the spirits of workers. He knew that much of their work was tiresome but critical to the success of the campaign. Even with that limited contact, she felt that there was something special about this man. And it was more than charisma. Ali attended a couple of Tim Sullivan's talks in some of the district's struggling towns.

She admired his knowledge, but felt, like others, that he wasn't getting his message across…policies that would actually result in economic benefits. His wording, she felt, was too aloof…not reflecting his empathy in a down-to-earth manner.

Ali wrote a draft with suggestions: *Linda, This past Wednesday I attended Tim's talk at the Chelmsford gathering. I thought Tim's method of communication…choice of words…was too aloof, sophisticated for that audience. He's a more down to earth person than he's projecting. I hope I'm not offending, but I have some suggestions for the upcoming town hall gathering in Lowell. If you think they are useful, please share with Tim.*

These are earnest blue collar people. They're interested in working, feeding their families. They're not interested in Watergate. I suggest he start with one word: Jobs. Then pause. Repeat "jobs" again. And then proceed: I was raised in Lowell. It will always be home. Jobs. That is what I'm all about. You are the

*muscle of our country (appeal to the macho ethic of the growing
Hispanic community). Hard working Americans. I respect and
admire you. My goal on your behalf: good paying jobs.*

Ali continued her document with simple phraseology
designed to connect with people who are plain speaking, who
would leave the town hall session with a clear understanding that
Tim knows their needs and will fight for them.

She dropped the document on Linda's desk with a note:
*Linda, this might be a bit brazen, but please take a look. Let me
know what you think.*

A few hours later—11 p.m. to be precise—the Lyons' home
phone rang. Ali was certain it was the infamous Mrs. Webb. She
let Mike pick up.

They were both reading in bed.

"Hello." Mike was blind to the mocking look on his wife's
face.

"No, no it's not too late. She's right here. Yes. I look forward
to meeting you as well, Tim. Ali's very excited about working on
your campaign." He handed the phone to Ali.

*Tim Sullivan calling me? And at this hour? Maybe something
to do with my suggestions?*

"Ali, hi. Tim here. Really sorry if this is too late."

"Oh, not at all, Tim. Is there something wrong?"

"To the contrary. Linda shared the written materials you left
for her at the office. We love what you've done! Your ideas, some
of the phraseology…perfect. Solid, usable messaging written for
the very audience I'm trying to persuade that I can help. I think the
way you explain some of the policies and ideas can do nothing but
help uplift these folks."

"And get them to the polls," said Ali.

"Precisely. Any chance you could have coffee with us
tomorrow morning?"

"Of course. I'd be delighted."

"Great. How about Mel's Coffee Shop? I assume you're familiar with the place. Seven okay, or is that too early?"

"That'll be fine, Tim. I'll see you and Linda tomorrow morning."

She turned toward her husband. Her smile was brighter than any he had seen in weeks. "Hey, Mike, he likes my stuff." Her excitement, if only for the moment, suppressed her underlying sense of having been betrayed by her husband.

"That's great, Al. I'm really happy for you." And Mike was happy for himself.

Ali's involvement with this campaign stuff is lighting her fires. Maybe it's the spark that'll bring her back to me. I hope it's not an infatuation with this Sullivan guy. He is a handsome dude. No way. Ali's just not the type. We're not the type.

I've got to figure when and how to get something on the table. There's just too much distance between us now. Maybe this is a good time to talk to her.

* * *

Camp ended for Hillary and Michelle, and the Lyons family settled into a last minute change of location for their annual month on the Cape. Ali found a beautiful cottage in Chatham near a lake and close to where the Prescotts were staying. It was larger than what they used to rent in Wellfleet.

Why the change? Mike thought. *Of course, the Sullivans have their place in Chatham. Get off that kick, Mikey. Nothing's going on. It simply makes more sense to be close to the headquarters. And June and Stanley and their kids are nearby.*

Although Mike might do some occasional shuttling to his office, he was determined to spend as much time with his family as he could manage for the month of August. In fact it became a necessity because Ali maintained a hefty pace regarding her volunteer efforts. He ventured into his office only on those days when the weather turned gloomy and the kids joined Ali to do envelope stuffing.

"Mike," Ali said as her husband was tending to burgers and hot dogs on the grill one glorious Cape evening. "Tim is having a fundraiser this Sunday. I think it would be wonderful if you would come. Give you a chance to hear him and get to know a little more about what he stands for."

"And the kids?"

"Up to them. They're perfectly capable of taking care of themselves. If they want to go to the lake or beach, I can arrange for them to join the Prescotts. But the weather outlook is not so great for Sunday. So, they might want to come along with us," Ali responded.

"Sure. Why not? And I suppose I should bring the checkbook."

Ali thought she detected a note of resentment in Mike's reply. Maybe she was right.

"No way, Mike. This has been my caper. Donation comes from my side of the ledger," said Ali.

"I thought we were in this together...life...the kids...college...finances. No?" Mike asked.

"It just seems there's been so much expense, particularly the college fund, that it'd be a help if I dove into my trove. Just want to do my part."

"Thanks, Al. Okay. Whatever you feel is best. How much were you thinking about?" Mike asked.

"I don't know. What do you think?"

"Well, you certainly have donated several grand with just the time you've put into this thing. Maybe a couple of hundred?" Mike's tone betrayed his resentment. *I know damned well Ali wants to write a bigger check. I'll be a prick and just make her say it.*

"Oh, I think at least five," said Ali. Mike was silent as he handed the platter of grilled goodies to Ali.

"Mike?"

"Five. No more than five. You think he's going to get the nomination? I see Kerry as very strong. Vietnam, Yale, tossed his medals…and a family with big bucks," said Mike.

"Don't be so sour, Mike."

She's right, Mikey. You're only digging a bigger hole. Come out with it. Tell her you're jealous…well, not now…maybe tonight after the kids have gone to sleep. It didn't happen.

* * *

A light rain and heavy sky blanketed much of the Lower Cape that Sunday. It resulted in a large turnout at the Sullivan home.

Ali introduced Mike to Tim and his wife as well as other staffers and spouses. Mike hit it off immediately with one of the volunteer's husbands. They stepped onto the porch of the Victorian house, spotted a cooler and opened a couple of bottles of Heineken. Their conversation quickly morphed into the loss of their wives to the campaign.

People came and went. The candidate was a master at working the crowd and remembering names. As six o'clock rolled around, not only did the house clear of well-wishers, but the Cape sky rid itself of its gloom and slowly was replaced by a glorious mixture of rainbow colors.

"Well, thanks to your efforts, Ali, we had a terrific crowd today. So much better than I had anticipated," said Tim as he opened his first beer of the afternoon.

"Mike, your wife has been just amazing."

"Thanks, Tim. It's really been nice meeting you. I join Ali in wishing you great success with the campaign," said Mike. "But I can't wait to get her back."

Everybody laughed.

"And you kids," Tim said to Hillary and Michelle, "have also been an enormous help this summer. I've got a proposal. How about persuading your folks to join our kids and the old people for dinner at the Chatham Bars Inn. Great make-your-own-sundaes. That's my bribe."

"Tim, that's really nice of you but..." Mike was interrupted.

"Come on, Dad, it'll be fun," implored Michelle.

Ali smiled, nodding her head.

Mike was aware of his wife's excitement. There was a schoolgirl quality about her demeanor and conversation during dinner. He thought, *Ali's got a crush on this guy. I can see it in her face. She keeps blushing.* As they all left the restaurant, Mike observed Ali lifting a check from her handbag.

"I forgot an envelope. You think it's okay if I give it to him this way?" she whispered.

"Of course," said Mike, noticing the amount was one thousand dollars. He wrinkled his eyebrows and cocked his head to the side.

"Mike, come on. Don't be like that. This is important. He's got a real chance. And he's honest. He'll be a great Congressman."

Mike shrugged.

"Tim, forgive me. Mike and I wanted to give this to you earlier," Ali said as she handed him the check.

Without looking at it, Tim turned to Marilyn, his wife, and asked that she put it in her handbag.

"Ali, thank you so very much. And Mike, I appreciate yours and Ali's generosity. I'm grateful for your supporting Ali's dedication to the campaign. Once we lock up this primary she'll be yours once again."

Mine? I hope so. Mike offered a weak smile.

"You're lucky, Mike. You get Ali back. I lose Tim to Washington," Tim's wife said.

"Well, first we've gotta top Kerry for the nomination. And then dig in and handle our Republican opposition. Long way to go before we get to the House."

Laughter. Mike observed what he thought was an extra long handshake between Tim and Ali. He watched as his wife kissed

Mrs. Sullivan. Tim turned around while he and his wife walked toward their car. "Ali, if you have any time the day after tomorrow, we could use some help getting the Wayland headquarters in shape for election night. I'm hoping Linda and a few others will be able to lend a hand. But we need to spruce up the place—give it a winning feeling."

"That'll be fine. Maybe Mike and the kids will join the party," Ali said.

She knew that wouldn't happen. It would be one of their last days on the Cape. The kids would want to enjoy some time at the beach before ending their vacation.

She was right.

* * *

When Ali drove along Boston Post Road on her way to the Sullivan headquarters in Wayland, the place felt like a ghost town. The local affluent citizenry were all at their Cape Cod, Maine, Berkshires summer places squeezing in the last days in advance of Labor Day weekend. She would sleep in Sudbury that night, then head back to Chatham in the morning. She was excited about seeing Tim. *I feel like a giddy teenager,* she confessed to herself. But she also looked forward to seeing Linda and whoever else would be there. The staff and volunteers had become a new family for Ali. They had injected a fresh breeze into her life. It would be difficult, she thought, once this all came to a close. She would miss them…the charged atmosphere…the sense of community purpose. *But if Tim wins the primary, I can continue to help. They say that Paul Cronin is the likely Republican and that he'll be tough to beat. Just hope for now that we can top Kerry. Then Washington? Now that would be exciting! Take a leave from work and join Tim's DC staff. Presumptuous, Ali,* she thought.

After brushing her hair and putting on some lipstick in her car, Ali walked into headquarters. Tim greeted her. It was just the two of them. No one else was there. She was surprised and thrilled. Was it wishful thinking that prompted her to bring along her diaphragm? Ali thought to herself: *Does Mike ever go through my things when I'm not around? I know I sometimes flip through his papers. Would he notice that my diaphragm's not in its usual place? No. He's not the type to snoop around. And much too self-confident to even think about me with anyone else. Besides, he'll be on the phone for hours with that Webb slut. I know they're messing around. I just know it.*

Mike remained at the Cape with Hillary and Michelle. His mind was on Ali. His maleness and intuition resonated with a message that something was going on between Ali and the candidate. He remained afraid to confront her. Fearful that she might lie or even worse, tell the truth. *And then what,* he asked himself. *Divorce? No. I couldn't handle that. And what if nothing's going on between the two of them? She would be furious if I confronted her with such an accusation. No....not now, anyway.* Fear won the day. Not denial...fear.

* * *

The thought of being intimate with Tim was exhilarating for Ali. It wasn't long after they exchanged some ideas about changes to the interior of the headquarters that Tim slowly locked the door and confessed that he had not asked anyone else to stop by.

"I need to be with you, Ali. Just you. I confess that I deliberately didn't ask any of the others to help out. Ali, we're drawn to each other." He furrowed his brow, raised his eyebrows and opened his eyes wide. She could feel the excitement. She had never been unfaithful but she felt herself nodding. *It's okay,* she signaled. Not since before her marriage had she made love with anyone other than Mike. But her husband had been disloyal. *With that damned Webb woman. Women know,* she persuaded herself as she rationalized her desire to have sex with Tim. It wasn't long ago when the two of them were having a late night chat after a work session that Tim revealed that his marriage was unhappy. "My wife is a wonderful person, but the excitement has left our marriage. And frankly, Ali, there's no longer any intimacy." Ali

was flattered that he confided in her so personally. And she knew
that he was delivering a message.

Ali's brain had maintained her very own treasure box ever
since she was a child. Although she opened it and shared much
with Mike over the years, she never totally allowed all to escape.
She never gave away the key to that box. There were always
thoughts, happenings that must remain just hers.

* * *

Within moments, Ali and Tim embraced. And after sharing
soft kisses, their mouths opened. Tim slowly guided Ali to the
couch. He undid his trousers as Ali reached behind and unfastened
her bra. She felt his hands move slowly up and down her sides and
then softly caress her breasts. There was a moment of exhilaration
and then something heavy grabbed at her. A disruption to that
sacred place within her heart that defined and spelled her love for
Mike. She realized what was happening would crack the lining of
the unique bond she and Mike shared.

Her desire to have sex with Tim Sullivan was strong. But not
as powerful as the image of her husband that made its way into the
centerfold of her mind.

*I want this, but oh Mike… I just can't. I don't want to destroy
what we've built…our kids, us. Maybe you've been loyal after all.
Maybe this is just what you experienced.*

Ali, beneath Tim's body, moved his hands away as he groped
to remove her denim shorts. She then pressed her palms against his
chest. He felt the message and raised himself.

"I'm so sorry, Tim. I'm just not ready. I'm so very sorry."

Tim was startled, disappointed, but he was not about to force
himself upon Ali. He slowly backed off.

"I understand, Ali. I'm the one who owes an apology. I just
thought…"

Ali gathered herself and started toward the door. "I
apologize, Tim. I feel like such a fool. I had no right…"

"Ali, please. We're adults. Imperfect at best. This isn't a question of fault. The chemistry is genuine and strong between us. Please don't leave, not yet. Let's sit…talk a bit…let's at least be friends."

Ali nodded, tears starting down her cheeks. She sat, lowered her head and put her face in her hands. Tim gently placed a hand on her shoulder.

"I think we could both use a bit of a drink," he said. "There's a bottle of Chablis in the fridge. Friends?" He cast a warm look into Ali's face. She nodded, responding to his gentle manner.

Tim poured the wine into a pair of paper cups.

"This is really crazy," he said extending a cup to Ali.

She frowned, tilting her head to the side, as if to speculate that he was referring to what had just happened between them.

"Oh, no, I don't mean us. I mean it's crazy that such a classy operation as ours doesn't have some proper glasses for our libation," he said. He flashed a broad reassuring smile.

Chuckling and appreciating his lightening the charged atmosphere, Ali responded: "I'll get right on that, sir. Top priority…first thing tomorrow."

Tim raised his cup, ready to make a toast. Ali followed.

"Friendship, Ali. It's a precious commodity. Let's not allow each other to part on negative terms. I admit I'm vulnerable and craving intimacy. And I suspect your story may not be very different. Each of us is married to a wonderful person, but the relationships are growing stale. At least, that's what's happened between Marilyn and me. Am I close? You and Mike?"

"Close?" Ali asked absentmindedly.

"Close in terms of your story, Ali?"

"Ah," she said focusing on whether or not to launch into her feelings for Mike, their distancing relationship, her fears. "My story?"

"I'm a good listener," Tim said.

"You are. I've seen it with your constituents. And you're kind and very wise."

"Please tell that to the Kerry supporters," Tim chuckled.

"Are you worried?"

Tim stood, sighed. "Honestly? Yup. I don't like polls. They're giving me an edge, but I'm concerned." Tim sat near Ali, resting a hand on her knee. "Ali, that's not what I want to talk about now. It's you…you and Mike who are center stage."

Ali held out her cup for a refill.

"Just a half, madam. We'll each be driving. All either of us needs is to get pulled over," said Tim.

"Just a wee bit," Ali signaled. "I still feel like such a fool for what I did. Can you forgive me?"

"What *we* did. Not what *you* did," said Tim. He wheeled away from her.

"Tim, I've been with Mike for a long time. And I realize how much I love him. I'm afraid I was allowing myself to fall in love with you…for all the wrong reasons." She looked into his captivating blue eyes. "Retribution."

The silence was heavy.

"Ah," Tim broke in. "Mike's been unfaithful?"

"I have a strong suspicion. I don't know for a fact, but there's a big part of me that believes he's been having an affair with a client."

"A client? Mike? He would take such a chance? Jeopardize his license to practice law? How do you know this? Or what is it that makes you suspect you're right?"

Ali launched into a description of Danielle Webb without mentioning her name. She shared what she had heard about Danielle from Mike and Jane. She unleashed her frustration about the endless hours Mike has devoted to the case, the constant phone calls, including most every weekend. "We were at a friend's house for dinner one Saturday last May. He gets beeped, leaves the table and returns her call. Can you imagine? Takes her call in the middle of dinner with friends. I've never seen him so obsessed with any one case. He talks nonstop about her and her outrageous behavior and theatrics in court. I begged him to get out of it. So did wonderful Jane, his secretary, who has good judgment. But he insisted he couldn't quit...couldn't run from a fight, he said. I've listened to some of the phone calls. He's so damned deferential. I tell you, Tim, she's seduced my Mike and he hasn't had the guts to tell me. To be blunt, we hardly ever have sex anymore."

Ali wept. Tim placed a hand on her shoulder.

"And I thought *I'll show him,*" Ali said.

"I admire your candor, Ali."

"You shouldn't admire anything about me. But please understand, Tim. I have real feelings for you...beyond my crazy way of thinking that I'd get some satisfaction by getting back at Mike by sleeping with you. The truth is I really would like to make love with you, Tim. But the confusing truth is that despite my suspicions about Mike and my genuine attraction to you, I realize that we have such a strong bond. And the kids. I'm just so crazy about them. The thought of interfering with their happiness...the four of us...our lives together. I can't, I won't jeopardize all of that."

"I hear you, Ali. And I respect your thinking. But let me ask a crazy question," Tim said. "Have you ever considered confronting Mike?"

"Considered? Sure. But we've allowed ourselves to avoid each other. He's all wrapped up in that stupid divorce case...and other cases, too. I kept my head buried in my work. Then when the school year ended, I turned to your campaign. Selfish? Yes. But I'm also passionate about everything you stand for. You'll be a great congressman."

"Thank you, Ali. So you and Mike, not unlike Marilyn and me, and scores of other married couples, get all wrapped up in diversions so that we don't face the emotional deterioration in our marriages. We awaken in the middle of the night with angst. We know something's wrong. But we're afraid to face it or just plain filled with denial. It's so much easier to just go on pretending."

Ali nodded. She placed her cup on a table. "Tim, you're a wonderful, caring, and handsome man. But it just wouldn't make any sense for us to get involved. It would, I'm afraid, end badly. We must stop before it, whatever it might be, gets started. A different time in our lives and who knows what might have been." She reached for her handbag, shook her hair, and gestured to give him a meaningful hug.

Tim said, "Please, Ali. Know how deeply I care for you. But I understand. And maybe I understand what I have to do. Marilyn and I could use some therapy after this campaign is over, win or lose. Maybe, just maybe, she and I can rekindle the spark that was once there. But I do want to see you."

"And I want to see you, Tim. But if we're to save our marriages, that just can't happen. It would make everything a big lie. As difficult as it is, we have to make a clean break and be thankful a sexual relationship never…"

"Got off the ground," Tim finished her sentence.

Ali nodded. Tim extended his arm. Their hands touched.

"Ali, confront Mike. You have it in you. Don't be afraid. As for us, I realize this is somewhat of a goodbye…before we even said hello." They laughed.

"Tim, you're a very kind man. Right now my head is scrambled."

"Ali, I'd be so grateful if you would stay with the campaign. We're close to the finishing line. I'll keep my distance." He raised an arm. "Scout's honor."

They walked together to Ali's car. After opening the driver's door, Ali turned, raised herself on her toes and kissed Tim gently on the cheek. "Thank you for understanding. Your kindness makes it all the more difficult for me to say goodbye. But we must."

* * *

As Ali drove back to the Cape the next day, she felt relief. *One of these days after Mike's Webb trial is over one of us will break the ice and ask the question each of us has been afraid to ask. But unless Mike initiates something earlier, I'll wait until that case has come to an end.*

* * *

Ten days later, Tim Sullivan lost the Democratic primary to John Kerry.

Excepting for one chance meeting, Ali and Tim never again had any direct contact.

CHAPTER TWENTY-ONE
MIKE AND ALI

Mike ruminated over the disappearance of the tall man after spotting him at the close of the last session before the Thanksgiving break.

"Christ, Sean, how does a tall, conspicuous guy like that disappear so easily?" Mike had just rushed out of the large double door of the courthouse in Pemberton Square. Sean, breathless, was a few steps behind.

"For crap's sake, Mike, who the hell is this guy? What are you so damned excited about?"

"There!" Mike pointed straight ahead down the exterior escalator leading to Cambridge Street. He was certain that he saw the tall man bending into a taxi, ushering somebody ahead of him. But in an instant his peripheral vision spotted an equally tall look-alike entering a CVS.

Mike dashed into the store, his swinging briefcase almost cutting down a customer at her knees. He spotted a man at least six feet three inches, but other than his height and trim build he bore zero resemblance to the mystery person Mike had met at the hospital the day of the shooting – the one he was certain had been stalking him later when Ali picked him up, and now showed up in the courtroom.

The lawyer turned to his colleague.

"I don't know about you, Professor, but I sure could use a nip."

Sean replied, "Oh, well, if that's an order…yes, sir."

During their Scotch time at Patten's Bar & Grill, Mike rehashed the entire hospital scenario involving the tall man and then spotting him later when Ali came to drive him home.

Sean asked an obvious question: "Tell me, Mr. Trial Lawyer, why do you give a damn about this guy? You and your esteemed Mrs. Webb came so close to being shot. The two of you are at the Mass General ER. She told you that he was a friend. He's a friend hovering about her. And why not? She just had the hell frightened out of her. Later, you think he's stalking you because you happen to see him or someone who looks like him…what, two hours later…when you're in your car and God knows in what kind of state after damn near getting killed? Anything since?"

"No. Nothing, Sean, until spotting him in the courtroom," Mike replied.

"And didn't you ask her about him during any of your office sessions?" Sean asked.

"She said something about his being a friend of her husband. And she remembered him saying one day when he came to the apartment to meet her husband that if she ever needed help, any kind of help, he would be there for her."

"So…

"So, she told me she remembered the offer and called him from the ER," said Mike.

"So, my friend, end of story. Go home. You're on overdrive. This guy is inconsequential. Your imagination is creating something that doesn't exist. Take the weekend off. Maybe even be real smart and patch things up with Ali," said Sean. "The two of you have been on the outs much too long. And don't give me 'this is none of your business' crap. She's much too good for you and you know it. Now get home and take care of what's really important."

"That, Counselor, is the best advice you've given me all week."

The friends shook hands outside on blustery Court Street.

Mike said, "And don't forget. Thursday. Thanksgiving, in case you've never heard of it. Ali wants everyone there by five. And if you want to bring whoever it is you're romancing with these days, be sure to call and let Ali know. The kids are gonna make place cards."

Sean had been a regular at the Lyons home on Thanksgiving and Christmas ever since Sean's wife and sons were murdered.

"Thanks, Mike," shouted Sean as he hustled by the site of the 1770 Boston Massacre where British militia fired upon several unarmed civilians. "I think you should invite your client," he added playfully.

"Forget our invitation, wise guy. Take yourself to a movie instead," Mike hollered back, turning in the direction of his office building.

Two close colleagues…two dear friends…releasing tension after two long weeks of a gritty trial.

* * *

Mike walked into his reception area. He mouthed the words in her direction: *"go home."*

"Must have been a good day in the life of Attorney Michael Lyons," Jane said.

"Au contraire," said Mike, flinging his briefcase on a chair. "We really ended on one awful note, but my dear Miss Jane, the weekend is upon us, I am fueled with Scotch, having had a couple with the professor *and* no court next week."

"Messages on your desk. I've been explaining that you've been tied up in court. And by the way we could use some greenbacks. The account's getting a little low and I'm due for another gigantic bonus." She paused.

"Webb is behind. We'll get a check next week. I'm going to add something for combat pay. What a piece of work. Go have fun with Phil this weekend. I don't know how that handsome dude stands you."

Jane started to gather her coat and handbag. "Love to Ali and the kids. We're off to my folks' for the holiday. Can't wait."

Mike planted a platonic kiss on his loyal friend's cheek.

The lawyer stretched back in his chair, rifled through messages. Nothing earth-shattering. Buoyed by not having to face the dreary courthouse next week, he looked forward to some family time and alone time with Ali. *Time to do some mending.*

* * *

When Mike arrived home, the kids were on the way out to join friends. Quick hugs and they were off.

"Have fun," Mike hollered. He turned to Ali, a closed mouth smile on his face.

"Hello, Mike." Ali turned and went toward the kitchen. Mike followed. She pointed to the kitchen table. "Your favorite tumbler is at the ready."

Ali's up to something, Mike thought. *Very serious look. And she hasn't had a drink at the ready for me in months. Is this the day she breaks it to me…wants to split? Let me see if I can chip away at the ice.*

"No kiss?"

Ali ignored his playfulness. She poured herself a glass of Chablis. "It's good to know you're not on trial next week. You must be relieved."

"Oh, Ali. I can't tell you how freeing it feels. I've got a reprieve until after the holiday. My briefcase is in the car and that's where it's staying all weekend. What about your workload?"

She shrugged her shoulders. "I've got some psych tests to interpret…nothing urgent." Ali gestured with her wine glass toward the family room. She had placed a plate of hors d'oeuvre on the coffee table.

"Ali, the shrimp look fantastic." Mike reached for the plate.

They stood quietly, looking at each other.

"Mike…it's time. We need to talk."

He sighed. "It is, Ali. You're right. We need to get it out."

Ali sat on the couch, placed her glass on an end table. Mike straddled the ottoman so that he sat opposite her.

"Mike, our discontent has been festering for too long. We're each to blame for not dealing with our...fears. So I'm going to come right out with it. Are you sleeping with Danielle Webb?" Ali's penetrating gaze messaged her purpose.

Mike shook his head slowly. He closed his eyes for a moment, leaned forward. "Ali, I beg of you. Hear me. On the lives of our children...NEVER." He put his drink on the floor and placed his hands on his wife's knees. "Al, I care so deeply. I have never strayed. Not with Danielle Webb...not with any other woman since the day we connected."

Ali took a deep breath and reached for Mike's hands.

"Semper fidelis, Ali."

Her eyes welled. Slowly, softly, Ali acknowledged the deep significance of Mike referring to the Marine Corps motto. He never invoked those words lightly.

"Thank you, Mike. It's just that you've been so obsessed with..."

"The case, Ali. The challenges of the case. Not her. Is she attractive, flirtatious? Yes. But I have kept the desk...and always will...between her and me...between any client and me. I am unreservedly faithful."

Ali squeezed her husband's hands.

"And you, Ali? Since we're putting everything out on the table. Tim Sullivan? I've been tormented for months at just the thought of him...scared to ask."

Shaking her head, Ali responded: "I'm relieved. We've each been faithful after all."

Ali candidly confessed her "crush on Tim" and the unconsummated liaison. She admitted that beyond finding Tim attractive, she was seeking vengeance because "I was so certain that you were having an affair with Danielle Webb."

The heaviness lifted from their lives. Everything felt lighter...the room, the furniture, the air...and, most importantly, their hearts. Mike put steaks on the grill. It was the first time they enjoyed dinner together in months.

CHAPTER TWENTY-TWO
KATHERINE

"Mike, your three o'clock is here," Jane called on the intercom.

"Could you come in for a moment?" Mike replied.

Jane addressed the new client in the waiting area: "Pardon me for just one moment, Miss Hennessey."

The secretary stepped into Mike's office, closing the door behind her.

"I don't have anything in my book," Mike said quizzically. "Who is she?"

"Donna Anderson's client. Donna called last week. Wants you to take over the case. Coming up for trial in a few months. This is the one, coincidentally, where Dr. Armont is involved. I booked the appointment and also told you that you have the client's permission to talk with Dr. Armont. *Ricordare?*"

Mike slapped his forehead. "Of course you did. And I discussed the matter with Larry Armont the other night. I totally forgot about the date of the appointment. Early dementia, my dear Ms. Donnell. Dock my pay. She's the nun." *The shooting. It's had an effect on my short-term memory. I need to see someone. And I've got to have Sean riding shotgun with me in all trials. I can't risk messing up because of memory issues.*

"Ex-sister of the church. Shall I bring her in?"

"I'll come out."

The few steps from Mike's office into the reception area allowed him to make the transition from the repetitious thoughts of the shooting.

"Hello, Mi…Ms. Hennessey. I'm Mike Lyons. Please." He gestured toward his office.

Katherine Hennessey nodded. Obviously ill at ease, she slowly shook his hand and in a soft voice, simply said, "Hello." She was wearing a tired looking black straight skirt, white blouse with a button undone at her midsection, and a faded ill-fitting blue blazer with a school emblem over the left pocket area. *Probably a parochial high school,* Mike thought. She was not wearing any makeup. She carried a briefcase and had a tattered winter coat draped over an arm.

Times have been tough for this woman, Mike thought. *Larry Armont mentioned some serious depression...mood swings.*

"I'm pleased to meet you, Ms. Hennessey. Attorney Anderson spoke very highly of you. And I gather from what she said, you don't particularly like coming into Boston. Thank you for making the trip. Perhaps during future meetings we can arrange to meet someplace more convenient for you. Did you drive?"

Katherine responded with a close-mouthed smile. "I took the train, Mr. Lyons. But I'll soon be moving into the city. May I?" She reached into her blazer pocket and pulled out a pack of cigarettes.

Mike nodded. No time to lecture about not smoking. "How about some coffee?" He nudged an ashtray toward Katherine.

"Thank you, Mr. Lyons, but I'm fine. I drink too much coffee as it is." Her hand trembled as she struggled to light a cigarette. Not wanting to embarrass her, Mike did not offer assistance. Deep lines extended from the corners of her mouth. Her brow was furrowed. She looked like someone who was aging beyond her years, a fearful young woman filled with self-doubt.

* * *

The client's lawyer, Donna Anderson, was among the coterie of attorneys who referred their trial work to Mike. Katherine's psychiatrist, Dr. Larry Armont, was a highly regarded clinician at McLean Hospital in Belmont, Massachusetts, one of the world's leading psychiatric institutions. Coincidentally, he and Mike were longtime friends ever since their teammate days on the Dartmouth basketball team. They went their separate ways following graduation, but reconnected years later when Dr. Armont accepted a position at McLean Hospital after practicing in New Jersey and serving as editor of the *American Journal of Psychiatry.*

During their recent phone conversation about Katherine Hennessey, Dr. Armont spoke frankly about his disillusionment with many lawyers. "Mike, I'm so happy you're stepping into this one…or at least considering it. Donna's a fine person and lawyer, but the courtroom's not for her. Unlike you and Donna, I've found many of your fellow lawyers with whom I've worked on custody cases too cavalier and disconnected from the emotional turmoil of their troubled clients. They're primarily interested in the god-almighty buck. They lack passion and genuine caring. You and I go back a long way, Mike. I know what a compassionate and honest guy you are. I only hope you're a lot better at trial work than you were at hoops!" Good-natured ribbing between two pros with genuine mutual respect.

The doctor explained that he met Katherine when she was transferred from the Psychiatric Section of South Shore Hospital three years ago. He was intrigued by her story and the challenges her emotional state presented. Consequently, he agreed to take her on as a patient. After several outpatient sessions, he felt that Katherine might have the basis for legal recourse regarding Father Thomas Riley's deceit and his devastating impact upon her. Dr. Armont was of the opinion that "Katherine's emotional turmoil, including two suicide attempts, was directly related to maltreatment by Father Riley."

"This priest, Mike, was a Svengali-like person. He controlled this naïve woman, twenty years his junior, and deceived her about their having a life together. He lied when he promised that he would resign as a priest and that they would marry. In my professional opinion, his actions were absolutely causally related to her suicide attempts. I suggested that it would be helpful to her if the priest were held accountable; that she might want to consult with a lawyer. Katherine asked that I recommend a female lawyer. I immediately thought of Donna," Dr. Armont said. "But I have every confidence that Katherine will be totally at ease with you, Mike. She understands that Donna doesn't do any trial work. And I think she's come along sufficiently so that having a male attorney will work. Let me know how it goes after you've met with her."

* * *

The client fidgeted with her lit cigarette, inhaled deeply, and nervously flicked it although ashes had not formed.

"Dr. Armont called me a few days ago," Mike said. He turned and faced her. "Obviously, with your permission, he spoke briefly of your situation."

She responded, "Did he tell you just how fu…messed up I am?"

They both smiled at her near indiscretion with language. Some of the tension lifted. Mike thought it bizarre for the "f" word to even be on her mind, let alone slip from the tongue of a sister of the church, even an ex-sister.

"No. I wouldn't put it that way. Not at all. Donna Anderson and Dr. Armont each said you're a smart, talented, and marvelous woman. They said you've literally been to hell and back. I got the impression that the doctor is quite proud of the progress you've made." Mike intentionally used the word *hell*. And he hoped he didn't sound patronizing.

Katherine crushed her Marlboro into the ashtray.

"I don't know if I'm 'back,' Mr. Lyons. But I'm a lot better than I was when I first met Dr. Armont. But the nightmares persist."

Mike nodded.

"The doctor also explained that you had requested a female lawyer and that's why Donna was recommended. Do you think you can be comfortable with a male attorney trying your case?" Mike pointed to himself.

"Oh, yes. Donna and I discussed this. She and Dr. Armont were both so reassuring about you after she explained that she doesn't go to court," said Katherine. "I like to think I've gotten over that hurdle. And Donna said that you have the respect and admiration of the Women's Bar Association."

"Well, that is flattering," said Mike. "But it's critical that you have total confidence in any lawyer who's going to try your case. And that you're comfortable with him."

Katherine nodded. "Absolutely. I suppose we'll see how we both feel after this consult?"

"Yes. So tell me a little about yourself," Mike said.

"I assume you know that I was a sister here in Boston. A teaching order in the archdiocese."

"Yes. Donna told me that you had resigned from your position as a nun."

"Not a nun. I was a sister. There is a difference. Are you Catholic, Mr. Lyons?"

"Not really. A story for a different day. But, tell me Ms. Hennessey, what is the difference?"

"That can get complicated. Like everything with the church. But essentially, nuns lead a more secluded life than sisters. Our vows are pretty much the same, but sisters don't live in monasteries and are often committed to community tasks. I was a teacher. I apologize, Mr. Lyons. I had no business asking about your religion."

"Not at all, Ms. Hennessey. As I said…"

"You became disillusioned and stopped going to church?" she interrupted.

Katherine self-consciously fidgeted with the lapels of her blazer, which probably fit her just fine years ago.

Mike said, "The fact is I'm half Catholic, half Jewish. I've got a corner on the world market of guilt."

Katherine leaned back, exhaled, choking while she laughed.

Mike said, "My dad was Jewish, my mom Catholic. They never made an issue of religion. Well, I didn't go to church much at all, and synagogue on just a few high holidays when I was very young." Mike shrugged.

Katherine turned and stared toward the large window overlooking Court Street. She said softly, "I was once a devoted Catholic, but now..."

After allowing an appropriate space of silence, Mike asked, "So now that you no longer serve as a sister, just what kind of work are you doing?"

"I have a scholarship at Simmons College School of Social Work." She lit another cigarette. "I want to get my MSW." She turned her head and exhaled smoke away from Mike. That small but considerate gesture was not lost on the trial lawyer. It was a subtle but important indication of his client's character. Like any seasoned litigator, Mike was already projecting his client onto the witness stand, imagining just what kind of impression she might make upon a jury. Success in a courtroom frequently hinged upon the demeanor and body language of one's client. All part of a trial lawyer's obligation: listen unreservedly and observe even the smallest expressions and idiosyncrasies. Sometimes subtle mannerisms, gestures, facial expressions carry much weight with jurors and judges as they wrestle with a witness's credibility.

"That's terrific, Katherine. Simmons has quite a strong reputation. I think I remember reading that its social work program is the oldest in the nation."

She responded, "Yes. It's just outstanding. And I'm trying to be useful at Rosie's Place. You know of it?"

"Certainly. My wife and I donate clothing there throughout the year. My kids keep outgrowing everything. So you're commuting from the South Shore?"

"Not much longer, Mr. Lyons. As I mentioned, I'll be moving into the city...an apartment not far from Rosie's Place in a couple of weeks."

"Just what is it that you're doing there?" Mike asked.

"I counsel abused women." With that, Katherine's eyes filled. She paused. "I have firsthand experience."

Mike leaned forward. "I want to help you. Donna Anderson sent over the file dealing with your case, but I need to get as much information directly from you as you're comfortable giving me."

Mike thought about some of what he had read in Attorney Anderson's file and his own observations: *She's a scared soul. Deeply wounded. Abuse of power. Abused outcome. Attempts to take her own life. The darkness beneath her eyes…telltale signs of someone sleep-deprived and troubled.*

There was a knock on Mike's door.

"Yes," Mike raised his voice.

Jane opened the door slowly. "May I?" She entered with a plastic tray balancing two coffees and some pastries. "I'm sorry for interrupting. I just thought you might enjoy some fresh coffee. And there's some milk there as well." This was common practice for his secretary, who frequently offered refreshments of her own volition. Mike's theory was that it wasn't just that Jane Donnell was the most thoughtful and loyal secretary in all of Boston, but that she was filled with curiosity, if not a tad intrusive.

Mike smiled. "Thanks, Jane." Katherine seemed less tense. The interruption, the cordiality of Jane's gesture and manner lifted some of the heaviness in the room.

"Does your secretary always do that? So thoughtful. And I've changed my mind. I will have coffee after all."

Mike said, "And don't be shy about the coffee rolls. My favorite. Perfect texture, not too sweet."

After they each had a chance to enjoy some coffee, Mike said, "Whenever you feel like talking, that's fine with me. And by the way, let's get back to the difference between a nun and a sister as we progress. I'm curious."

"For a long time, Mr. Lyons, I seldom felt like talking…about *it*, I mean. I had several sessions with Dr. Armont before I finally began to open up. I was ashamed, scared. He's a true professional."

"What was it, specifically, that brought you to McLean's?" Mike needed to hear it from her.

"Suicide, Mr. Lyons. I tried to kill myself." She paused, stared at the lawyer, attempting to gauge his reaction. Mike's expression passed the test. It was serious and concerned, reflecting exactly how he felt.

"Someone had the good sense to transfer me to McLean after I had first been taken to a local hospital. Not that I deserve much of anything from our Lord, but He delivered Dr. Armont when there was little left of me."

There was a necessary silence.

"I'm sorry to hear that. I mean, I'm pleased that Dr. Armont has become a part of your life, but obviously very sorry to hear that your difficulties resulted in your attempting suicide," Mike said, shaking his head as if to signal compassion.

"Thank you. Shall I begin?"

"Please." Mike leaned forward.

Katherine launched into her story. Her voice for the most part was monotone, haunting in its matter-of-fact delivery of intimate details, including two efforts to take her own life. Mike was concerned that it might be a distraction if he took notes, so he decided against it. And he had a necessary ingredient that helped make him one of the very best trial lawyers: the art of listening and absorbing. One of Mike's mantras: *forget about yourself and concentrate 100% on the client. I want her to just go with her story. I want as much detail as she can give. I'll dictate after she leaves.*

Katherine related much of her situation in chronological fashion. She spoke of Father Riley having been designated her private mentor prior to her teaching assignment at an elementary school in Brighton.

"I'm not sure if it was the Bishop himself or one of his underlings who assigned him to me, but Father Riley told me on more than one occasion he had requested to work with me. He said that there was something special about me," she added with self-mockery. "I had taken a course he taught at Chestnut Hill."

She described his method of private instruction, which included the use of audiotapes that he recorded. She told Mike that she became infatuated with him and that he proclaimed his love for her. She described the lunch that the priest had prepared. "An afternoon that culminated in our making love for the first time. I was scared, but I acquiesced. I thought he genuinely cared about and loved me." She spoke of his repeated requests that she resign as a sister. Believing his promises that they would have a life together and that he truly loved her, she submitted her resignation. "He made me feel special. He resurrected some repressed emotions deep within my being." Katherine was becoming comfortable. Because of Mike's ability to focus solely on his client, together with his calm and sincere demeanor, she found talking with him to be freeing, therapeutic.

Katherine went on. "I was thrilled, ashamed, and scared all at the same time. My mind obsessed about our having sex." She stared open-eyed at her lawyer. Her expression telegraphed the messages: *You do get it, don't you? And please don't be judgmental.* She sensed that Mike did indeed "get it" and that he was not a critical person.

Mike said, "It must have been bewildering."

"I tell you, Mr. Lyons it was all I could think about. A man of God…a priest…telling me that he loved me…that he desired me as a woman." Katherine shook her head from side to side.

She then mumbled, "I was so needy, overwhelmed with a desire to be loved. I was taken with what I felt was kindness and warmth. Then something strange happened. There was a recording on which he told me how much he wanted me." She swallowed

and crossed her legs. "At least I *thought* there was such a
recording. But…"

"A tape recording?"

"I think so. I…I get so confused about it. Sometimes I fear
that I hallucinate. I think I hear or even see things that are just not
there. Dr. Armont says this is all part of post-traumatic syndrome."

"These tapes, what were they all about? Did they remain with
Father Riley?"

"Oh, absolutely," Katherine said and then added in a faint
voice, "He was very possessive of them. More than once he told
me how hard he worked to prepare them. They were examples of
difficult classroom scenarios…about twenty minutes in length. I
would listen while alone in his study. Then he would come in and
we discussed the issues raised in the tapes."

Katherine reiterated Father Riley's proclamations of love for
her, his desire, "Indeed, his command that we each leave our
positions with the church. He drafted my letter of resignation. He
told me over and over, not just that day, but for months after that,
that he was going to break away. He talked about how he had
served and served well. He said that it was time for us to enjoy the
gift of God, the gift of each other delivered by Jesus. I believed
him. I hung onto his every word. Like a fool, I trusted him. I
actually thought that he really loved me."

Katherine leaned back, lit another cigarette. "I dutifully
submitted my resignation as a sister." Tears. "What a fool. I threw
away all that I had cherished." Shaking her head, she added: "I just
so *believed* him…held onto his every word."

Mike said: "It was all part of his scheme. He wanted you to
believe him. I think, Katherine, that it was all about control
without regard to the destructive emotional impact on you."

She said, "For two years it went on. He used some friend to
get a condominium in Hingham. It was en route to his sister's
home on the Cape. He insisted that we always enter the building
from the rear. And he never showed up wearing anything but

civilian clothes. After a short while, he didn't ask but insisted I move in…by myself. He said this would be our little love nest."

"And you did?" Mike asked. "The two of you lived together?"

"Oh, no. As I said, I moved in by myself. He remained at the house in Newton. I was to live in the so-called love nest and just wait for him to stop by as he chose. What a fool. I was under his spell."

She described how excited she had been during the early months but then boredom and a sense of uselessness dwarfed the novelty and thrill. "I came to realize how empty I felt. I wanted to move back to the city. He would have none of it."

She spent her days in the apartment, playing piano, reading, writing, but for the most part, waiting for Father Riley to appear. "At first he came almost every day, late in the afternoon. We would have cocktails, talk of marriage, make love, have dinner, which I always prepared. For awhile he would stay and help clean up. Then that changed."

Katherine lit a cigarette and paced in silence.

Mike asked, "Are you okay? Would you like to stop?"

"I think I'm ready, at long last willing to go ahead with a trial. But, yes, for the moment I'm kind of drained."

"Understandable."

"How does this all work? Are you now my lawyer? Is Donna no longer involved?" Katherine inquired.

"As I explained to Donna, before I agree to take on your case I want to gather more information. Then I can advise you for certain whether or not I would be willing to undertake the trial."

"If you do take it on, Mr. Lyons, do I pay a separate fee?"

"Absolutely not. It remains as a contingent fee case. The fee remains the same. You pay one-third of the amount I actually recover for you…no matter how many lawyers are involved. But it is important that you understand that I would pay one-third of my fee to Donna as a referral courtesy and compensation for all the work she has done up to this point," Mike explained.

"And if there is no money at the end?"

"In that case, there is no fee," Mike answered.

"That's quite a gamble for you and Donna, isn't it?" Katherine asked.

"Quite frankly and selfishly that's why I'm very careful about which cases I take on when the fee is contingent upon the recovery. Another reason for my wanting to reflect about the law and facts before plunging in. Works both ways. Certainly is unfair for a client to chase false hopes."

"So should I come back?" Katherine asked.

"Definitely. I need to hear more of your story. Tomorrow's a heavy day for me, but what about the following day?"

"I'll make it my business to be available. What time?"

"How about 10 a.m.?"

"I'll be here. He used me, Mr. Lyons. Used me until the life was gone out of me. He stole from me." Katherine took a deep breath. "He manipulated my being. It took hours of work with Dr. Armont for me to be able to admit to myself that I had been...used."

"Abused, Ms. Hennessey, abused." Mike said. "Just awful. I think you just might have a triable case. See you day after tomorrow."

CHAPTER TWENTY-THREE
KATHERINE

Many tools are available to litigators for use prior to a trial in order to discover as much as possible about their adversary's case. Trial lawyers master the *Rules of Discovery* and *Rules of Evidence* so that they have a good handle on what is admissible and what is not permitted during the course of a trial. Trial by ambush is largely reduced by what is referred to as *pretrial discovery.* Methods are provided so that a lawyer, if he/she prepares properly, will be able to reduce the element of surprise at trial. One of the tools, *A Notice to Produce,* enables each side to get from the other copies of documents and other tangible items that each attorney suspects the other side might have. This helps to curtail, if not eliminate, either side from suddenly springing a movie-like surprise with a document during trial.

Mike's thought was this: once he agreed to take the case, he then would send a *Notice to Produce* to the attorney for Father Riley and the Archdiocese requiring them to make and send copies of all instructional tapes and any personal recordings the priest may have made.

As it turned out, Mike then would receive copies of the teaching tapes but no personal tapes. Their reply stated: "All tapes were prepared solely by Father Thomas Riley and for the sole purpose of instruction. There are no personal recordings."

* * *

Katherine returned for her second appointment with Mike.

"I've made fresh coffee. May I offer you a cup?" Mike asked.

"Oh, that would be wonderful, Mr. Lyons. I take it black. Are you okay if I smoke?"

Mike nodded and went to the reception area to get the coffee.

As Jane got up from her chair, she said, "I'll take care of that, Mike."

"Absolutely not. I'm more than capable. Your job description says nothing about being a waitress," Mike said.

His secretary smiled and said, "Well, since you're pouring..." She held out her mug.

As Mike complied, he added, "Don't forget to remind me to fire you."

* * *

"Here you are, Katherine. And I hope you don't mind my using your first name. We're pretty casual around here. Please call me Mike."

Katherine smiled, lit a cigarette, inhaled deeply, then waved her hand as if to clear the smoke. She was better groomed and more relaxed than during her first visit.

"My associate and I did some research with respect to the type of lawsuit Donna started on your behalf. And we agree that Donna properly framed your case as one seeking monetary compensation for *intentional infliction of emotional distress.* As Donna no doubt explained, a major requirement is that we must show that the priest's conduct was extreme and outrageous. I certainly don't think that's a problem in your situation. The payment of money by the priest and archdiocese for your hospital, medical, psychiatric expenses together with compensation for your extreme emotional abuse is what we can attempt to accomplish for you. I assume Donna explained all of this?"

"She did. She also brought up...I think she called it...charitable immunity?"

"Exactly. There's a law in Massachusetts that limits the amount one can recover from charitable institutions, such as an archdiocese, for torts committed while carrying out their charitable purposes. It's quite obvious that Father Riley was not furthering any charitable purpose of the church..."

"Hardly."

"Yes. As you know, Donna has sued the priest and the archdiocese. Father Riley is a defendant both as an individual and as an employee of the archdiocese. And the archdiocese is a defendant because as an employer it can be held responsible for certain acts of its employees. More importantly, somebody high up in the archdiocese may have been aware or suspected that Father Riley was behaving reprehensibly. Consequently, the archdiocese should have taken action long before it finally transferred him to Fitchburg. If so, that strengthens our argument that the monetary limit should not be applicable in your case."

"I think I understand. The law is inundated with exceptions. No?"

"Absolutely. All part of the intellectual challenge. And I should add that the archbishop has taken the high road with some other abuse cases and settled for amounts beyond the statutory limits. There's never a guarantee that a case will be settled, but he may well want to reduce the likelihood of negative publicity and be willing to resolve your matter for an amount greater than the twenty thousand dollar limit," Mike explained.

"Thank you for the explanation, Mike. Donna did discuss some of this."

"There's more regarding this issue, but no need to discuss it any further at this point," said Mike.

"Mike…and I hate to sound so vindictive…is it not possible to extract some kind of apology from them?" Katherine asked.

"Technically, no. But we'll certainly try to make that part of any settlement," Mike answered. "If we're unable to get a strong offer to settle, we'll go forward with a trial. A jury is not empowered to include a mandate for an apology. But I've got your message."

"Thank you, Mike. I so hope that there'll be a settlement," Katherine said. "May I assume that your decision is to go ahead and represent me…to try the case if it has to go that way?"

"It will be my honor," Mike replied.

Katherine gestured her thanks.

"Donna is disappointed that the archdiocese did not make an offer to settle. But that can all change as we get closer to trial. The ball's now in my court. One step at a time. For now I'd like more information. Tell me about the condo, where it is, who owned it, your thoughts about living there," Mike said.

"Well, I learned that he chose a place on the South Shore because it was far enough from the college and en route to his sister's year-round home in Wellfleet on the Cape. He used to go there often, particularly on weekends. His sister is married, three kids. In his diabolical way, he calculated just how convenient a small South Shore town would be for him. How sexually convenient. Many a Friday night he would come down, always insist upon sex, sometimes stay for dinner, other times not, and then would…escape, yes, that's how it felt…as though he was running away." Katherine shook her head. "He would leave and go to Wellfleet. And there I would be. I felt abandoned."

"Did he ever stay with you for the weekend?" Mike asked.

"Yes. Early on…just a few times. And we would actually have fun, but he would always insist upon eating in. Anytime I would suggest going out for dinner, he would wave me off. He'd say something like I'm such a good cook…that it would be more fun to make love, stay home, drink wine, listen to music, and read."

"And that was it? Just a few weekends?" Mike asked.

"Later, there would be another stretch of three weekends."

Mike asked, "Did he come to the condo during the week?"

She answered, "During the first few months Father Riley would come one or two evenings a week. He never slept over during the week. Said it was dangerous; that because of his housemate and the housekeeper, he had to sleep during the week in Newton. And I understood that. But then he stopped coming during the week at all, claiming that his teaching and administrative duties at the college were too burdensome. His visits during the final months were limited to Friday and Sunday evenings, on his way to and from the Cape."

"We're going to need a little detail regarding those visits. I'd like you to prepare, as best you can, some kind of calendar. Enough to give us an idea of when he was there during the week and the weekends when he stopped in on Friday night, but didn't stay over…instead, went to his sister's place in Wellfleet."

"I think I have what you need. I kept a diary throughout most of our time together," Katherine said.

"Fantastic," Mike said.

Katherine bent down and removed a spiraled notebook from her handbag. She placed it on Mike's desk.

"Thank you. This will be very helpful," Mike said as he flipped through a few pages.

"I made daily entries. In a way it felt therapeutic. And I worried about what was real and what wasn't. What I might be imagining. Writing things down helped. I felt as though I was losing my mind."

Katherine continued: "You'll see many times when he would stop on Friday on his way to the Cape and then again on Sunday night on his way home. He would insist upon sex. It stopped being lovemaking. It was on demand. He became cold and harsh," Katherine said.

"Would the two of you have dinner together, a glass of wine?" Mike asked.

"That all changed after the first few months. Sex. He would always demand sex. Strictly for his own gratification. It mattered not what I wanted or how I felt about it."

Mike shook his head and asked, "What about his promise that he would leave the Church and no longer serve as a priest?"

"Oh, my. Now you've asked *the* question, Mike."

Mike signaled with his hand, encouraging her to continue.

"He was an expert at inventing excuses. 'Oh,' he would lie, 'just as soon as the college comes up with the right Jesuit to replace me.' Another line was 'there's a crisis at the archdiocese' and they desperately needed his presence. He would speak of how difficult his resignation would be for his sister. 'I've got to wait for the right time,' he would say."

"And that time never came," Mike said, getting up and pacing behind his desk.

She looked up at him and said, slowly and emphatically, *"Never."*

"Terrible. The revelation that he was lying about resignation had to be so very difficult for you."

"One could say that. *Difficult.* One might also say *ruinous.* I spun out of control, Mike. I was simply being used. I felt dirty and degraded. But at the same time, in a state of denial."

Mike shook his head, the look on his face revealing empathy.

"To put it simply and pathetically, I started watching the clock each day waiting until five so that I could have some wine. It wasn't many weeks before two o'clock became the new five o'clock. I was young, lonely, felt abandoned, full of self-hatred."

"You held onto the belief that he would one day surrender his collar and that you would marry?"

"I did. I was totally taken in. Dr. Armont helped me to realize I was under his spell. I was in a fog as to what I had become. Things were actually blissful those first few months. And then it all changed. He changed."

Katherine went on, "He used to proclaim his love for me all the time. He would tantalize me by speaking of marriage, even having children. We would laugh and talk about names for the kids. And then he would suddenly demand sex. As I said the other day, my feelings didn't enter into the equation. I gradually became aware of his nasty side. He would arrive on a Friday, late afternoon, and insist upon immediate sex. Sometimes he would call and tell me to have dinner ready. But then, after sex, he would simply say that he had to get to the Cape. He would chastise me for not keeping the apartment clean. And then he started in with my drinking too much." Katherine leaned forward and buried her face in her hands.

"I feel terrible for you, Katherine. You've been through a lot," Mike said.

"I felt isolated, so alone. I found myself wandering through the center of town, sometimes going to the local coffee shop. I admit that I was always one to slip into a fantasy world but this was different. I was zombie-like. I became aware of another woman who was at the coffee place most every time I went in. One day she asked if I minded if she joined me. A friend! I was desperate for a friend. I was too ashamed to reach out to any of the sisters in my Order."

Mike said, "I get that…about the sisters. Shame is very powerful. Let me ask a blunt and tough question. You were aware you were being used and that Father Riley had no intention of resigning. Why didn't you just get out?"

Katherine welled up. She raised a hand, palm facing Mike, as if to say: *You've hit a nerve. I can't go there.* "

"I'm sorry," he said. "But we're going to have to get into some difficult areas. Perhaps this is too soon. We can come back to it another time," Mike said.

"I understand that you have to probe," she said. After gaining her composure, Katherine responded, "I was spinning. Spinning out of myself. I was becoming somebody I didn't recognize…far beyond the fantasy life I used to create. It seems clear now but believe it or not, I was so in love with that man, and obsessed with the idea that he could love me. I kept hoping, deluding myself that each time would be different and that our relationship would get back to where it once was. I wanted so much to believe that he would keep his word."

"I get it," said Mike. "Easy for anyone outside to suggest that you just leave at that point. You were, Katherine, his *prisoner*. He deliberately isolated you and made you emotionally dependent upon him."

"I just couldn't face reality, Mike. My work with Dr. Armont revealed exactly what you say: he imprisoned me and stripped me of my being. I was nothing more than an object for him to control," Katherine said.

Mike thought: *This is a strong infliction of emotional distress case. She'll be a good witness on the stand. She's honest and it shows in her bearing. And that counts for a lot. But we're going up against the archdiocese as well as the priest, and that could be daunting. Through it all, though, a jury can relate. I'm beginning to feel my final argument.* The trial lawyer instinctively leaped ahead in his mind and envisioned what the trial might look like, including possibilities for his summation after all the evidence had been presented. Courtroom litigators frequently think first about what they want to say in their final argument. Then they work backwards to work through all the testimony and pieces of evidence that must be presented during the trial so that they have the basis for a strong and convincing summation. *Here's what I want to be able to say to them, but I can't unless I've presented the evidence to support my final argument. That's what the law requires. Can't just make up a bunch of stuff like the courtroom movies.* Preparing properly for trial is grueling. Trial lawyers calculate each piece of testimony and other evidence necessary to present so that they've established the foundation enabling them to deliver a powerful and convincing final argument.

After a pause during which Katherine lit a cigarette, Mike asked that she tell him about the woman in the coffee shop.

"We talked. She told me that there was a terrific bar, women-friendly, in one of the nearby towns. I can still remember her eyebrows raising, knowing indeed that I was interested. I can only imagine, Mike, how desperate I must have looked."

Katherine spoke of her frequent trips to the tavern that her new friend suggested, sometimes the two of them, sometimes on her own. "I switched from wine to beer and then to the hard stuff in the middle of the day."

Mike shook his head, not in a judgmental manner, but signaling that he understood.

"And I confess, Mike, I actually enjoyed the leering of some of the young men. I was slipping and I'm not sure that I knew how to stop. I was medicating myself with the alcohol and seedy atmosphere. I had become plain and simple an alcoholic."

"Did you confide at all in your new friend?" Mike asked.

"A couple of drinks and I was loose-tongued. I think I let out much of my stuff. She was a good listener. A drunk maybe but compassionate."

"Name and address?" Mike asked.

"Certainly. But do you think she'll have to be involved?"

"Maybe. I'd like to meet her. Speak with her. And then we'll decide whether or not we might need her," Mike said. "She may be able to corroborate much of your story. And at the very least describe just how you appeared, how down, upset, and on a path to self-destruction you were. But I'd need to learn about her skeletons before making a decision about getting her involved."

Katherine pulled an address book from her handbag.

"Money...what about money?" Mike asked.

"Are you ready? He actually provided me with an allowance. Always cash; never a check."

"An allowance? Now that's surprising," Mike said.

"Not at all. It wasn't generosity. When I look back it was pure and simple hush money. Did I just use the word 'pure'?"

They shared smiles.

"He didn't want me turning to anyone to try and borrow money. I might say too much. I drank my days and nights away, until..." She stopped.

"Until?" Mike asked.

Katherine's eyes were teary. She turned her head toward the window.

Mike asked, "Drugs?"

She fixed her eyes on Mike. "Quaaludes. Cynthia, my new friend, became the source."

Katherine then related the first time she attempted to take her life.

"I had lost all faith, both in the Lord and certainly in Father Riley. Do you know that practically each time before he would have sex with me, he would bend by the side of the bed and pray in thanks to God? He would sprinkle holy water over the sheets. How bizarre is that?"

"What would you do?" asked Mike.

"I would stand numb. Sometimes I would try to engage him and suggest that maybe we could make love later. I would tell the truth…that I wasn't in the mood."

"How would he react?" Mike asked.

"As though I wasn't there…only my body. He would insist. And I was caught under his spell and afraid that if I didn't respond as he demanded, something awful would happen. There was a look in his eyes and a smirk on his face that frightened me."

"You spoke of suicide, Katherine. If you can please tell me."

"There was a Friday when he called and said he would be at the apartment by five that afternoon. Nothing else. His conversations had become terse and cold. I became angry. I wanted to die. I wanted him to suffer and feel responsible. I wanted him to experience real guilt. So about an hour before I expected him, I took a 'Katherine Cocktail.'"

"Booze and drugs?" Mike asked.

"Double dose this time. I was done. Even if it meant an eternity in hell I needed to end my life. I wanted him to find me dead. I wanted to shake his tidy hypocritical world," Katherine said.

Mike asked, "A note?"

"No, but I wish I had," Katherine said.

"What happened?"

"I went out. *Out cold.*"

She explained that when Father Riley arrived and found her unconscious and saw the bottle of Quaaludes, he tried to wake her.

"It's dim but I remember starting to come to, his yelling my name, slapping my face, putting cold washcloths on my face. He finally got me up on my feet. I could barely stand. I was a mess. Disoriented. Needed a doctor."

"Did he call for medical help? Take you to a hospital, call an ambulance?" Mike asked.

"Absolutely not. His priority was protecting his own hide. Through the haze I became aware of how scared he was and how happy I was that he was so frightened. I'm sure he just wanted to leave but that would have gotten too messy for him. He must have been afraid that someone might find me and that I might tell all. He pulled me to my feet, made me drink coffee. I wretched. He dragged me outside, the back way, of course, once I was able to stay upright."

"Did he say anything, Katherine? Did he talk to you?"

"I remember him telling me how we would walk it off and that everything would be fine. His voice was so kind as we walked. Like it had been way back in the beginning. I realized that I had yearned for that soothing and convincing tone. In my stupor I thought that he loved me once again. I hated what he had done to me. But I wanted his love so badly. Denial, Mike, is a powerful force."

"Katherine, thank you for being so forthright. This is a lot for you to relive and deal with. Would you like to stop now or are you okay to go on?" Mike asked.

"Mike, you're just like a shrink. I told that to Dr. Armont when I called to tell him of my meeting you. He laughed. I asked how the two of you knew each other. He mentioned that you were good friends at Dartmouth and that you were always a good listener. But he told me to remind you what a lousy basketball player you were."

Mike laughed. "Next time you speak with the doctor please tell him that I told you to remind him of his nickname on the basketball court: *Mr. Double-Dribble.*"

"He's an excellent psychiatrist and a real human being. He's not rigid, if you know what I mean. I know that he has his reasons for the tones that he sets. On occasion, parts of our sessions feel like casual human conversation. It's nice that the two of you have such a good rapport. And reassuring," Katherine said.

Mike nodded. "And regarding your compliment about my being like a shrink, thank you. But this is all part of my being a lawyer on your behalf. I'm not trained to offer any psychological guidance. You know that. But to represent you, I need thorough and complete knowledge of everything that you endured."

"I'm fine to continue," Katherine said.

Mike nodded and then asked, "Your wanting his love so badly, as you put it, changed, didn't it?"

Katherine frowned.

"Your need for his love, his affirmation. That changed, or am I wrong?" Mike asked.

"Oh, Mike, I hope so. I've been working hard with Dr. Armont to rid myself of that sick need for him." She paused and then added, "My self-esteem was dead. My soul was dead. I really wanted to be dead."

"He imprisoned you and was killing your spirit," Mike offered.

She's convincing. Her suffering will be clear to any jury. It's more than half the battle...having an honest and naturally persuasive client on the stand, Mike thought.

Katherine got back to the incident when the priest found her comatose. "When I began to come around, he said that he had to leave. The coldness and stern persona replaced what I kidded myself into believing had been genuine caring. He admonished me 'to get a hold of myself.'"

"So mercurial," Mike said.

She continued with how the priest threatened that he wouldn't see her at all if she didn't give up the pills and alcohol. She told Mike that Father Riley called her weak and a disgrace to the Church. "And this was after I had just tried to take my life!"

Mike shook his head. *She said it a few minutes ago...half of this job is being a shrink. I so hope she's going to be okay. I'll make an appointment to sit and talk with Larry.*

Katherine continued. "Then, on a dime, he slipped back into a soothing tone."

"Sounds like classic split personality disorder," Mike thought aloud.

"Dr. Armont certainly referenced that disorder," Katherine said, reaching for her package of cigarettes.

Mike got up from his chair, walked to the windows overlooking Court Street.

Katherine continued: "He assured me that everything was going to work out. When I questioned what he meant by 'work out,' he renewed his promise to resign and marry."

"Just like that?" Mike asked.

"Yes, and I was fool enough to believe him. I was that desperate. My suicide attempt succeeded in my gaining the upper hand, or so I thought. For a change, I thought, I had manipulated him. I had so frightened his exposure that he decided his only way to keep everything from getting out was to mollify me. He actually called throughout the weekend. I fell for his fake caring voice and what turned out to be hollow words."

Mike echoed her thought, "'Hollow words.' Promising a future for the two of you together. So how was his behavior toward you after that? What happened?"

Katherine spoke of a few weeks when Father Riley spent time with her during the week in addition to three consecutive weekends. She described his demeanor in retrospect as "syrupy." At the time she tried to convince herself that he was changing, "coming back to me. He lied about how he had inquired about the most expeditious way of resigning and that he was waiting to hear back from the archdiocese."

"Did you realize at the time that he was lying once again, or…?

"I was trying to convince myself that he was being sincere but then one evening he showed his true colors."

"How?" Mike asked.

"I told him that I had not had a drink or taken any drugs in over a week. It was the truth. I asked if we could get away for a weekend. I explained that I was a little shaky and anxious, having stopped cold. He burst out at me saying that it was absurd to think that we could be seen together in public. I told him that I felt like a prisoner. I thought he would understand."

"How did he react when you used the term 'prisoner'?"

"He showed his true colors. He screamed. He told me that I was selfish and I had never served Jesus properly. Can you imagine? That hideous hypocrite accusing me of abandoning Jesus? 'Beg for forgiveness,' he said. 'You have created our sin.'"

Katherine stared, her face in disbelief at the memory of all that had happened.

"Unbelievable," said Mike.

"And that's when I lost all faith in everything. His leaving the apartment…the next several days and nights are all one major blur. Alcohol, Quaaludes, and yes, I even got access to cocaine. Just like a bad movie. I was spinning out of control, picking up young men and begging for love. A nightmarish cliché. Weekends came and went without a word from him. I telephoned and he didn't take my calls, didn't return them. He knew that I was under his control. He came to believe that I wanted him so badly that I wouldn't utter a word and that his dirty secret of imprisoning me was safe. Oh, I think at this point in time he was sure I would be driven to do away with myself. I don't think he was worried anymore that my killing myself would expose him. And he nearly got his wish."

Mike asked whether Katherine made another effort to take her life.

She got up from her chair and excused herself to use the restroom.

* * *

Mike stepped into the reception area. After his client left to go down the hallway, he stared at Jane. She looked up and read his face. "That bad?" she asked.

"As bad as it gets," he said shaking his head. "I'll need to do some serious dictation after Ms. Hennessey leaves."

They had a brief conversation about some messages regarding other cases and the need to hire a young attorney to assist Sean with his research.

"When you do," Jane said, "what about considering a woman?"

Mike pointed a finger toward his secretary. "You're right on. When the time comes, we'll hunt for a 'she.'"

* * *

Mike returned to his desk while waiting for Katherine. *This priest abused his badge of power. His conduct, no question, was blatantly extreme and outrageous, beyond all bounds of decency. Katherine was abused. She trusted him. He used her, plain and simple. This hypocrite destroyed a huge part of her life. She'll be left with permanent scars. This is a strong case of intentional infliction of emotional distress. Thankfully she's under the care of a first-rate psychiatrist. Larry is outstanding.*

* * *

When Katherine returned she spoke of the night she had slit one of her wrists and then wandered outside. Discovered by police who were driving by in a cruiser, they rushed her to South Shore Hospital. A few days later she was transferred to McLean Hospital.

"That's when Dr. Armont came into my life. God bless him," Katherine said.

She explained that as a result of her work with Dr. Armont she was able to face all of this and resurrect what had happened. "During my therapy I learned that the second time I tried to commit suicide and went outdoors, I did so because there was a part of me that still wanted to live…to be found. I wanted help."

Katherine leaned over and opened her briefcase. She removed a sheaf of papers. "Here, Mike. It's all here. Copies of the hospital records and a narrative that I prepared as part of my therapy, which is pretty much taken from my diaries."

"Thank you," Mike said. "These documents will be most helpful. Is Father Riley aware of the second attempt? And I must tell you that I cringe at using the title 'Father'."

Katherine answered that she doesn't know and that she's not had any contact with the priest since before that last attempt to do away with herself.

"The police, the hospital personnel? Did you tell them about him, about the relationship? If you did, there will be references in their records which could be useful."

Katherine responded, "Oh, no. And not out of any sense of loyalty. I felt it was my fault. I was consumed not only with a newfound hatred for him, but with self-hatred. I questioned myself. I was consumed with shame. I thought I was to blame, just as he had said."

Mike shook his head. "Katherine, what's the age difference between you and this man?"

"Twenty years. I put the birthdays in my notes." She gestured to the papers she placed on Mike's desk.

"Tell me a little bit about your background? Please." Mike gestured toward Katherine.

"My own father was verbally and emotionally abusive, particularly after my mother died while I was in high school. In later years I learned that he had been unfaithful to my mother, who was a woman he referred to as a saint. He was always suspicious of me. During high school if I came home from a date later than his curfew he would call me 'whore.' He was certain that I had had sex with my boyfriend and then insisted that I become a nun. 'Lie about not being a virgin,' he would scream. I shared all of this and more with Father Riley. He took advantage of my vulnerability. This and much more came racing into the light after working with Dr. Armont."

She leaned back, lit another cigarette, and sobbed.

"I'm so sorry, Katherine. What you've been through is horrific. And hearing so much more from you today buttresses my opinion that Father Riley's corrupt conduct was so egregious that the Archbishop will feel morally obliged to settle your case for more than any possible twenty-thousand dollar limit. In short, we can overcome the charitable immunity cap…even if we have to go to trial."

"Thank you, Mike. But this is more than about money to me."

"I understand. But as I mentioned earlier, monetary compensation is what I can accomplish for you."

Katherine nodded.

Mike said, "This is probably a good place to stop. I want to take the time to read through the hospital records and, of course, your narrative. I'll call you in a couple of days. We'll arrange a meeting. In the meantime I would like to speak again with Dr. Armont, with your permission, of course."

"By all means," Katherine said. She stood and extended her hand. She thanked Mike, paused on her way out to thank Jane.

"I'll wait for your call, Mike. Dr. Armont was right about you," Katherine said. "I feel safe with you. You're an excellent lawyer…and shrink."

She opened the suite door, turned around, and added, "It was as though I was infected by him and he excised my soul."

CHAPTER TWENTY-FOUR
KATHERINE

"Rosie's Place. Hang on. I'll get her."

"Hey, Sister K, call for you."

"Deleanor Smith Washington, how many times have I asked you not to shout. I can hear you just fine. Too loud, Ms. Deleanor. And how many times have I told you I'm not a sister anymore."

Katherine Hennessey paused, looked into the wide reproachful eyes of her volunteer office helper.

"Well," said Katherine, "what I mean is not that kind of sister. I used to be a sister of the church. But not anymore. The other kind? Yes, of course. And you know that very well. We women are all sisters here."

Ms. Washington, her head high and tilted back, grinned a grin of satisfaction and held the phone toward Katherine, who mouthed the words, *"Who is it?"*

Deleanor shrugged, then said, "Sound like a Mr. Lyin'."

Katherine took the phone, shaking her head.

"All men are liars," Deleanor said.

"Hi, Katherine, Mike Lyons here. I hope I'm not interrupting anything."

"Hello, Mike. No, you're not interrupting. I don't start my next session for another twenty minutes." She waved her hand, signaling her assistant to leave.

"How are you?" she asked.

"Great, thanks. And you? How are things going for you over there?"

"All peace and tranquility," Katherine answered jokingly.

"How's your program going? Are you getting some decent feedback from the powers that be?"

"It's a project in the making, Mike. But I think it's going to work out. With all lack of modesty, I sense the women are getting something positive from the sessions. Anything new with the case?"

"Yes. I got a call from the trial clerk. We can expect to get started with trial in two months. And you recall that we talked about depositions. I'm going to take Father Riley's dep and they're going to take yours prior to trial."

"Just the word 'trial' makes me jittery," Katherine said.

"It's going to go great and you'll be terrific," Mike said. "And the depositions will be like a rehearsal. They've agreed to take your deposition first. Then I'll take Father Riley's."

"Part of your strategy?" Katherine asked.

"Yes. I know you're going to be impressive. By their taking your deposition first we'll be hitting them hard and fast with the real substance of our case. Let them know just what you've been through. I'll also get a feel from their questions just what their strategy might be. It'll give us a leg up to go after 'you know who' when I take his dep."

"I think I understand," said Katherine. She felt anxiety welling up within her. "When does this happen?"

"In ten days. Plenty of time to get you well prepared. I know this is short notice but any chance that you can come in tomorrow or the day after?" Mike asked.

* * *

Katherine arrived at Mike's office the following afternoon.

"Good to see you, Katherine. Come in. Please make yourself comfortable."

She lit a cigarette. "I must say, Mike, I'm kind of nervous about this." Her voice was a tad shaky.

"You're going to be fine, Katherine. You and I will go over all the issues and questions that are likely to be asked. Be yourself, tell the truth, and we're on top," Mike said. "The dep is really a mechanism for them to find out what kind of person you are; what kind of witness you're likely to be should the case actually go to trial," Mike advised.

"I'll do my best. Where will it take place? In the court?"

"Oh, no. It's an important part of the case, of course. You'll be placed under oath by a stenographer who will take everything down that is said. But it's done in a rather informal setting. It will take place at Attorney John Colello's office. He's representing Riley, and one of his associates will technically be representing the archdiocese. When I take Father Riley's dep, it'll take place here."

"Is the judge present?" Katherine asked.

"No. If there's a need for me to object to any questions, I'll do so. And if the matter to which I object is very significant, it's taken up with the judge in her lobby prior to trial and after transcripts are prepared. Highly unlikely, though," Mike answered.

"I understand," said Katherine.

"By the way, Father Riley's been placed on leave from the College. He was transferred to Fitchburg some time ago…before Donna started the lawsuit. As I mentioned when we first got together, somebody in the archdiocese knew something was going on," said Mike.

"Fitchburg? Ah, yes, the Church's way of slapping his wrist. They ship out *'priests in need of assistance'* to small parishes. He'll probably be there for all of a one-year sentence before returning to his comfortable home and beloved Chestnut Hill College," Katherine said sarcastically. "Totally rehabilitated, of course."

Mike replied, "It'll be more than a slap on the wrist once we're done with him. He's never going to be returning to his position at Chestnut Hill…not after we get through with him."

"Should I be worried about his lawyer? You mentioned that he's a real pro."

"John Colello is an excellent lawyer and an honest man. He and his firm handle just about all the archdiocese's litigation. He's 'old school.' For the most part, a gentleman. But he can be clever and lull an unsuspecting witness into a false sense of security. He and I both use the 'kill *'em with kindness'* technique. No nonsense. Honest. If after the dep he recognizes just how meritorious your case is and realizes how you have been suffering…and I know he will…he'll urge the archdiocese to settle for significantly more than the forty-five thousand they recently offered. He doesn't want a story like this getting into the newspapers," Mike said.

"I should hope not," said Katherine. "I would dread having this in the papers. You did mention, Mike, that you would do everything possible to keep this out of the limelight. I'm very nervous about all of this."

"You're going to be fine. We'll get you well prepared. You'll simply tell the truth. You'll do very well."

"You have a reassuring manner about you, Mike," said Katherine.

"We're going to have at least three good prep sessions. If we need more, we'll do it. We'll be asking every possible question that I think John Colello might ask. In fact, as we're rehearsing, I'm going to do my best to imitate his grandfatherly style. And yes, I certainly did promise that I'll make every effort to settle your case but only if the terms are reasonable. I'll give you my honest opinion regarding any future offers they may make. But right now we've got to proceed to prepare for trial so that we can be in the perfect posture to negotiate a maximum settlement. You and I both agree that the forty-five thousand dollar offer they proposed is far from reasonable."

"Why do you suppose they did that?"

"It's just a matter of strategy. They're hoping you'll get cold feet and not be willing to go forward with trial. But they don't know the *real* you. They've gotten a distorted view from Riley. When Mr. Colello takes your deposition he'll discover how honest you are and that your integrity will be apparent to any jury," Mike said.

"I have such confidence in you, Mike. I'll do my best. I don't want to let you down," Katherine said.

"Any case, Katherine, can be settled short of trial. But the trick is to get the *maximum,* and a key toward that objective is to thoroughly prepare for trial so that the other side knows we're serious and ready to go the distance. My experience tells me that after they take your dep and certainly after I depose that excuse for a priest, they'll raise the ante. Sorry to make this sound like a poker game, but it's part of the business of settling and trying cases."

He looked into her eyes. He read her concern. She focused and felt his enthusiasm and integrity. Katherine knew she had first-rate representation. Nonetheless, she was apprehensive. *Still frightened of him?* she asked herself. *Or am I still in love with him? Am I doing the right thing...suing him? Actually suing the man who I made love with? Get a hold of yourself, Katherine. He abused you. He abandoned you. And never once expressed remorse.* She took a deep breath and reached for a cigarette. *If only he would apologize.*

"Katherine," Mike interrupted her thoughts. "This is all about you and how you were emotionally damaged by this man. You trusted him. You admired and looked up to him. He's a priest. To you...to *the followers*...a man of God. He was your mentor. You believed him. He lied. He broke his promises to you, just as he broke his vows. You were vulnerable and he deliberately took total advantage."

Mike clenched his fist and nodded emphatically.

"Let's get started, Katherine. I've carved out the afternoon. Anytime you need a break just say so. Have you had lunch?"

"I'm fine, thank you."

"Coffee?"

"An iced coffee would be perfect."

* * *

The question and answer session proceeded smoothly. Mike was methodical. His tone, for the most part, was easy and calm. Then it changed, quite deliberately, as he delved into Katherine's past. Sarcasm accompanied by a harsh expression as he asked about her sexual history before becoming a sister.

"I thought you said he had a grandfatherly style, this Mr. Colello?"

Mike replied, "He does, but even grandfathers can get angry. He's a trial lawyer. There's an actor in him. If he thinks some righteous indignation might rattle you, he'll spice his style with it. It's posturing. An integral piece of the gamesmanship involved in trials and depositions."

"But Mike, how could he possibly know about…well, you know what I mean?"

"Katherine, he may not know anything about your one-time episode with that lad in high school. But then again we must assume his investigation about you has been thorough," said Mike.

"Zachary lives in Atlanta. As I told you, I last saw him at our high school reunion a year ago. He's married, kids. Truly blessed. I'm certain he would have contacted me had anyone talked with him."

"So you want to lie? If you're asked about any sexual intercourse prior to your becoming a *sister*, you, Katherine Hennessey, are going to sit there, under oath, and say 'none'?"

Mike tipped his head as if to say, *come on Katherine, that's not you.*

He continued. "The worst thing you could do to your case, to yourself as a person, is to lie. Don't allow yourself to corrupt your own dignity, your own sense of integrity. Remember my opening advice?"

"I know," she said. "Just tell the truth and everything will be all right. But, Mike, this is embarrassing and don't you think it's a stretch to think Mr. Colello might possibly know about Zachary and me. Zach's a good person. I know he would have contacted me if anyone got in touch with him about the case, about us when we were kids in high school."

"You may be absolutely right. But why take such a chance? You might have confided this in Father Riley and forgotten that you did. The fact that you had sex on just one occasion prior to representing to the Church that you were a virgin may be a weak spot in our case but it's not a fatal one...not if you're forthright about it. On the other hand, our case could be wrecked if the opposition knows about you and Zachary and you deny having had intercourse with him. They'll produce Zachary as a witness to contradict you...and thereby attack your credibility," Mike said.

"I could call Zachary," she said.

"You're fighting me, Katherine. None of us is perfect. If you tell the truth, the jury will understand. They'll admire that you're being candid about such a personal matter. And it gives me an additional basis to argue what an open and honest person you are. But if you were to get caught on that stand lying about this, our case will be damaged. They'll have the basis to argue that you're probably lying about other things regarding Riley. It will cast a shadow on your credibility. And trust me, you're not the first woman to become a sister who has misrepresented her virginity. That reality will be in the minds of the jurors. They'll reward you for your honesty."

Katherine got the point. She nodded. "I understand."

"Okay. So, we're back at the deposition. Colello asks: 'Ms. Hennessey, did you ever have sexual relations with a man prior to representing to the Order that you were a virgin?'"

"Yes, sir. I had sex on one occasion when I was a teenager in high school."

"And did you lie about that to the Order?"

"What do I say, Mike?" Katherine asked.

"Simple. The truth. And here is where you can volunteer something. Say how you felt about that," Mike counseled.

Mike repeated the question.

"I was embarrassed and still am?"

"Did you lie about that to the Church?" Mike repeated.

"I didn't tell the Order that I had had intercourse as a teenager. I was ashamed. And I regret that."

"Perfect!" Sean, who had been observing, exclaimed. "Perfect. Colello will know that you're being forthright and that's major. He'll know he's dealing with an honest person and that he's not going to be able to trap you into lying," Sean added.

Mike nodded in agreement.

* * *

And so it went. Mike, Sean and Katherine worked an additional pair of three-hour sessions going over every possible line of questioning that they could anticipate. Mike wanted his client to be thoroughly prepared.

* * *

The deposition went smoothly, except for Katherine's equivocation about an alleged "personal" tape recorded by Father Riley.

Attorney John Colello, carefully calibrated, spent a great deal of time getting as much detail as he could from Katherine about what she alleged to be the medical and emotional consequences of "your mutual relationship," as he repeatedly characterized it. Katherine did not hold back. Attorney Colello's strategy of emphasizing consent was designed to show he had some arrows in his bow; that if consent didn't exonerate the priest, it may well serve as a mitigating factor.

Attorney Colello: "Ms. Hennessey, did you at any time refuse or decline to have sexual relations with Father Riley?"

Katherine: "Yes."

Attorney Colello: "And when was that?"

Katherine: "Several times. Once I began to feel that Father did not really love me and that he wasn't going to resign, I tried to stop having relations."

Attorney Colello: "*Tried* to stop? What does that mean? You're an adult. Are you implying that he forced you?" Colello's stoic expression morphed into one of staged indignation.

Katherine: "He would insist." She paused. "He had a way of making me feel it was my obligation."

Attorney Colello leaned forward, a feigned look of confusion on his ruddy face.

Katherine did not wait for the next question. She broke Mike's admonition about only answering questions and not volunteering. She added: "There was something always so commanding about his persona. And he would lie and speak again of our getting married. I would be confused, wanting to believe him, yet knowing in my heart that he was just using me, using me for sex. I didn't have the emotional strength to ward off his insistence, hoping against hope that his tenderness would return. And that he would keep his promises."

Mike hid his smile. His client may have broken his rule, but she had struck a chord, getting across the fact that she literally was under the priest's spell and physical power. Dr. Armont had helped Katherine see that she had become mesmerized by the priest, by his repeated expressions of love for her combined with his authoritative position as a priest and mentor. This came across during her testimony.

Attorney Colello, masquerading his chagrin with what Katherine had just volunteered: "Let's try to be more specific about just when you claim to have attempted to decline to have relations."

Katherine was well prepared for this line of questioning. She answered truthfully and with specific time periods.

Katherine: "I remember that first Thanksgiving after I left the Order. Father Riley drafted my letter of resignation. My dad, furious with me for having done that, said I was not welcome to spend the holiday with the family. I was devastated. Father Riley came to the apartment…"

Attorney Colello interrupted: "Ms. Hennessey, my question was a simple one. *When* was it you say you attempted to keep Father Riley from having relations with you. *When?"* He was probing to determine if there was a boiling point…something he might want to use at trial.

Mike, whose strategy was to be as low profile as possible in order to convey the correct impression that his client is honest and strong and can handle these questions without her lawyer jumping in, nevertheless decided this was a good point to make a little noise.

"Come on, John. This is a depo. No need for theatrics. And the fact is, Ms. Hennessey kept a diary, which is loaded with dates on which he forced her to have relations. I provided your firm with a copy long before you sent out a *Notice to Produce*. We've nothing to hide."

Trial lawyers love the gamesmanship. The adversaries looked at each other, doing their best impersonation of anger, but neither was capable of rattling the other. There was too much mutual respect and experience for that sophomoric strategy to go anywhere between these two pros. And they each knew it.

Colello turned to Katherine: "You may continue."

Katherine: "Well, the day before the holiday, Father Riley came to our apartment. I had hoped he was going to stay with me. I was bereft. I had already told him about my father banning me from my own family. I broke into tears when he arrived. I so needed him." Katherine swallowed hard. "That man, that man, Mr. Colello, stepped into the apartment and hugged me. I was so relieved. I never knew what to expect from him. I thought he was being kind. I thought for sure he was going to say that we would spend Thanksgiving together. But within moments it was clear that all he wanted was sex. I tried to make him understand that I simply couldn't." Tears came to Katherine's eyes. She struggled to compose herself.

Colello: "How did he, as you put it, *insist?"*

Katherine: "He sprinkled holy water on the bed. Unfastened his pants. Looked at me with that commanding way of his. It was as though I was under his spell, Mr. Colello. He made me feel it was my obligation."

Colello: "And what happened?"

Katherine: "I succumbed. I was afraid if I didn't, like so many other times, he would get angry. I felt I had no choice. I had been cut off from everyone. Now that my own father had cut me off, Father Riley was my only contact with the world. I was his prisoner."

Colello: "What if anything did he say to you?"

Katherine: "'Come now, Katherine' he would say to me. 'This is us. This is our private expression to each other.' Words, he was so good with words. And his tone and penetrating eyes were…well, it was getting to be threatening, intimidating. He was brilliant at making me feel it was actually my obligation to submit. And that if I did, he would love me."

Colello: "But he never physically forced you to have sex, did he?"

Katherine: "Well…"

Colello: "Oh? Did he physically force you…on any occasion?"

Katherine: "No, not physically. But he is so strong."

Colello: "And he never physically prevented you from simply leaving the apartment, did he?"

Katherine: "No, but…"

Colello: "My question is, did Father Riley ever stop you from leaving the apartment?"

Mike: "Come on, John. There's no allegation of physical harm in this case."

Colello: "I take it that's an objection to my question?"

Mike: "It certainly is. Irrelevant." He then advised Katherine that she may answer the question.

Katherine: "He did not."

Colello: "And just so we're clear, did Father Riley ever once strike you?"

Katherine: "He did not."

Colello: "Did he ever physically push you onto the bed?"

Katherine: "Not exactly 'push.' Sometimes he would put his arms around me and lower me to the bed. As I said, he's very strong. And I was too intimidated and afraid to resist."

Colello: "Did he ever push or shove you at all?"

Katherine: "No."

Attorney Colello was doing what many skilled trial lawyers do. He was asking a series of questions that during the actual trial would require a one-word answer and an answer that was favorable to his case. And he was ruling out definitively any allegation of physical harm.

Mike shrugged, as if to say, *"I just said there isn't any claim of physical harm in this matter."* He also knew exactly what his adversary was doing.

Toward the end of the deposition, Katherine testified about her downward spin: the alcohol, drugs, one-night stands, the breakdowns, and the attempts to take her own life. She also answered questions regarding her psychiatric care with Dr. Larry Armont. Attorney Colello was matter of fact in learning as much detail as he could. He had two goals: In the event this case actually went to trial, he did not want any surprises in the courtroom regarding the damages aspect of Ms. Hennessey's case; and with respect to potential settlement, John Colello wanted ammunition with which to persuade the Archbishop that settlement may well require more than the current offer.

Attorney Colello concluded the deposition: "Ms. Hennessey, you're an adult. You were an adult when you first had relations with my client. Excepting for the few occasions toward the end of the relationship when you say you tried to decline sexual intimacy, you gave your consent. In fact, there were many times when it was you who initiated, isn't that the truth?" His point was made. He didn't care what Katherine's answer might be. In fact, he concluded his questioning before she had a chance to answer. Mike simply held up a hand as if to say, "It's fine; don't bother with an answer."

As they left the conference room, Colello suggested that he and Mike talk. Mike took this as a clear sign that meaningful settlement was in the offing. Excepting for some muddled answers when Colello asked about the "mysterious personal cassette tape," Katherine had done a first-rate job. Mike also felt that the Archbishop wanted to keep this case out of the news.

Mike turned to Katherine. "You did great. Truth always prevails. I know you're probably exhausted, but would you mind waiting in the reception area? John and I are going to talk a bit."

"Not at all," she said.

* * *

"Mike, I'm going to be candid with you. Katherine Hennessey has a lot of emotional issues. But I'll be damned if I buy into your claim that her mental state is all as a result of her love affair with my man. She lost her mother when she was a kid. She had a terrible relationship with her father. Her psyche was a mess long before she decided to seduce Father Riley. And you know I'll go after all of that. But, nevertheless, give me a decent figure, something reasonable, and I'll see what I can come up with over and above the forty-five."

"What! Seduce Father Riley! John, your good priest is the one with the messed up psyche. And he has some serious memory problems. When he told you that he never made a recording on which he proclaims his love for Katherine, he's either outright lying to you or has damaged memory cells," Mike said. "Dr. Armont is going to have some interesting things to say about that," Mike added.

"Come now, my friend, have you ever actually listened to this mystery tape? Did you see her face when I asked questions about it? Did you hear her equivocal answers? That's all because she invented the recording. Pure fantasy. She herself used the word 'hallucination.' And she mumbled something about not being certain. That's on the record now, and you know it," Colello responded. "And as you are well aware, our expert, Dr. Cohen, will have a field day with your client's world of fantasies and hallucinations...particularly when it comes to the invented tape thing."

"No, John, I've not heard the tape because your guy has it or destroyed it," Mike said.

"Wrong. It never existed. With all due respect, Mike, you have a delusional client on your hands. She fantasized about hearing a tape and about much of what she says Father Riley promised. She needed to convince herself that Father Riley wanted her. And when she realized he was not about to stray from his calling and devotion to his responsibilities as a priest, she couldn't handle it and has come up with a lot of *imagined* material. Dr. Armont is too honest not to deny that about her when he's up on that witness stand."

"John, Katherine Hennessey is an honest woman. And a jury's going to see that. She's more than just credible. Your guy's going to walk into that courtroom with 'hypocrite' written all over him," Mike said. "And by the time I'm through with him, the jury will see the words 'vile,' 'immoral,' and 'evil' written all over him."

"For God's sake, Mike," Colello said. "She just admitted that she experienced hallucinations, went on 'imaginary trips.' Those were her words, not mine. Don't delude yourself, Mike. She may be a nice person but she led the priest on because of a fantasy life she created and wanted. And I know you've got Doc Armont who'll testify about the emotional stress she's endured, but as I just said, he'll also have to testify about her hallucinations and fantasies."

"John, I have infinite respect for the Church. Your priest demonstrated that he does not. He broke his vows. He led this woman, twenty years younger, down a path that resulted in not one, but two suicide attempts. He abused and isolated her, all to exercise control and satisfy his sexual cravings. I look forward to taking his dep."

Mike stood and extended his hand. John reciprocated and said, "Think about a figure, a reasonable number that I can work with."

"The forty-five the archdiocese offered is chump change. It's going to take a lot more. Looks like we're going to trial," Mike said.

"Well, without a decent number from you, Mike, maybe that's so. You know how I love the drama of the courtroom," Attorney Colello responded.

"And so do the newspapers." Mike wasn't through, not yet.

"The Archbishop is not afraid of her claims. In fact, he just might relish a story about a disturbed former sister seducing and now trying to destroy a victimized priest."

"She didn't exactly force him to penetrate her on at least a weekly basis," Mike said.

The lawyers smiled, each fully aware that the settlement dance was underway. And at the same time, each was concerned that the other just might be stubborn and take this thing into the public arena and go forward with a full-blown trial.

"I'll call you," said Mike as he left.

* * *

Mike and Katherine stopped at a local coffee shop. Despite his assurances that she did a fine job, the emotional impact of five hours of questioning and reliving this dreadful chapter of her life had taken its toll. She was filled with self-doubt.

"I just don't know if I can go through with this. Maybe we should just take their offer?" Katherine asked.

"Katherine, you did a great job. I've been through a ton of depositions in my career. You're temporarily down because you're wiped out. You did nothing but help our case. And, yes, I'm quite confident that they'll increase their offer. In fact, that's what my talk with John was all about. Cutting through his posturing, I believe he and the Archbishop have a strong desire to resolve this short of a courtroom. But as I've said before, no guarantee. We need to continue to be strong and prepare for trial."

"I so hope they'll settle. Because the way I feel now, I just couldn't bear to talk about this before a jury."

"You're exhausted. I totally understand. Get a good night's rest. Then we can talk about any potential settlement parameters," Mike said.

They shook hands in front of the Government Center subway entrance. Mike patted her shoulder. Katherine turned and started inside. She stopped abruptly, pivoted, facing her lawyer. She diverted her eyes downward and said: "I'm not sure that I've been totally forthright with you. There's something I need to tell you. But I'm just too tired now. I'll call tomorrow."

CHAPTER TWENTY-FIVE
DANIELLE

Mike interrupted what had been a satisfying and relaxing Thanksgiving holiday with his family to meet with Danielle Webb on Saturday in order to conduct a final preparatory session for her testimony on Monday.

Danielle was all business. Mike was pleased with his client's uncharacteristic serious and straightforward demeanor during the question/answer drill. She shrugged off Mike's inquiry about her Thanksgiving celebration, other than to say that she made a great dinner and how much she loved being with her kids.

"But as for their father," she said, "he...well...not important."

Mike frowned. "What are you talking about?"

Danielle waved Mike off as if to repeat *not important.* "Let's continue, shall we?"

Mike did not press her. Instead, still obsessing about the tall man he had seen in court at the end of the last session, he asked: "What's with that tall guy? He was there in court during our last session. At least I saw him and a disheveled woman come into the courtroom together at the end of the session. Did I see you leave with them?"

"That's the guy you met in the ER the day of the shooting, don't you remember? I had called and asked that he come to the hospital. I certainly wasn't going to ask for Brooks' help. He's sort of a friend of my husband. Has been to the apartment. A little strange, but a nice enough guy. Not sure exactly what his connection was with Brooks. Once he casually said if I ever needed anything I should call him. Said he'd be happy to help. So I decided to take him up on it. I called and he came to the hospital," said Danielle.

"That's it? Good friend...a little creepy...wanted to help?"

Danielle answered: "Yes, that's it." She obviously did not want to elaborate.

No messing around today. This has been a productive session. She's serious and just answering the questions. May it carry over to Monday, he thought as he said goodbye at the conclusion of their preparation session.

* * *

"ALL RISE," the adrenalin-pumping call to arms for trial lawyers and the traditional opening words of the court officer as the judge enters the courtroom.

Some judges, in their arrogance, actually think that the proclamation is for them personally; that the courtroom is their fiefdom. Not the Honorable Kelvin Henry. He was ever mindful that courts belong to the people; that he was honored to serve rather than serving to be honored. He never forgot that the opening broadcast of each court session was not for him personally but part of the tradition of respect for the office he held.

Attorneys Mike Lyons and Kelvin Henry met each other as trial lawyers a half dozen years before Kelvin was elevated to the bench. They formed an instant friendship, particularly after they became aware of some commonalities in their backgrounds. For one, they were both combat veterans. Judge Henry was a pilot with the Tuskegee Airmen during WWII. They also learned that each had lost his father when they were teenagers, were raised in inner city neighborhoods where drugs and crime were prevalent, but nevertheless they each obtained a fine education. They knew about the hardships of life. There was a mutual respect and admiration, an unspoken camaraderie. When Mike appeared before Judge Henry, the judge was always careful to specify that he had a "professional friendship with Attorney Lyons" and offered to recuse himself should Mike's adversary have any concern. But

Judge Henry's well-deserved reputation for *"calling them like he sees them,"* regardless of who the lawyers were, seldom resulted in a request for recusal. Sofia Vasquez was advised by her firm not to raise objection to Judge Henry. The lead partner was not only aware of Judge Henry's reputation for unbiased decision-making, but more importantly did not want to take the chance that such objection might obligate "Lyons to get into the Mahoney mess. Sofia should have let it be known that we did his estate plan," one of the senior partners lamented.

* * *

The tall athletically built judge stood. His face stern, he gestured to all in the courtroom to take their seats. But he remained standing and glared directly at Danielle Webb. Mike turned. His client, her face crimson, avoided Mike's eyes. Without saying a word, Judge Henry flashed his gaze upon Mike. It was unmistakable: *Good friend, I think you've got some trouble here.* Silence.

Holy shit, Mike thought, *Kelvin's pissed. That stupid ass rolling of her eyes at the end of the last session ticked him off. I was so hoping it would blow over during the holiday break. Gotta battle through this. She's entitled to counsel...and she's paying full freight and dammit, she's the better parent. Look at the self-satisfied smirk on Vasquez. Insufferable.*

"I'll see all counsel in my lobby...now!" Judge Henry barked.

Mike, hoping to pick up a signal, glanced at the court officer. There was just a shrug, as if to say *I can't say a word.* Mike's adversary feigned a troubled look as they followed the judge and court officer.

The judge's office, also referred to as *lobby,* was laced with a dusty set of the *Massachusetts Annotated Laws* and an incomplete collection of grimy beige books containing Massachusetts Supreme Judicial Court cases. Close to his desk was the complete set of *Massachusetts Family Law*, an updated compilation and synopses of cases and statutes dealing with the myriad issues facing judges and lawyers who handle divorce cases. The judge was a contributing author. A smell of pipe tobacco and coffee permeated the room. The large bare windows overlooking the street were in dire need of gallons of Windex. The fluorescent lighting overhead flickered.

Mike had formed a coalition that frequently lobbied the Massachusetts House of Representatives and Senate for more funding for courthouse improvements and maintenance throughout the Commonwealth as well as salary increases for court personnel. Bogged down in the political quagmire, politicians seldom prioritized these issues…they lacked voter appeal.

Judge Henry poured a mug of coffee from a thermos. Mike was aware of the judge's habit of biting his lower lip when he was troubled about something or about to make a major point. And the judge was indeed biting his lip. He gestured toward some mugs on a tray. He got up and walked over to the coffee pot, straightened a photo of his Tuskegee Airmen squadron.

"Fresh this morning from the Golden Dome Coffee Shop," His Honor said. He looked at Mike as if to ask if he would like coffee. Mike declined.

"Ms. Vasquez?"

"Why yes, thank you, Your Honor."

Vasquez knows something I don't know. She's wearing that holier-than-thou, arrogant, know-it-all smirk, Mike thought.

The judge slowly sat, his hands curled protectively around the coffee mug. He stared with an unfocused gaze. Then said, "Mighty fine. Mighty fine coffee. Now tell me, Counsel, did you both have an enjoyable *family* Thanksgiving?"

Uh, oh. Emphasis on family. Could it be…?

"Ours couldn't have been nicer, Your Honor. We were doubly thrilled that the Senator was able to join us this year," Attorney Vasquez replied.

The Senator? I think I'm going to throw up...all over her,
Mike thought.

Sofia Vasquez's brother-in-law was a one-term United States
Senator some ten years ago. Attorney Vasquez landed a position in
a large corporate-oriented firm because of the Senator's
connections. And one could not have a conversation with Attorney
Vasquez without her dropping his name.

Kelvin Henry was a man who disdained pretense. "How
nice," he said, failing in an attempt to mask sarcasm.

"And you, Attorney Lyons. I trust that you and Mrs. Lyons
and your children had an enjoyable holiday?" the judge asked.

'We did, Your Honor. We had quite a family gathering.
Sixteen in all. My wife did an incredible job. And you and Mrs.
Henry, Your Honor?"

"Well, we had a double celebration this year. Not only was it
Thanksgiving, but this year it fell on our tenth anniversary."

"Congratulations," both lawyers said.

"As I've mentioned, Mrs. Henry and I do not have children.
Married too late in life for that. Most every Thanksgiving we travel
to Santa Monica to join her family. But this year we decided to
stay put. Too much going on for each of us. So we treated
ourselves to dinner at the Ritz-Carlton. It's where I proposed
marriage." He smiled.

"Now let me tell you," he went on, "about the strangest
happening." He arched an eyebrow and looked at Mike.

The judge's upper canine tooth started to nibble on his lower
lip. Mike felt something ominous was about to unfold.

"Well, there we were...Mrs. Henry and I, finishing dessert. It
was five o'clock. Remember the song? The one with the lyrics
"Guess who I saw today, my darling?"

*Jesus, please dear God, don't tell me. Don't let me hear this.
It can't be true. Holy fuck.* Mike struggled to remain poker-faced.

Judge Henry continued: "The one and only Danielle Webb.
Your client, Attorney Lyons." He nodded a couple of times. "And

she wasn't alone. Not with her children. Not with Mr. Webb. It was Thanksgiving."

The judge took a sip of his coffee, dabbed his mouth with his handkerchief.

He continued: "I thought I remembered clearly directing both parents to stay home with their children. Am I in error?"

"You did, Your Honor," Mike replied. His innards felt hollow. "Your Honor, I, I…"

"Counsel, I specifically directed that she, that both parents spend the *entire* day and evening *at home* with their children. Crystal clear. No?"

"Oh good Lord," Attorney Vasquez said, her tone oozed with condescension.

Mike brushed his hand through his thick black hair. He crossed and uncrossed his legs. "Your Honor…"

The judge interrupted: "Are you telling me you're unaware of this breach?" the judge asked Mike. "Now I know that I didn't issue a formal Court Order. Instead, in the spirit of the upcoming holiday, I wanted to give the Webbs a clear message without the necessity of such a formality."

"Your Honor, I'm shocked by this. May I have a few minutes with my client? I'm sure there's an explanation," said Mike.

The judge's broad, lined face said it all: *she's dug herself into one deep hole, Counsel. I can't wait to hear this story.* He turned to Mike's adversary.

"Ms. Vasquez?"

"No objection, Your Honor."

Judge Henry turned his attention to Mike. "Let your client know, Counsel, that she's lucky it wasn't a formal Order, because if it was I'd hold her in contempt. I'll give you fifteen minutes. And be certain you cover this caper during the balance of your direct examination. I look forward to hearing what she comes up with."

"Yes, Your Honor. Trust me. I'm equally curious."

"Your Honor," Attorney Vasquez started, "you still have the right to issue a Contempt."

Kelvin Henry was never one to worry about being politically correct. He said what was on his mind, directly and clearly. "Attorney Vasquez, why don't you leave the judging to me and you just take care of your business."

"Certainly, Your Honor, I just..."

"You're a fellow lawyer, Ms. Vasquez. I don't know how much trial work you do, but this is a precarious business...the business of trying cases. Never forget that you don't know when all hell might break open regarding your own case. Now, if you would like to present a formal motion to hold Mrs. Webb in contempt..."

"Oh, no, Your Honor. I'm certainly guided by whatever course of action the Court thinks best."

"And, by the way, Attorney Vasquez, I suggest that you have a similar talk with Mr. Webb."

"Of course, but I can assure you..."

"I hear your assurance," the judge said. "But I want Thanksgiving out in the open, under oath. And you both can be certain that if you don't get into this out there with each of your clients, I will. Clear?"

Both lawyers nodded.

"All right. Fifteen minutes," the judge said.

Mike left the lobby and went directly to Danielle Webb.

"Follow me," he directed.

When they reached the corridor, Mike pointed to a corner. The antiquated courthouse was sparse when it came to bathrooms and conference rooms, a matter of poor planning on the part of the architect and court advisors.

Mike fired away. "Ritz-Carlton? Not with your kids? Defied the judge? That, madam, was a high decibel fuck-up. I don't want any bullshit. Listen to me and listen to me very carefully. The judge and his wife saw you in the hotel dining room on

Thanksgiving Day with some guy. For crap's sake, you were directed by the judge to spend the entire day and evening with your kids...*entire*. You do remember that, don't you? You defied that direction. And you didn't say a word to me. We're fucking drowning. Now tell me what this is all about. Be quick and to the point."

Danielle Webb's mouth dropped open. She was obviously unaware that she had been seen by anyone who knew her, much less the judge who was presiding over her divorce and custody trial...the one person who held the key to her financial future and the care and custody of her children. She had never seen her lawyer this angry.

Mike leaned back against the wall.

"I'm listening," he said.

Wide-eyed, face the color of a blinding sunset, Danielle Webb stuttered: "I can explain. I can explain everything."

Mike beckoned with his hand. The expression on his face said it explicitly: *this better be good. And it better be the truth.*

She spoke at the speed of a machine gun blazing from the sands of a Normandy beachhead on D-Day.

* * *

Conference over, Mike and his client headed back into the courtroom.

"Let's hope your entire case hasn't gone down the toilet," Mike whispered as he held open the door.

* * *

Danielle Webb took the stand, raised her right hand and took the oath.

"You may proceed," the judge said peering at Mike.

Mike Lyons had been in many a storm during various trials. If he had learned anything, it was to ride them out with as much cool as he could muster.

Keep your wits about you. Don't quit when your client tosses the ball out of bounds…when a happening during trial blows a great big hole in your case, rise to it, keep calm and get right back up on that horse, he had admonished fellow trial lawyers when lecturing at continuing legal education seminars. *That's part of what we get paid to do: be resilient…bounce back.*

"Mrs. Webb," Mike started, "you have just taken an oath to tell the truth."

His client nodded.

"A nod is insufficient, Mrs. Webb. Please answer the question verbally," Mike directed.

"Yes," she answered.

"Please tell the court, Mrs. Webb, what did you do on Thanksgiving?"

Mike wasn't going to pussyfoot around. He was diving headfirst into the cesspool created by his client. *When you've got a problem,* Mike thought to himself, *get right at it.* And he knew that despite the mutual respect and friendship between him and the judge, Kelvin Henry was going to decide this case as he saw it…based on the credible evidence, the parties' demeanor, his conclusions about character, and what's best for the children.

Attorney Vasquez rose to her feet. "Your Honor, I object. This question calls for a narrative."

Judge Henry replied: "Indeed. And that's just exactly what I wish to hear. If Mrs. Webb strays, I'll put a stop to her testimony and direct Counsel to break it up with a series of questions. Objection overruled."

"Mrs. Webb," he said, indicating that Danielle was to proceed with her answer.

She testified: "We had our Thanksgiving dinner around one-thirty. I had gotten up around six that morning. Mrs. Jensen, our nanny, arrived around seven-thirty. The two of us began to get things organized, stuff the turkey, cut vegetables, set the table…that sort of thing. My husb…the children's father was watching the Macy's Thanksgiving Day Parade on TV with the kids. I thought that was so great. He never spends that kind of time with the kids."

Clever…nice little add-on, but don't go overboard, Mike thought.

Again, Mike's adversary leapt to her feet.

"Objection, Your Honor. I move to strike."

Attorney Vasquez may be technically correct, but strategically inept. Too many objections, whether or not they are consistent with the rules of evidence, annoy a trial judge, particularly when he/she is presiding without a jury. With the exception of Georgia and Texas, matrimonial cases are tried before a judge presiding without a jury.

Judge Henry: "I suppose you are quarreling with that part of her answer when she testified that her husband hardly ever spends that kind of time with the kids? Am I correct?"

Attorney Vasquez, succeeding only in emphasizing a point that did nothing but harm her case, said sheepishly, "Yes, Your Honor." She sat. The judge nodded ever so slightly.

Judge Henry: "Technically, Attorney Vasquez, you're correct. Consequently I will grant your evidentiary motion and strike from the record that part of the answer that references Mrs. Webb's statement to the effect that Mr. Webb 'hardly ever spends time with the kids.' I'm confident that the issue of how much time Mr. Webb does or doesn't spend with the children will be brought out in your direct examination of him, as well as challenged during cross-examination." The judge made his point, hoping that maybe Sofia Vasquez learned something about when and when not to raise an evidentiary objection.

Mike loved it. He recalled the oft-repeated question put to him over the years by clients: *when a judge strikes an answer that has just been given, how does he actually strike it from his mind?* Every trial lawyer has been asked this question and every trial lawyer has the same straightforward response, *he/she doesn't.*

Judge Henry: "Let's move along. Please proceed with your questions, Attorney Lyons."

Mike: "Thank you, Your Honor. Mrs. Webb, did Mrs. Jensen at some point leave your home to be with her family?"

Danielle: "Yes. Mrs. Jensen took the kids to a nearby playground around noontime and when she returned, I insisted that she leave and join her own family."

Mike: "And did she leave?"

Danielle: "Yes."

Mike: "So, for awhile anyway, you and Mr. Webb and your children were at home together?"

Danielle: "Well, I wouldn't exactly say 'together.'"

Mike: "I understand. But it was just the four of you. Mrs. Jensen had left. Isn't that correct?"

Danielle: "Yes."

Mike: "Please proceed with what the rest of the day was like."

Danielle: "Everything was really beautiful. I was very proud of myself. We sat down to have dinner around three o'clock. The dinner was perfect. It felt like we were a family again until..." Danielle Webb stopped, blinking toward the ceiling as though she was suppressing tears.

Mike: "Go on, please."

Danielle: "The phone rang. My husband started to get up from the table. Even though I was expecting the possibility of an important business call, I shook my head signaling that we shouldn't answer it. He ignored me and got up from the table. I asked that he just let it ring. I didn't want our time interrupted."

Mike: "Then what happened?"

Mrs. Webb: "He took the call in the kitchen. He came back and said that it was urgent, something about one of the people he works with; that he had to leave, but would be back shortly."

Danielle had never said a word to Mike about this until the recent break.

He looked at her, tipping his head and frowning as if to say: *This sure as hell better be the truth. Representing you, Danielle, is like walking through a fucking minefield. Worse.* But he loved hearing his adversary whisper just loudly enough to be heard: "*What?*" He saw her lose her composure and turn toward Brooks Webb, whose face remained inscrutable.

If it's not bullshit, and I don't think it is…not at this point… this will neutralize her caper at the Ritz.

Mike: "Excuse me one moment, Your Honor." He turned toward the counsel table, feigning to collect some nonexistent notes. *Stall a little bit longer…let this register with Kelvin.*

And then Mike noticed the tall man sitting next to an unkempt woman near the back of the courtroom. And he remembered that she was the one who came into the courtroom with the tall man at the end of the last session.

I know her, Mike thought. *And not just from the last time. But where? Who is she? Why are they here?*

The woman looked at Mike, nodded and smiled knowingly.

CHAPTER TWENTY-SIX
DANIELLE

Distracted by the unkempt woman's smile, Mike struggled with his memory. *Where have I seen her?* He fumbled with his legal pad.

"Counsel?" Judge Henry said.

"Yes, of course, Your Honor. Forgive me."

Mike: "Now, Mrs. Webb, I'm going to ask you some questions about your having left your home despite His Honor's admonition that you and your husband were to stay at home with your children the entire holiday. You did leave, didn't you?"

Danielle Webb remained silent. Then tears. She groped into her handbag for Kleenex. Judge Henry, eyebrows arched, cast a skeptical glance at Mike. Sofia Vasquez muttered, just loud enough to be heard, "Oh, come on."

Mike did not play into the tears. *Could be real. Could also be a bit of histrionics. Next time around, I'm gonna be a shoe salesman.*

Mike: "Mrs. Webb, at some point in time you left the apartment?"

Danielle: "Yes, but first I would like to say…" And then she stopped.

Mike: "What is it that you started to say?" *No, dummy…Rule One: Never ask a question to which you don't know the answer.*

Danielle: "Oh, no, well, what I was going to say…"

Attorney Vasquez: "I must object, Your Honor. This is hardly a response to the question."

Judge Henry: "For Lord's sake, Attorney Vasquez, give the witness a chance to finish." He turned to Danielle and indicated that she was to continue.

Danielle: "I just wanted to say that when my husband returned, he seemed very…spirited. And strange, but I recall that he was sniffling a great deal…like he had caught a cold or something."

Mike, pleased that his client reminded the judge that her husband had taken a foray away from the family contrary to the judge's direction, continued: "Well, all right, Mrs. Webb, please tell His Honor your best memory as to how long your husband was gone before he returned."

Danielle: "A good hour and a half before he came back. We had barely started to have our dinner when he tore himself away. The kids were very upset."

Mike: "I'm sure. So, it was after your husband returned before you left?"

Danielle: "Absolutely. I would never have left the children alone."

Mike: "Please tell His Honor why you left the apartment and where you went."

Attorney Vasquez: "I'm sorry, Your Honor, but that is multiple questions."

Judge Henry: "You mean *those* are multiple questions. You're quite right, Counsel. But I'm going to allow them. We're getting into the narrative that I've already ruled upon. Go on, Mrs. Webb."

The judge cupped his chin with his hand.

Danielle: "Well, as I testified before, I've been working as a part-time real estate agent for the past year. The agency does lots of high-end properties. I was representing a couple who were selling their luxury condo on Marlborough Street near Arlington Street and the Public Garden. Mr. George Taylor, a gentleman who lives in London, had come to see it in October. He has a daughter who's a student at Boston University. He was interested in buying a condo for her to live in as well as for investment. The asking price is in the six figures, so if it were to go through, the agency and I would earn a nice commission. "

Mike: "Go on, please."

Danielle: "I showed the condo to George…I mean, Mr. Taylor, back in October. He was handling things himself without a broker of his own. Then I brought him a second time with his daughter. Mr. Taylor told me that he was very interested and that when he returns to Boston in November he would probably be ready to make an offer."

Mike: "And did he return and contact you?"

Danielle: "Oh, yes. He's a very nice man. Also very busy with a tight schedule, it seems."

Mike: "And just when did he contact you?"

Danielle: "Well, that's the thing. He called me from London on Monday of Thanksgiving week and said that he was flying into Boston on Thanksgiving Day and wanted to take another look. I said that…I mean…well, I told him that I would be celebrating the holiday with my family and suggested we go to the unit on Friday. He said that would be okay."

Mike: "And then what happened?"

Danielle: "He called on Thanksgiving. It turned out that he changed his plans, had to fly to Paris that night, said something about a big deal that was 'breaking fast,' is how I think he described it. At any rate, he said that it was urgent that he see the apartment for a quick final look today…Thanksgiving…and would need to talk with me about making an offer."

Mike: "And so you left your home?"

Danielle: "I felt terrible. I couldn't tell him…I didn't want to get into my personal life and tell him about the trial and all. But I did say, absolutely, that I didn't want to leave my family on the holiday even though the kids and I had finished dinner by the time Mr. Taylor called."

Mike: "And then what?"

Mike glanced at Judge Henry. He couldn't read the jurist's expression.

She's not fluttering those eyes. She's got a good solid demeanor going. And I'm gonna make damned sure she continues with the straight, true story. Just a little tough to read Kelvin at the moment. Hearing that hubby left the home is a great shot in the arm. Takes the sting out of Danielle's caper. We've gotta turn Kelvin around completely. He's only human. Unfortunately, his actually seeing Danielle at the Ritz is a lot more powerful than just hearing that Brooks also had left the family.

Mike looked down at his legal pad, caught his breath, placed the pad back on his table, glanced at Sean, and then returned to his direct examination.

Mike: "You did leave the house?"

Danielle: "George…Mr. Taylor…said that he was also considering a place in the South End. He emphasized that he wanted to make a decision and make a decision ASAP. I didn't want to lose this opportunity."

Mike sent a clear message with the expression on his face: *For crap sake, answer the question. It calls for a 'yes' or 'no.' Don't dodge.*

Danielle: "Yes, I did leave our home."

Mike: "And you remembered Judge Henry's admonition that you and Mr. Webb were to be with your children the entire day and evening?"

Danielle: "I did." She looked at the judge apologetically.

Mike: "Clearly, Mr. Webb, who you testified had left the home earlier, had returned by the time you got this call?"

Danielle: "Oh, absolutely."

Mike: "And just as you stayed with the children while Mr. Webb was gone, I assume he remained with them during your absence?"

Danielle: "I made certain of that. No way would I even think of leaving the children without at least one of us being with them. I explained the situation to Brooks. He said he understood and it would be perfectly okay for me to leave."

Mike: "I'm sure he did. Where did you go?"

Danielle: "Directly to the condo Mr. Taylor was interested in."

Mike: "And where did you say it's located?"

Danielle: "On Marlborough Street near the corner of Arlington…close to the Public Garden."

Mike: "You met Mr. Taylor at this property?"

Danielle: "Yes. It was a short visit. He more or less went quickly through the entire unit. Very similar to other clients when they return for a second or third look at a place they're interested in."

Mike: "By the way, Mrs. Webb, you testified that your husband was gone for about an hour and a half?"

Danielle: "At least."

Mike: "When he returned did he tell you where he went, what it was all about?"

Danielle: "No. And I still don't know the truth as to why he had to leave."

Attorney Vasquez leaped to her feet. "I move to strike, Your Honor."

Mike glanced at Sean. Their facial expressions: *dumb…easy lay-up for us.*

Judge Henry: "You mean you move to strike that part of her answer: *and I still don't know the truth as to why he had to leave* as not being responsive? Technically, you're correct, Attorney Vasquez. I'll strike that portion of her answer about *the truth.*"

Once again a blatant example of a trial lawyer trying to show that she knows the rules of evidence but ends up making a tactical error. She wound up emphasizing testimony damaging to her own case. There are times when it's valuable to object to certain questions and to move to strike answers that may not respond to the particular question. And there are times when doing so can backfire. It's more than *knowing* the rules; it's about *how and when to use* those rules.

Mike felt this was a good time to cut to the chase.

Mike: "But you wound up with this gentleman at the Ritz-Carlton dining room. Please explain to His Honor why."

Danielle then testified that Mr. Taylor said that he was hungry and that "he wanted to discuss what kind of offer below the asking price I thought might seal the deal. He said that he was prepared to leave a 'good faith' check with me before heading to the airport."

Mike: "And then what happened?"

Danielle: "I wanted to get back home as soon as possible, but I didn't want to lose this deal. I thought about inviting Mr. Taylor to our apartment, but with the kids around and all…I just didn't think it would be appropriate. The Ritz-Carlton is just a ten-minute walk from the condo he was interested in, and about the same from the hotel to my apartment."

Mike: "Mrs. Webb, how long were you gone from your home?"

Danielle: "I would say less than an hour. At the hotel, we ordered coffee. I gave him a new purchase number and he countered with a figure that I knew would be acceptable to my client. It was all pretty quick. He wanted to seal the deal and then be on his way."

Mike and his client were aware that Mr. Webb hurriedly wrote a note and passed it to his lawyer. And he saw the scarlet begin to rise from Danielle's neck. He had seen this telltale sign before when she strayed from the truth both in court and during their office prep sessions.

You're screwin' around, Danielle Webb. How can you say you were gone less than an hour? All the walking time was at least a half hour. You're messin' with the wrong judge. He's been around the block…and then some. He knows bullshit when it's hitting the barnyard.

Mike: "Are you sure that it was less than an hour?"

Danielle dug in her heels: "I'm certain of it. I remember when I got home. Brooks was napping in front of the television set. The kids were excited to see me."

Throwing in that napping stuff isn't too over the top, but the less than an hour bullshit is fucking impossible. If only she had told me all about this when I was prepping her…we could have thought it through and determined what the actual amount of time had to be.

Judge Henry interrupted: "Maybe we all need a…nap. I think this is a good time to stretch and take a break. We'll resume in twenty minutes."

Mike ushered Danielle to a different floor. He didn't want the opposition to view his frustration with her. He didn't want to risk being overheard.

"Are you kidding me? Less than an hour?" he confronted Danielle. "Just be straight with me. That's friggin' impossible. Do the math, for chrissake."

"Mike, I swear. No more than an hour. The guy and I had a cup of coffee. He had some dessert. He's a no nonsense guy, I can tell you that. It didn't take long at all for the two of us to come up with a number. I had an offer form. He signed it and gave me a check. I was home by six, six-thirty."

"What about all the walking time…to get to the property, then to the hotel…coffee…then back to your condo. And time-wise, which is it? Six or six-thirty?"

Danielle Webb shrugged.

"Come on. You're much too sharp not to know you screwed up and not to know exactly what time you got home. I don't buy that shrug stuff."

"Okay, okay, don't get so testy. Six-fifteen."

"Testy?" Mike exclaimed. "This is about *your* kids, not mine. I have a habit of cottoning to the truth. And so does this judge."

* * *

When they resumed, and after Danielle testified that she had made a mistake earlier; that "I was gone a little more than an hour. I left the house at about five and returned home around six-fifteen," Mike moved into a different phase of the custody case. He launched into a series of traditional questions about her relationship with the children, the daily routine, health issues, the amount of time she spent with them, the activities she did with them when they weren't in preschool, her observations about Brooks Webb's lack of time with them. At the conclusion of her testimony regarding the interaction between her and the children, Mike probed into the financial side of things in support of their case for child support, alimony and a division of the assets. Danielle Webb was all business as she displayed intricate knowledge about the Webb family fortune, revealing familiarity with items that her husband had omitted in the financial documents that each of them was required to file with the court.

Mike: "That's all, Your Honor."

Judge Henry: "All right, we'll commence with cross-examination in the morning."

* * *

"Wow," Mike sighed looking at Sean as they packed up their briefcases. "What do you think?"

"Well," Sean replied, "she was well prepped and did a good job touching all the necessary *I'm the better parent* bases. As for the trip to the Ritz? That's tough, in large part because of her inconsistency about timing. But hubby took off, too. So, maybe the score is even. Now, Mikey, we'll have to see how she holds up tomorrow on cross."

"I'm worried. I wanna go over another cross drill with her. Are you up for it? I'd like you to play Vasquez. Put her through the paces. Be nasty."

"In other words, be myself," Sean quipped. "I'd actually love to. Let's see, it's one fifteen. Let's hold off until three…give her a couple of hours to recoup. She had some heavy duty testimony this morning."

"Did I hear the two of you talking about a cross drill with me? Does that mean yet another rehearsal? You guys have to face it…I'm up for anything, but let's grab coffee first," Danielle said.

Mike decided to let *I'm up for anything* pass and noted that her accompanying wink was directed at Sean. The professor was oblivious.

Her husband is a drag, totally vanilla. There's something weird, almost spooky about him. He's hiding something. He's got that inscrutable Boy Scout face. She may be a bit over-the-top, but at least she's got some life to her…much better for the kids.

The three of them went to a cafe in Faneuil Hall.

* * *

The preparation session went well. Sean fired away with as many leading questions damaging to her case as he could conjure. It wasn't the first cross-examination prep, but since it was on the heels of her actual direct examination and they were headed into battle the next day, the adrenalin rush was far greater for each of them. Danielle actually seemed to enjoy it…a competitive gleam in her eyes.

"Don't be overconfident," Mike cautioned. "And don't be a smartass up there. Judge Henry's interested in the real you…your character as a person, as a parent. That's what cross-examination is all about…probing for the truth…trying to catch witnesses in inconsistencies and exaggerations. I know he doesn't buy your attempt to fudge the amount of time you were away from the kids on Thanksgiving. He's gonna be scrutinizing every look on your face," Mike cautioned.

"And Vasquez is going to be a hell of a lot nastier than I was today," Sean added. "Ignore her contemptuous smirk. She'll use that to try to get under your skin so that you'll get nasty on the stand. Be cool. Wide-eyed. Make sense?"

Danielle grinned. "Got it."

"And don't forget…" Mike started.

"I know, just tell the truth and everything will be okay." She sighed a sarcastic sigh.

"And just answer the question…don't add a bunch of stuff. If I think we need clarification or more testimony about any issue, I have the right to do a redirect examination and that's when we'll clarify any point that needs elaboration. Understood?" Mike added.

"I'll be a perfect Girl Scout…What?" she said and asked with alacrity.

"I said it a moment ago and time and time again: do not be a smartass on that stand. Humility will go a long way. Be open and honest. Cross is to test your integrity…what kind of character, quality of parenting and morality you bring to your children. Judge Henry will see right through any attempt to exaggerate or avoid a question. You're a competitor. Save it for the tennis court…not this court. Try to volley with Vasquez and you'll be playing right into her hands. She'll have a field day."

"Just answer the questions…truthfully," Sean repeated.

Danielle extended a hand toward Sean.

"I'll be the best cross-examined student the two of you have ever had."

* * *

When the trial resumed, Judge Henry advised everyone that he had two emergency hearings starting at eleven thirty. "Consequently, we're only going to have time for limited testimony today. And I've got a series of adoptions and a crucial hospitalized near-death witness whose testimony I must hear this week. And there's an administrative conference next Monday. So, we won't be able to convene on this matter until next week. But let's get started and see what we can accomplish in the next hour, hour and a half."

The first hour and a quarter of Sofia Vasquez's cross-examination reflected what Mike saw as her lack of experience as a trial lawyer. Her questions were mundane, merely repeating much of what had been established on direct examination. Danielle Webb was starting to get bored.

And then things got interesting.

Attorney Vasquez: "You said that when you met your real estate client, leaving your children at home in violation of the judge's Order..."

Mike: "Objection."

Judge Henry: "You're quite right. It wasn't a Court *Order*. However, it was a strong *recommendation*. Point made. Continue, Counsel."

Attorney Vasquez: "Let's see now, you testified that you were gone less than an hour. You remember that?"

Danielle: "I corrected that and said that it was slightly more than an hour."

Attorney Vasquez: "You changed your mind after a break and consulting with your lawyer, isn't that correct?"

Danielle: "I didn't change my mind, I..."

Attorney Vasquez: "That's okay, Mrs. Webb. Two different answers. Where would you like to leave it now with His Honor? Less than an hour or slightly more than an hour?"

Danielle: "I wasn't really looking at my watch."

Attorney Vasquez: "You weren't aware of the amount of time you were away from your children in violation of Judge Henry's recommendation?"

Danielle: "It was slightly more than an hour."

Vasquez: "So, thirty minutes became sixty minutes...and as you say, 'maybe'?"

Mike: "Objection. Mrs. Webb said nothing about thirty minutes and she has legitimately corrected her answer."

Judge Henry: "Sustained. I get the point, Attorney Vasquez. Let's move along."

Attorney Vasquez: "Let's see. You walked to the apartment on Bay State Road, met your client there; he walked through the apartment, maybe scrutinizing it more than his earlier visits…considering making an offer…being more thorough, perhaps? The two of you then walked a quarter mile to the Ritz-Carlton. You were seated. You placed an order and then waited for it to be served. You and your client had coffee, dessert, and a conversation about a six-figure real estate deal, and you returned home *all* in just forty-five minutes…or, excuse me, I guess you now say it was an hour? That's what you want us to believe?"

Danielle: "Slightly *more* than an hour. The condo's on Marlborough Street, not Bay State Road. And as I said, Mr. Taylor's inspection of the condo was just a quick walk-through. It, as well as our coffee at the Ritz-Carlton, was all very quick."

Vasquez: "Including the sex you had with your client?"

Mike: "*Objection*!" Mike was on his feet.

Judge Henry cocked his head to the side. His facial expression said it all: *this is heating up and this lawyer Vasquez is stepping over the line unless she's got something.*

Judge Henry: "Ms. Vasquez, you are going on a wild fishing expedition unless you've got something specific and convincing to support the accusation in your question. There's no basis of which I'm aware for your question. I don't tolerate such a tactic, Ms. Vasquez. I'm going to call upon you to make an *offer of proof*; show the court specific evidence that you have to back up your assertion. I'll hear you, Attorney Vasquez."

Sofia Vasquez was flustered by the judge's admonition and her lack of any such evidence. She was going on an old-fashioned fishing expedition and got nailed by Mike's objection.

"Ms. Vasquez?" the judge asked, his tone clearly signaling that he knew all too well that she had no such proof to offer. She had stepped out of bounds.

"I'll withdraw that question, Your Honor."

The judge said: "I think this is a good place to stop for the day. We'll resume next week."

Mike turned to his adversary and whispered: "Sophomoric." She pretended not to hear. Mike observed her swallow hard.

"Cheap foul," Mike added as he turned to Sean.

"A bevy of slam dunks for the good guys," Sean said.

"All net," Mike said with a triumphant grin.

CHAPTER TWENTY-SEVEN
KATHERINE

The former sister, unable to sleep, turned and stretched her arm to reach the nightstand clock which read 3:07 a.m. Testifying at the deposition that prior day had been emotionally traumatic.

My god, I'm sweating. She toweled herself and put on a fresh top, then went into the galley kitchen of her two-room apartment. She opened the Valium and Tylenol PM, which were conveniently placed on the countertop. Without hesitation she poured some water and swallowed hard. Her throat tightened when she was overwhelmed with anxiety.

I shall forever be his prisoner.

The process of the lawsuit, including the deposition, was arduous. Details of the destructive relationship had come roaring back as she was compelled to recall and articulate the grand larceny of her soul.

Katherine imagined herself in her habit, kneeling before the crucifix in St. Thomas Aquinas. The image was finer, clearer than the one in her recurrent dream in which she sought but never received His forgiveness.

She crossed herself and returned to her bedroom. She knelt and once again made the sign of the cross.

Hypocrite, cheat, liar, she admonished herself.

She leaned back against cropped pillows and allowed the day's deposition to replay itself. She had been compelled to testify about so many parts of the relationship…the thrill and comfort of finally being loved. A caring paternal figure had at long last come into her life. And he was a man of God. She relived Father Riley's soft seductive tone, his words of reassurance that their lovemaking was God's work. She testified about the first time "he took me. He said to me it was as though God himself guided him into me."

She swore under oath that the priest had said on more than one occasion that "our love and our beautiful expression of it is His will; that we have served faithfully. It is our time. We shall resign and marry."

She recalled her testimony about *their* apartment, how Father Riley called it "our own little love nest." She described his demand that they each submit their resignations. She emphasized his promise of marriage…of an eternal love for each other.

She replayed her testimony of Father Riley's drifting away from her, his warmth morphed into cold, his broken promises, his betrayal. She testified about the priest's demands for sex despite her protestations. She succumbed out of hope and fear. She recounted her spin into the world of drugs and alcohol, her one-night stands, her desperation, her efforts to take her own life.

The nightmare of what had deteriorated into a sinful affair with Father Riley, "rather than genuine love he had once expressed," all came gushing out in response to Attorney Colello's questions. She recoiled when he implied that it was she who seduced Father Riley; that she was more than a consenting adult.

Perspiring again, she kicked off the top sheet. She could still hear some of the questions:

"Father Riley never once encouraged you to drink beyond a social cocktail, isn't that correct?"

"When you were aware, as you put it, that he no longer loved you, you stayed on at the apartment. You could have left, couldn't you? You called him numerous times asking that he come to be with you. Isn't that correct?"

"And you knew that might well result in your seducing him, your insisting upon having relations in an effort to make him come back to you. Isn't that correct?"

"And wasn't it Father Riley who said that he finally garnered the strength to break away from your spell. Isn't that what he said to you, Ms. Hennessey?"

Katherine pulled the sheet over her head but could not erase Attorney Colello's expression of disbelief and disdain when she testified about the tape. She was aware of his glance toward Mike and could see Colello shaking his head in disbelief. And then his mocking words: "This tape…this alleged tape…" He interrupted himself and gestured as if to say, "such a fantasy isn't worth the time."

"Well, strike that," he said, while beginning to gather his papers. "I have no further questions regarding this preposterous…" She was haunted by the intimidating manner in which the skillful Attorney Colello allowed his thought and message to fall off the page without spelling it out any further.

Katherine sprung from her trance. "The tape," she said aloud to nobody. "Why didn't I explain everything to Mike before? Why now? Why didn't I tell him before? I'm a flawed person…damaged." She plunked her head back on the pillows.

Tears formed as the tranquilizers finally did their job.

* * *

Mike's night was restless. Katherine's parting words *I'm not sure that I've been totally forthright with you* not long after John Colello's assertion that the tape never existed repeated itself throughout the night.

He had called his friend, Dr. Larry Armont, as soon as he returned to his office after his client's parting words.

"One thing is certain, Mike," Dr. Armont said, "she has been permanently scarred by this man. Her efforts to do away with herself were cries for help, genuine evidence of her utter despair and loss of hope. Could she be fantasizing about the tape? Yes, it's possible. She was in a vulnerable state when being mentored by Riley. She took it all in and needed to believe that he truly loved her. Her thirst for his love had been repressed into her unconscious and this talk about a tape in which she says he proclaimed love for her might be nothing more than a wishful fantasy."

"Hallucination?" Mike asked.

"May very well be. And then again, Mike, it might be real. It's unclear. Katherine becomes silent with any mention of such a tape. There's still much work to be done, much to unravel. Mike, she was young, naïve, and vulnerable when she came under his spell."

"Tell me something, Larry. What's this priest all about? What did you learn when you met with him?"

"That, by the way, was a great idea, Mike. Good lawyering to get the judge to order that each side have the right to have its psychiatric expert meet with the other party. Riley was a star-studded priest at Chestnut Hill College. But he's also a tormented, needy soul, haunted and at the same time titillated by his father's abuse of his mother. Speaking of hallucination, I think he saw Katherine as his mother and consequently had a need to mimic his father and abuse her. This is not an excuse for his behavior, just an explanation. Make no mistake about it, Mike, he damned near destroyed her."

Dr. Armont paused and then added, "She became a sister of the church for all the wrong reasons."

"What do you mean?" Mike asked.

"Her father pushed her into it. He had his own issues. Probably frightened about the thought of his daughter being loved by a man and having a healthy intimate sex life. And he was trying to assuage his own sense of guilt about the way he treated Katherine's mother. From all that I learned from Katherine, her mother was a person born to serve. She married Katherine's father, forsaking a dream to become a nun. He demanded that Katherine fulfill the mother's dream. She complied, desperate for her father's approval."

"Complicated stuff," Mike offered.

"Mike, that's putting it mildly. Here was a young woman hungry for a father as well as a lover."

"And along comes a predator, one Father Thomas Riley."

"Yup. And he was, no doubt, sending suggestive messages during his mentoring sessions with her. He knew exactly what he was doing. He saw her vulnerability. He couldn't resist his need to control and take and dominate. She had sexual fantasies, parental fantasies about this man. Even if she did invent the tape recording that doesn't erase or excuse what he did to her," said Dr. Armont.

* * *

It was 5 a.m. Mike noticed the first splinter of early morning creeping through the bedroom curtains. He went downstairs, did some push-ups, and then some more thinking.

Colello's not a bluffer. He's a pro. A practicing Catholic. Is he right? Did Katherine create that whole tape story? Would the priest actually have been so carried away with her that he would record his feelings on a tape? Does sound preposterous that he would do such a thing. He's much too wily. And it's easy to imagine her naivete when she fell under Riley's spell. But was there a spell? Is the tape thing a figment of her fantasy life...her desire and deep craving to be loved? Would he have actually thrown caution to the wind and recorded his love for her on a tape...risked his entire reputation, his position at Chestnut Hill? Is this what she says she wasn't straight about? Or am I way off base? The good priest may well have lied to his own lawyer...destroyed the tape long ago and now denies that it ever existed...that he ever said such things. Or have I been played by my own client? Wouldn't be the first time. Or better yet, has she been played by her own fantasy? No doubt if there ever was such a tape, the priest would have destroyed it. Her psyche was crushed by this so-called man of God. She may well have invented the whole recording thing. Or is it the old pro, John Colello, who's the one led down a path? Will a jury believe her story about a tape we can't produce?

Mike needed relief. He went upstairs to get his running shoes.

I'll go for a run. That'll either loosen me or kill me. Hell, with either option, I'll be relaxed. A win-win.

Ali stirred. She glanced at the clock, 5:40 a.m. She frowned.

Mike whispered. "The ex-nun. I've been up much of the night. Go back to sleep. You've got another hour plus. A good run will do me good. I'll make the coffee."

He heard the kids stirring. They had a 6:30 bus to catch.

"Hey troopers," he said as he knocked on their doors.

"Dad, don't forget. Tonight's the play."

"Worry you not. I wouldn't exchange this performance for a...a Red Sox World Series win."

"Lie, Dad. You'd make that deal in a heartbeat."

* * *

The lawyer barely put down his briefcase when he reached for his office phone and made contact with Katherine. She said that she could meet with him at three o'clock that afternoon.

"Mind telling me what you meant by your parting remark yesterday?" he asked.

"It's best that we wait until I get there." Her voice was hesitant, thin.

Mike hung up and grabbed his suit jacket. "You know what, Jane? I'm betting there never was any such tape. That's what she was talking about yesterday when she said there's something she needed to tell me. She's coming in at three."

"And the mystery will be solved. You're probably right. At least you'll know how to proceed once she tells you," said Jane.

Mike nodded. "It's beautiful out there, Ms. Jane. More like a late day in May rather than April. Think I'll go out, enjoy the warmth. I've got some thinking to do."

Instead of a sandwich, he bought an iced coffee and took a long walk to the end of Cambridge Street. He debated whether to turn left and amble along Charles Street with its strolling tourists and multiple antique shops or head for the river. The latter won. Mike crossed the footbridge to the banks of the Charles. He stood at the edge, felt himself transforming as he stared at the river's rolling surface.

He was no longer Attorney Michael Lyons. He was the eighteen-year-old Marine, enveloped by ominous mountains and the bitter cold of Korea, fighting in a questionable war. His mouth hung open as he gazed at the sparkling silver caps on the surface of the Charles. He didn't see them as the gentle tips of modest waves created by the river's currents and the gentle breeze brushing along the surface. They were the ice-covered helmets of the hordes of Chinese and North Korean troops coming at Mike and his fellow Marines in the black of night. It was uncontrollable. His mind was gripped by the terror, understandable only to those who had served in combat...only they could comprehend the numbing fear...the rush of adrenaline to defend oneself...to kill. His mind was locked into that death-enveloped nightmare of his young life. He and his gritty fellow Marines of the First Division were fighting for their survival in the unforgiving mountainous terrain near the Chosin Reservoir. It was November 1950. The reservoir was frozen. He was just a young rifleman who volunteered to be part of the group to launch a rescue effort. Fox Company, near the Chosin, was completely surrounded by Chinese troops who had entered the war in October when General MacArthur had ill-advisedly ordered that American forces approach the Yalu River at the border of North Korea and China. Fox Company had already taken horrendous losses and was struggling to survive. Its CO managed to get word to Mike's commanding officer, General Smith, who quickly organized the rescue effort. Mike and his fellow Marines trudged six miles in darkness through deep snow with temperatures and wind chill *twenty-five degrees below zero.* And they obeyed the order to maintain absolute silence.

Each man could barely see the Marine ahead of him. They climbed sharp-edged ridges through the icy landscape, at times an inhuman challenge. Not a man would escape some degree of frostbite. As they closed in toward their destination, they came under attack and were vastly outnumbered. During the fierce firefight, Mike became aware that two Marines manning a critically important machine gun had been hit. He rushed to the position, mindful that once he started to use that automatic weapon he would be a primary target. Another Marine dove next to him to feed the ammunition. Glued to the weapon, and despite being hit by shrapnel, he stayed the course and doggedly fired every round fed into the weapon. For his courage, he was awarded the Navy Cross.

A loud splash in the river…some kid throwing a stone…allowed Mike to escape and return to the present. He wiped the perspiration from his brow.

Jesus, it's a beautiful warm day. That was decades ago. Why? Why did I just go back there? Shit, why did I survive that night…the whole damn thirteen months? So many…so many great Marines were taken that night…and later during General Smith's valiant move to the sea.

Mike's shirt was soaking wet and it wasn't because of the balmy weather.

The river was a jewel on this early spring day. Its rippled surface embraced the sun's offerings, showing off thousands of dashes of silver…shapes changing and constantly animated. And yet this tranquil scene masqueraded as *the* nightmare of his life. Strange. But now he was back. The sparkling tips of the waves were no longer enemy soldiers' helmets. He smiled at the realization that he survived…that he was alive. The trial lawyer's gut relaxed.

He gazed to the Cambridge side of the river and stared at a luxury apartment complex. This daydream would be pleasant.

What a cool place to live. I can see us there after the kids have flown the nest. College behind us. Off our payroll. Those apartments must go for a bundle. But who knows? Two or three major scores and we could be lazy grandparents one day. I see us. We're having breakfast...no, no...nightly cocktail on our terrace enjoying the Boston skyline. Hell, not so crazy.

Mike shook his head, not unlike the family standard poodle coming to shore after a dash in the ocean, his quest for a seagull an expected failure. *Time to get back at it. Enough with the dreams.* Refreshed and filled with anticipation, he returned to his office.

* * *

Katherine was seated in the waiting area, nervously thumbing through a magazine.

"Katherine, it's good to see you. Hope you had a decent night's sleep after yesterday's ordeal. You did a terrific job. Come in, please." Mike, with arm extended, shepherded his client into his office. He was aware of her unease, her distance...not unlike the first time she met with him.

The lawyer leaned back in his chair, stretched his arm, then pitched forward. Katherine lit a cigarette.

"Hey, I thought you got rid of that habit," he paused and then quipped, "No pun intended."

His comment evoked a modicum of a smile on the ex-sister's face.

"I'm not to be trusted," she responded.

Mike furrowed his brow. *A double entendre?* He tipped his head slightly. *Here comes the bombshell.*

"I stay off...sometimes a month, five, six weeks even. And then wham," Katherine said while holding up an unlit cigarette.

She looked as she felt...distraught.

"You have every right to feel stressed, Katherine. Litigation is never fun. Particularly when you're sitting all day being questioned about something so painful and terribly personal. But I repeat. You did a first-rate job. Why? Simple. You told the truth. You were authentic."

But I need the whole truth. Is the tape real or a part of her fantasy life? Sean's right. Riley is too cunning to write or record anything about his purported feelings for Katherine...some of which may well have been real until he yielded to his need to dominate. I'm going to gently bring up her parting comment, but I can't push her...not today. She seems particularly fragile. And I don't want to add to any doubts she may have about continuing with her case.

Katherine crushed the cigarette and thanked her lawyer for the compliment.

The room was still. Mike knew the value of silence. Let his client ease into whatever it is she needs to say and he needs to hear.

After what he felt was an appropriate amount of pause time, Mike said, "Katherine, as you were leaving yesterday, you said something about not being totally forthright. I'm pretty sure that's how you put it. You mentioned that there was something you wanted to tell me?"

Katherine nodded.

Mike gestured, hoping to encourage his client to open up.

"Mr. Lyons," she started.

Uh, oh, this must be serious, the lawyer thought to himself.

"*Mister?* I'm always Mike, Katherine."

"I'm not sure I know how to start," she said. Her hands were trembling.

Trial lawyers don't like it, but they learn to expect the twists and turns of their clients' stories. Litigation is more often than not much like the proverbial roller coaster ride. The lawyer struggles to keep his gut even-keeled and assure the client that the ride will come to a successful ending as long as she is truthful and not withholding. It's an evolving art form to learn how to do the dance and encourage a client to be forthcoming about *everything*. It's all too often an impossible task. Shame, embarrassment, fear are powerful human characteristics.

Some clients garnish the truth, some outright lie, some withhold information, some get cold feet. Mike was concerned that Katherine might have exaggerated about the existence of a personal tape recording; that she may be so consumed with shame she might want to quit; that she couldn't bear to go on, brought down by her own fantasy, her distortion.

I'll try to be patient. She'll tell me when she's ready. Let me shift things.

"So," he said, "tell me about the counseling sessions you're leading over at Rosie's. They must love you."

"I'm a good actress. They trust me. They think I'm…pure…that I've got it all together."

"None of us is pure, Katherine. We're merely human. Each and every one of us. But despite what you've been through, you really do have it together. And I'm sure you're great at what you're doing there."

Katherine wrinkled her brow and took another cigarette from her pack. She put it in her mouth, didn't light it.

She invented the story about the love tape. She made it up. She slipped into a fantasy and made the whole thing up. Colello is right. And now she's struggling to get it out.

Katherine placed the unlit cigarette on Mike's desk, grasped her hands in her lap, bowed her head as if in prayer.

Mike nodded, signaling that he understood. Nevertheless, he wanted to burst out: *It's about the sex you had as a kid in high school, isn't it? You're still unwilling to have me bring that out. Or is it the tape thing? The tape doesn't exist. It never existed. Is that what you're trying to tell me? Just tell me.*

He got up from behind his desk and sat next to his client.

Katherine raised her head, eyes staring toward the window. She said, "It's a strange story." She swallowed. "I'm so embarrassed. I just can't get into it now. I'm so sorry, Mike. Another time."

Mike could no longer contain himself. "Is this by any chance about the tape...the personal tape? Or are you still wrestling with the concern about having had sex back when you were in high school and our need to bring that up?"

"I don't, can't deal with this...not now...perhaps some other time. Is that okay?" Katherine said, getting up from her chair.

Mike nodded and sighed. "Of course. Some other time."

"So, what comes next, now that they've taken my deposition? Will they sit down with you and have another settlement discussion?" Katherine asked.

"Possibly. But I'm now going to schedule my deposition of Riley."

"I hope I'm not supposed to be present when that happens?"

"No," Mike answered. "But I will need you to be by a phone in the event I have any questions for you."

Katherine nodded. "I think I really should leave now. I'm just not up to this today. I'm so sorry I wasted your time."

"Never, ever a waste of time. I understand," Mike said as he escorted Katherine to the reception area. "I'll give you plenty of notice about the date of the dep."

"Thank you, Mike. Again, I'm so sorry."

"That's okay. Just call whenever you're ready to talk about whatever it is that's troubling you."

With that, Katherine bowed her head, gestured to Jane, and left.

* * *

"She seemed quite upset today, Mike," Jane said.

"Yup. Something's troubling her. I don't know if it's the mystery tape or the fact that I've urged her to be forthright at trial about having had sex with her teenage boyfriend. For some strange reason, Colello didn't go near that when he deposed her," Mike said.

"Probably saving it as a bombshell at trial," Jane offered.

"You're brilliant," Mike responded.

"Forget the accolades," Jane said. "I can't deposit those in my bank account."

"I've told her that I want to avoid a bombshell on cross-examination by our bringing that stuff out when I do my direct exam of her rather than take the chance that Collelo doesn't know about it. Because if he does know, and we say nothing about it on direct, he'll destroy her credibility on cross…accuse her of trying to hide the truth. I've explained the dangers of avoiding it. But she seems so ashamed…"

"She'll come around," said Jane. "Probably what she's wrestling with. Probably wanted to tell you that despite your advice, she just can't go there. But seeing you is making her re-think. That's why she had to cut this meeting short."

"Enough," said Mike. "Let's go to Brigham's and get hot fudge sundaes. We both need a break."

CHAPTER TWENTY-EIGHT
KATHERINE

Locke-Ober, a stately Boston restaurant since 1875, was often a place of celebration and strategy sessions among trial lawyers. Attorney John Colello, his two assistants, and the Archbishop of Boston dined in a private room on the eve of trial.

After wine was poured the Archbishop turned to Attorney Colello. "Remind me again, please, John, as a matter of law what specifically is the designation of the plaintiff's claim."

"*Infliction of emotional distress*, Your Excellency."

The Archbishop nodded, then looked expectantly at his lawyer.

"As we've discussed, there's no question that a sexual affair took place between the two," John Colello advised. "But we're prepared to show that not only was the relationship consensual on her part, but Ms. Hennessey was both delusional and the perpetrator. She was the seductress."

"And as you advised, John, it's likely that the jury will look unfavorably upon the party who they find instigated this nightmare," the Archbishop said.

"Father Riley is filled with remorse and that will become clear to the jury. He's a forthright and repentant man. He admits that he weakened, succumbed to her advances, but is steadfast that she was the instigator. The jury will hear that Katherine Hennessey abandoned both the church and her students, broke her vows, and out of a sense of guilt for having initiated the affair, turned to alcohol and drugs. Her long history of a weak relationship with her biological father will help explain her desperate thirst for a father substitute, driving her to create a fantasy of Father Riley, her mentor, as a lover and go so far as to imagine the existence of a tape recording in which he spoke of his desire for her. All her imagination."

"Father Riley has indeed been remorseful, John. I assume that you have not had any further talks with Lyons after they turned down our most generous offer of forty-five thousand dollars?"

"No further talks, Your Excellency. And as I reminded you at the outset, the doctrine of charitable immunity capping damages at twenty thousand could be invoked in this case."

"I'm fully aware of that, John. Of course. But I don't want to seek such protection. Just as I did in settling some of the other nightmarish abuse matters, I'm prepared to pay more to avoid any cloud of scandal. And it's the morally correct thing to do, as long as the settlement figure is fair. And I think our offer is reasonable," said the Archbishop.

"I think you're being most generous. I respect your thinking, Your Excellency. But understand that I've deliberately not responded to any of Lyons' recent phone calls, including today. They may be getting cold feet about going forward with the trial. Our shutting them out, so to speak, is a sound strategy. Our refusal to engage makes them uncertain about their case. I think they'll come to court with the proverbial tail between their legs…more than willing to fold for the forty-five."

"I'm pleased to hear that. As always, I admire your strategy, John. And you know if it needs to go to fifty thousand, I'd be willing to pay." The Archbishop leaned back and dabbed his lips. "But that's it."

"If we go to trial it will all come down to credibility. The issue as to who seduced who is key. The jury is much more likely to believe Father Riley. His repentance and suffering will be obvious. And by the time we're through, the jury will be convinced that it was she who seduced our client and inflicted emotional distress, not the reverse as she alleges," Attorney Colello said.

"And this judge, Leilah Giordano, what are your thoughts?"

"In a word, Your Excellency, the very best. Before ascending to the bench, she was a superb trial lawyer, honest and fair. Her evidentiary rulings are impeccable."

"Good to know, John. But you're aware that I loathe the fact that there'll be publicity. Surely this trial will be covered in detail by the press," said the Archbishop.

"I agree. And that's what our adversary's banking on. They're convinced that you'll cave in and pay more because of the prospect of publicity."

"Should we?"

"Oh, Your Grace, stick to your earlier thinking. Your very words: 'We will not be blackmailed.' If I thought Father Riley was the instigator; that he had made any such audio recording proclaiming his feelings for her, I'd advise that we get back to the table and raise the ante."

The Archbishop nodded. "Yes. And be certain that any allegations about this tape thing that she spoke of during the deposition is debunked. The truth, John, that's all I ask."

"Of course, Your Excellency. During a break in the deposition of the plaintiff, I called Father Riley and told him of her testimony about an alleged personal tape recording made by him. He reiterated that he made tapes for instruction purposes. His audio cassettes explored real and hypothetical classroom scenarios. After his student...in this case, then Sister Hennessey,...listened while alone, he would then join the student and discuss the issues raised in the tape. But in terms of such a recording about which Ms. Hennessey fantasizes, Father Riley's words: 'I know that I was a fool, an utter sinner to allow myself to be seduced. But I am not such a fool as to ever have said, written, or recorded anything of the sort alleged by Ms. Hennessey.' And then he went on about her frequent fantasies about the two of them resigning from the church and having a life together. All her imagination."

"And the psychiatrist whom you engaged to examine Ms. Hennessey," the Archbishop inquired, "you are satisfied with her conclusions, the basis of her opinions?"

"Nancy Cohen is one of the best, Your Excellency. She has a strong theory and much data to support her conclusion that Katherine Hennessey is delusional; and that her guilt about having seduced Father Riley is such that she had an overpowering need to invent the stories both about the tape and running from the house in a state of fear and outrage."

"And very clever, John, to have engaged a female psychiatrist, a non-Catholic, to testify on our behalf. I know you're a master when it comes to the courtroom," said the Archbishop. He nodded at the associates.

"Thank you, Your Excellency."

"No love notes, cards, letters?" The Archbishop asked seeking reassurance.

"No. We served a formal notice under the applicable rules for the production of all written materials furnished by Father Riley to Ms. Hennessey. Their response: 'None.'"

"And that prevents them from introducing any such written notes should they surface?"

"Absolutely. They're bound by that pretrial representation," Attorney Colello said. "And Father Riley's own words: 'I never wrote anything to Katherine Hennessey. And I never recorded anything other than the teaching tapes, which I kept in my office.'"

* * *

Mike was pondering the trial that would get started the next day. His adversary cut off all communication, and therefore any further settlement talks. He declined to return any of Mike's calls.

Katherine was worried, both about the stress of having to testify and the uncertainty of the outcome. And she was deeply concerned about talk of perjury charges raised by Attorney Colello during the sole negotiation session.

"Perjury talk is nothing more than posturing," Mike advised. "It's a scare tactic."

Mike was in accord and relieved that Katherine felt that the forty-five thousand dollar offer was nothing more than a cheap attempt to buy her off.

"I know that this is about money," Katherine said. "You've explained that that's how our system works...monetary compensation for physical and emotional injuries. I get that. The amount of their offer is insulting and it seems so crass and empty without any apology. Without any feeling for what this has done to me."

Mike replied, "Their offer is belittling and I'm totally with you in deciding to reject it."

After Katherine left the office Mike made one last effort to contact his adversary, not just about settlement but about an important development in the case.

"I'm sorry, Mr. Lyons, but Mr. Colello is not in. I'll give him the message that you called." In keeping with the strategy of silence, John Colello did not return the call. "Make 'em worry. It dampens their expectations," Colello said to one of his associates.

* * *

"ALL RISE," barked the court officer as the judge entered the courtroom. "All persons having business before the Superior Court, Suffolk County, Commonwealth of Massachusetts, give your attendance and you shall be heard. The Honorable Leilah Giordano presiding."

* * *

"...And so ladies and gentlemen of the jury, we are faced with two diametrically opposed stories. One is the truth, the other a sad concoction of Katherine Hennessey's thirst for love and her imagination in which she blames Father Riley. Rest assured that when all the evidence is presented, you will conclude, contrary to Attorney Lyons' remarks during his opening statement, that the sexual relationship between Father Riley and Katherine Hennessey not only was consensual on her part, but that it was instigated by her. Ladies and gentlemen, I can assure you that the evidence will be clear that Ms. Hennessey seduced Father Riley, initiated intimacy, proclaiming her need for him. I can assure you that the evidence will be such that you will conclude that if anyone inflicted emotional distress upon another, it was Katherine Hennessey who so harmed the repentant Father Riley." Attorney John Colello completed his opening statement to the jury. He glanced in Mike's direction expecting a signal that Lyons was ready to accept the offer of settlement. Was Colello acting counter to his clients' best interests by not engaging Mike in further negotiations? *I'm going to stay the course. Lyons is treading water. He'll fold before this goes much further. And I'm holding the line at our generous offer of forty-five. Certainly Lyons has a strong argument as a matter of law to get around the charitable immunity cap. But the facts are against him. Any publicity will actually be favorable to the archdiocese...Katherine Hennessey will come across as a greedy fallen sister of the Church. The truth will come out.*

* * *

The courtroom was filled with curious lawyers, members of the press, and the public. The subject matter was titillating.

Mike decided to lead off with Katherine. She was well prepared and presented as a strong witness, relating in appropriate detail the various stages of the affair with the defendant priest. Mike's style, as always, was a smooth, relentless rhythm. The jury listened attentively to Katherine's testimony of the priest sprinkling holy water on the bed before they would have relations, of his insistence and constant demands upon her for sex most every time they were together, and then of his coldness, withdrawal, and refusal to resign his position with the church after she succumbed to his demands to no longer serve as a sister. She understandably faltered during her testimony about the two attempts to take her own life and the uncertainty and anxiety with which she continues to live. This aspect of her case would be buttressed by the testimony of Dr. Larry Armont. During this stage of testimony, Mike stayed away from any mention of the teaching tapes or purported "love tape."

Day one was nearing an end.

"Ladies and gentlemen, it's drawing close to four o'clock," the judge said while looking at the jury. "Unless Counsel has an objection, I suggest we adjourn."

Lawyers never want to curry disfavor with the jury. Quite the opposite. When a judge gives jurors an opportunity to go home, seasoned trial lawyers agree enthusiastically.

"Fine. 10 a.m. tomorrow morning. I trust, Attorney Lyons, that you will conclude your direct examination of the plaintiff sometime tomorrow?" Judge Giordano asked.

"Yes, Your Honor. I expect to," Mike said.

* * *

As they were leaving the courthouse, Mike wished his adversary a pleasant evening. Attorney Colello's response was purposely remote, all part of his strategy of feigned disinterest, if not self-righteous disgust with the plaintiff's case. He managed a curt smile.

Mike said to himself: *noted.*

He shifted to his client.

"Katherine," Mike said, "you were fabulous on the stand. Honest, clear, and convincing."

"Thank you, Mike. You prepared me well. But it's the cross-examination and the tape thing I'm worried about. Should we do another prep session?"

Mike laughed. "We're both wiped out. You've been well coached by Sean and me for any cross that John Colello may throw at you. For now, rest is more important. Your brain is on overdrive. Let's meet tomorrow morning at 8:30. We'll both be fresh for a final tune-up."

"Fine. The tape thing, Mike? Are you going to lead off with that tomorrow?"

"I am, Katherine. Have a good evening. Take a long walk and have a good dinner with a glass of wine. Give your brain the night off. But if any questions, thoughts come up and you want to talk, please call. You have my home number. Call any time. I'm a night owl…rarely sleep…wastes too much time."

"I'm worried about the whole issue of my fantasies. Mr. Colello made a big deal of that during the deposition. I suppose he'll go after that during his cross-examination?

"One way or another, I expect so. Just stick to the truth. Jurors are human. They have fantasies. The jury will forgive most anything when they're convinced the person on the stand is telling the truth."

"I do feel ashamed about the tape thing."

"I can understand your feelings. You've been through so much. But we're going to handle that just fine."

Mike nodded reassuringly. "So, again, get some sleep. I need you fresh and alert. See you at 8:30."

"Yes, sir," Katherine said, feeling buttressed by Mike's confident style. Although embarrassed at times during her testimony, she felt relieved that she was getting to tell her story to a jury in open court.

* * *

Unable to converse with his adversary in the courtroom at the conclusion of the day's trial, when Mike arrived at his office just after 5 p.m. he placed a call to John Colello. The response was a recording that the office was closed. Mike left a message that this was an urgent call. He left both his office and home numbers. In keeping with the defense strategy of posturing that they had no interest in exploring settlement, John Colello took the extreme measure of not returning Mike's "urgent" call.

Mike felt that he had fulfilled his obligation as a fellow trial lawyer to make contact with his adversary. The next morning he and Katherine met in the courthouse and went over the anticipated testimony. They then went upstairs to the courtroom in sufficient time for Mike to have an opportunity to speak with his adversary before the 10 a.m. trial resumption.

At 9:45, Attorney Colello, his assistants, and Father Riley strolled into the courtroom.

"Hi, John, do you have a minute?" Mike asked.

"Sorry, Mike," John Colello said, busying himself with his briefcase. "We only have a few minutes before we get started. I need to go over my notes. I expect you'll be through with your client shortly and I want to be ready for my cross."

Bullshit, John. You've been ready for your cross-examination for days. You're salivating at the opportunity to get to Katherine. You're taking a hard line...shutting me out. Well, as Sean has said more than once, "what goes around comes around."

* * *

Trial advocates may be professional friends and respect and admire one another. But when they think the occasion calls for it they will fight like dogs...metaphorically of course...regarding strategy and tactics. On occasion a strategy may backfire.

The jury took their seats.

After the usual proclamation by a court officer, Judge Giordano greeted the jurors warmly. "I trust that you've all had a pleasant evening, a good night's rest, and are prepared to resume your civic responsibility."

Jurors nodded and smiled.

Judge Giordano gestured toward Mike. "Counsel, you may proceed."

"Thank you, Your Honor," Mike said while pulling something from his briefcase.

An associate sitting at counsel table with Attorney Colello watched Mike, and then his mouth dropped open. "Sir," he whispered to Colello pointing toward Mike's table. A tape cassette player was now visibly displayed.

Colello frowned. *What in the Lord's name is going on? What's he up to?*

Mike started: "If Your Honor please..."

"Your Honor," barked an irritated Colello, a look of consternation on his face. *Was there a tape? Or is this some kind of charade?* "May I approach?"

The judge beckoned both lawyers to the bench. Leilah Giordano was as savvy on the bench as she had been when trying cases. Colello's irritation was loud and clear and the judge was fully aware that Mike had placed a cassette player on the table.

Colello whispered, hoping to keep the jury from hearing any of this bench conference. "I'd like to know where Mike is going?" He faced Mike. "I like to think you're above game-playing. Are you trying to make me believe that you actually have something that you're going to try to play on that thing or is this a bluff?"

Mike was dying to challenge John Colello. *Are you calling my bluff? Because if you are...* But he didn't. He knew that taking the high road would serve his client better.

"Your Honor, may I suggest that we deal with this in your chambers?" Mike said.

"Thanks for calling it 'chambers.'" The judge chuckled, aware of the value humor played in an effort to ease tension. She turned to the jury and explained that she and the lawyers were going to retire to her lobby to discuss a potential piece of evidence. "I'm going to excuse you so that you might go to the cafeteria and have some coffee rather than have you just sit here in the courtroom. Please return in forty-five minutes." She nodded to the court officer who would escort them.

The jurist and lawyers filed into her lobby. Judge Giordano sat behind her desk and pointed to chairs on the other side.

"Your Honor, may I?" Mike asked, indicating that he wished to place the cassette player on the judge's desk.

"Of course," the judge answered. "What've you got? What's this all about?"

"*Res ipsa loquitor (the thing speaks for itself)*, Your Honor," Mike answered.

"Haven't heard that one since year one at BC Law."

"Your Honor," pleaded Attorney Colello. "I haven't a clue."

"Come on, John. You know damn well what it is," Mike said.

Colello's handsome face was scarlet, but he was struggling to remain his usual unflappable self. The highly regarded seasoned courtroom warhorse brushed a hand through his signature head of silver white hair.

Mike leaned toward his adversary: "I've been trying to talk with you these past few days but you wouldn't take my calls. I wanted to let you know about this. And yesterday, wow...cold shoulder. And this morning, you gave me the bullshit about needing to look at your notes. Sorry, Your Honor."

"Come, now, Mike. I may look like a choirgirl but after dueling with pros like you and John before taking this job, and raising a couple of teenage boys, *bullshit* will hardly offend me," the judge said. Somehow or other the word *bullshit* actually sounded noble coming from her lips.

The air lightened. The three of them enjoyed a round of laughter. Some judges, particularly those like Leilah Giordano who had experienced the hazards of being a trial lawyer, knew all too well the shock of the unexpected, the highs and lows, the complexities and tension involved in the business of trying cases.

"Your Honor, I plan to lay the proper foundation to introduce the contents of this audiotape into evidence," Mike said while waving a cassette. "I certainly think that the Court and John should hear this in advance before the jury has the opportunity to listen to it. My client will identify the voice of the defendant, Father Thomas Riley."

John Colello quickly rallied. "Judge, whatever this thing purportedly is, it will fail to rise to the level of admissibility. For one, authenticating that the voice on this tape is that of Father Riley is a major issue. He made it abundantly clear to me when I told him of Mike's client's assertion about some sort of…love tape, that no such tape existed…that he never recorded any such thing. And we have hearsay as well to contend with."

"I hear you, John. But Mike's suggestion that we listen to the content of this recording out of the hearing of the jury is appropriate. I can't possibly rule on its admissibility until I've heard it. Let's turn this on," the judge said. She gestured to Mike to start the cassette player.

The sound quality was crisp and clear. *Sister Katherine, I can't begin to tell you how much I have enjoyed working with you these past weeks. I know that you will be an extraordinary teacher. It saddens me to think of our sessions coming to an end. I would like this to be not an end, but a new beginning…*

Sister Katherine, I have fallen in love with you. I want you. I need to hold you in my arms…to stroke your beautiful face. You are like no other. My nights are torture.

I yearn for your lovely being to lie next to me…to kiss you…to explore the essence of you…I imagine and crave the touch of my hands upon you, upon your loving body…there is a future for us, for you and me, Katherine and Thomas as husband and wife…together…

John Colello, the consummate professional, knew when to fold his tent and not tarnish his reputation by wrangling when it was obvious that his case was sinking into the depths of the Atlantic. He sighed a sigh of surrender. He put up a hand, asking that the tape be halted.

"There's not much more," Mike said as he obliged and pushed the stop button.

Colello, embarrassed, looked past Mike. "I'm stunned. We screwed up. We took our client at his word. I should have known to doubt him. Dammit, the son-of-a-bitch…and I can't believe I'm saying that about a priest, Your Honor. You both know I've been representing the Archdiocese for years. I have nothing but love for the Church. He broke his vows by having this affair. I should have known not to simply take his word about the tape."

"Wait a minute. Mike, you weren't planning to ambush John with this, were you? I know you're better than that," the judge said.

Mike, thrilled that everything crystallized, did not want to rub it in. He knew all too well what it was like to get hammered when evidence suddenly turned dramatically against one's client. He and John Colello would have many more cases across the aisle from each other.

Mike said, "No way, Your Honor. If John hadn't requested a bench conference, I was all set to ask for one."

"But why didn't you tell John about this months ago? Surely it would have resulted in settlement long before trial."

"Judge, I only learned she had a copy of this tape three days ago."

"What! Not until three days ago!" the judge said.

"Your Honor, you know from your days out there that our people are not always forthcoming. I asked her about the whereabouts of the tape way back when she first told me about it."

Attorney Colello sat with his mouth open, leaning forward. He looked at the judge expectantly.

"And?" the judge asked.

"Your Honor, at that time my client merely shrugged. She shook her head and said that the priest kept all tapes in a locked desk drawer. Ms. Hennessey said nothing about having made a copy. Your Honor, she's been to hell and…well, I'm not certain that she is all the way back yet. Waves of shame overcame her better judgment. This relationship did a terrible number on Ms. Hennessey."

Mike turned to his adversary. "It's about this tape that I've been trying to get a hold of you these past three days, but…"

Attorney Colello turned scarlet. He shook his head as if to chastise himself.

"Judge, I guess Mike and I both were misled. I confronted my man and took him at his word when he said there never was any such tape. He said, and these are his words: 'Sister Hennessey is deceptive and delusional.' He's a priest, for God's sake. I believed him. Shame on me."

"Shame and denial are powerful forces," the judge offered. "Father Riley was too ashamed to admit that he had made such a tape. And Ms. Hennessey also too ashamed to reveal that somehow she had made a copy. Wow! Gentlemen, you're a couple of pros. Time to get this settled and keep this tape from the jury's ears, to say nothing of the press."

Mike said: "John, you're absolutely the best. And I'm not being condescending. You know me. We all get blindsided. We get taken in by our clients, despite everything we preach."

Judge Giordano nodded, her facial expression in full accord.

Colello continued: "At the deposition I took of Ms. Hennessey she testified about this tape. I thought it was preposterous. You remember, I'm sure, Mike, that I asked for a break. I called my client who we had on standby. I told him of Katherine's testimony. Again, he admitted to the affair. But he vehemently denied the existence of any such cassette. He said the only tapes were instructional which he gave to me long ago. He said that he never permitted her or any other mentee to take any cassettes home. He said he was always concerned about possible loss. I allowed the lawyer in me to slip. I naively took him at his word. My faith got the better of me. And that's why, during pretrial discovery, I never called for the production of any electronic recordings. As I said a moment ago, he said that she was delusional. Father Riley assured me that there never was a love tape or any love letters. I suppose you have a trove of those, too?"

"John, we've all been in this kind of situation. It's awful. I didn't want to ambush you. That's why I've been trying to tell you about this…to let you hear it before we got near a courthouse. And no, there are no love letters."

To say that the top-ranked lawyer, John Colello, was chagrined by all that had unfolded would be putting it mildly. He had taken his client's word. A priest. And the strategy to raise the plaintiff's anxiety level by not responding to telephone calls clearly had backfired.

"He's a very convincing fellow. Charming, to say the least. Nevertheless I should have known better. His character was already tarnished. I should have probed." Colello shook his head. He turned to Mike and asked: "How in the world did you get this thing?"

Mike replied, "Convincing? Charming? I should say. Just ask Katherine. As for the cassette, it's a copy. The morning after Katherine heard this tape in his home study, she returned. She told your client that she replayed the tape in her mind throughout a sleepless night. She asked him if he really did love her? He said that he did. She asked if she could hear the tape again…could she take it home. He was flattered. They kissed. She said it was passionate. My guess is that his thinking wasn't rational. He was consumed with his obsession to have her. At that moment, it may have been genuine love…before it morphed into sadistic control. Her life was upside down. He let her take the tape home. She told me that as she was leaving, he casually asked that she return it."

"And she didn't?" Colello asked.

"She certainly did. The next day, but not until she had made a copy with some equipment she had at home for recording music. As simple as that. She never told him that she had made a copy. She was embarrassed and thrilled and confused and excited. She wasn't being surreptitious. She wasn't thinking of ever holding it over his head. She revered him. She just wanted, as she told me, to luxuriate in his words. She fell deeply in love with him and with the idea of a life together. She never told me about the fact that she had made a copy…not until the eve of trial. She's truly embarrassed, maybe on some level ashamed, that she made and kept a copy. That's why it took her so long to tell me. I suppose it's like holding onto a love letter. She trusted and believed him."

"And so did I," said Colello. "My error. And here I am, decades at the bar. Shame on me. But one would like to think that a priest…Well, I should have known better. I should have explored this further, not simply taken his word. Your Honor…"

The judge interrupted. "You know, gentlemen, I'm reminded of Professor Sean Murray's words at law school and at many continuing education seminars. 'Remember, everybody,' he would start with a chuckle, 'there are many booby traps out there in the world of litigation. The most lethal? Sometimes, our very own client.'"

The lawyers nodded.

Attorney Colello asked, "Your Honor, may I use your lobby in private for a bit? I'd like to bring my client in and play this thing. After he's heard it, with your permission, Mike, I then want to take this to the Archbishop. And then let's meet there with our clients. We'll get down to business about resolving this mess."

Mike nodded.

The judge said, "Excellent idea. And John, you're one of the best. We've all made mistakes. Don't be too hard on yourself. I'm going to excuse the jury for the day. If the two of you can't work something out, and don't hesitate to call me while you're at the Archdiocese if you think I can be of some help, then we'll summons the jury back and resume trial."

CHAPTER TWENTY-NINE
DANIELLE

"December 7, surprise attack...Day of Infamy," Judge Henry said to Mike when the two of them ran into each other at 8 a.m. in the Golden Dome Coffee Shop on the anniversary of the 1941 Japanese attack upon Pearl Harbor.

Mike raised his mug.

They looked at each other. Not as lawyer and judge, but as men who had been *there*...the projects...combat.

Captain Kelvin Henry, a Tuskegee Airman during WWII, was a pilot with the 332nd Fighter Group. He distinguished himself in missions over Sicily, Anzio, and Normandy. He was part of the squadron that amazingly destroyed five enemy aircraft in less than four minutes.

Only the combat veterans knew. There were no words to explain to someone who has never been exposed firsthand to the horrors of warfare just what it's all about. Having been there, each of them knew that words were unnecessary.

* * *

When Mike stepped off the courthouse elevator, he spotted Danielle Webb chatting affably with her husband. Danielle was laughing. Her dour husband actually managed a smile.

This is a good sign, I hope. Maybe the two of them can soften toward each other so that Vasquez and I can sit down and work out a sensible resolution.

Sofia Vasquez arrived a moment after and quickly beckoned her client. She did not want Mr. Webb fraternizing with the enemy. They might be talking about reconciliation. That would be contrary to her firm's billable hours culture: *Keep this case going.* She would need her two thousand money-producing hours come

December 31 so that the powers-that-be at Weeks, Ward would include her on the bonus list. That was the new standard at Boston's large law firms: billable time carried the day.

"His Honor is ready to see all lawyers in the Webb matter," the court officer announced, pointing the way to the judge's chambers.

"Well, good morning, Counsel," Judge Henry said. "Please have a seat. I've pondered Attorney Lyons' objection to your last question, Ms. Vasquez. But before we launch into that evidentiary matter, I wonder whether or not during this interim time the two of you have had a chance to talk and discuss resolving this matter?"

Mike, in response to what he felt was his obligation to his client, had called his counterpart following the last session in an effort to initiate a settlement discussion. Sofia Vasquez would have none of it.

The judge looked at each lawyer expectantly.

Mike spoke up: "I'm always willing to explore settlement, Your Honor." He said nothing about his phone attempt. *Let Vasquez tell the judge herself that she has no interest. She's arrogant enough to walk into that trap. "Litigation rule 101": never, but never, turn down a judge's request or suggestion that counsel talk about exploring ways to settle a dispute.*

Mike turned to Sofia Vasquez. She feigned not seeing the challenging message on his face.

"Your Honor, my client and I don't see any way that we could possibly yield on the issue of custody. Nor would Mr. Webb be willing to share anything more than ten percent of the value of his assets, and I might add that that percentage, in light of everything that has transpired in this marriage, is more than generous. We also take the position that Mrs. Webb, fully capable of making her own living and solely culpable with respect to the destruction of this marriage, is not entitled to any alimony whatsoever."

Mike shot a knowing look at the judge and shrugged. "Well, Your Honor, I certainly would be willing to talk, but I think Ms. Vasquez is pretty clear."

Judge Henry said: "Attorney Vasquez, as I've mentioned before, one never knows what might come out of the mouths of witnesses once they're on the stand or what kinds of unexpected developments may take place outside of the courthouse. We've already seen one such happening in this matter, but certainly not in and of itself dispositive. I've always taken the position that most every matter can be settled. It usually inures to the litigants' benefit to control the outcome rather than put it in the hands of a judge. However, you and your client have the absolute right to continue with trial and you can be certain that I'll make the best determination I'm capable of based upon the evidence I hear and my observations." He looked at each lawyer.

"I hear you, Your Honor, but quite frankly I think it's impossible to put this case in any settlement category. Mrs. Webb's shameful adulterous behavior and her flagrant violation of your admonition that she remain with her family the entire Thanksgiving holiday is an example of her irresponsibility. And there's more." She turned and faced Mike with a self-righteous expression on her face. "We have impenetrable evidence that will show the court that Mrs. Webb is seriously deficient morally as a parent and a wife," said Sofia Vasquez.

"I'm sure that His Honor recalls that it was Mr. Webb who first left the family home in the midst of the holiday dinner," Mike said.

"Well, all right then, we'll proceed," the judge said, rising from the chair behind his desk and adjusting his judicial robe.

"Your Honor, the objection I raised when we were finishing the last session? I've of course spoken with my client and should she be required to answer any question about having had sex on that day…or any other day…with her real estate client, her answer would be an emphatic *no*. But because this question has zero factual basis, I renew my objection," Mike argued.

"Attorney Vasquez, as I made clear at the close of the last session, unless you make an Offer of Proof that Mrs. Webb was intimate with her client, I'm going to sustain the objection. I don't want a fishing expedition or any baseless accusations."

"That's fine, Your Honor. As I stated, I withdraw the question…for the moment."

For the moment? Mike asked himself. *Minor league bullshit bluffing.*

"Well, all right then," the judge said, "let's get started."

* * *

Danielle Webb resumed the stand, fixed her gaze toward the rear of the courtroom. Mike turned. There they were, once again, the tall man and the disheveled looking woman. They seated themselves in the rear. *The tall one is the guy who came to the ER. The lady…wait a minute…I do know where I've seen her…*

Mike's thought pattern was interrupted by the business at hand.

The clerk spoke: "You swear or affirm to tell the whole truth and nothing but the truth…"

And so Sofia Vasquez delved into her cross-examination of Danielle. She referenced the fact that she had been asking about Danielle's meeting with her real estate client on Thanksgiving and the amount of time Mrs. Webb was away from the family home in "defiance of His Honor's strong recommendation."

Mrs. Webb: "I feel terrible about that, but my husband also left our home."

Attorney Vasquez ignored that response.

Attorney Vasquez: "Mrs. Webb, I'm going to ask you some questions about your knowledge of your husband's financial portfolio. You seem to be quite familiar."

Danielle Webb's fair complexioned face and neck reddened. But as the questions poured out about the finances, including assets, income, the family trusts, and day-to-day expenses, she harnessed her poise and handled all with calm and self-assurance. The lengthy questioning was little more than a rehash of the information Mike garnered from her during his direct examination. Her answers were straightforward and informed as though she might have been the family accountant or tax planner. But Vasquez had a strategy. She doubted that she would catch Danielle in any meaningful inconsistencies with her testimony on direct examination. Instead, she wanted to impress upon the court this woman's all too detailed familiarity with the Webb fortune...that what Mrs. Webb was after was not really the children but rather a healthy chunk of her husband's inherited wealth.

"She's paintin' our lady like she's some whore gold digger," Mike whispered to Sean.

"But she's not," Sean whispered back. "And I think Kelvin senses that."

* * *

"How am I doing?" Danielle asked during the mid-afternoon break.

"You're terrific," Mike said. "As I've said before, I'm impressed with your knowledge about the trusts and other family finances. And why shouldn't you be? I liked your matter-of-fact style. Keep it up."

"Just stickin' to the truth," she quipped.

"If Vasquez doesn't ask anything about how you volunteered to help with the fall play at school..." Mike started.

"I know; I'll just stick it in."

"No. The judge already heard about your volunteering stuff on direct examination, but what I forgot to cover was the commendation you received from the preschool. I'll take care of that on redirect. You, madam, have an assignment: just answer the questions. And, by the way, do you have any hidden surprises I should know about?"

"Oh, Mr. Attorney Lyons, do I ever."

Mike blushed. *I walked into that one.*

"Save the surprises for your next husband," he said. "Okay, judge's coming out."

Judge Henry resumed the bench and gestured to Sofia Vasquez.

Attorney Vasquez: "Well, now, Mrs. Webb, I'd like to ask you whether or not you ever kept a diary?"

Diary?! Where in hell is this coming from? Oh, no. Do you have any hidden surprises I should know about? Oh, Mr. Attorney Lyons, do I ever. Mike's heart raced. *A diary?*

Mike: "Objection, Your Honor."

Judge Henry: "Overruled, Counsel. It's a simple question that calls for a 'yes' or 'no' answer."

Mike: "May I approach, Your Honor?"

Judge Henry: "You may not, Counsel," the judge ruled. He turned and nodded to Danielle as if to say, "Proceed and answer the question."

Mrs. Webb: "What do you mean?"

Mike squinted. He glanced toward Sean, his forehead furrowed.

Sean whispered: "She's just fishing. We served Vasquez with a Notice to Produce copies of documents that they intended to use at trial. An alleged diary should have been included with their response. It wasn't."

Attorney Vasquez: "A diary. You know, Mrs. Webb, some sort of log or writing about things that went on in your life."

Danielle Webb was wearing her playful expression. Mike shuddered. He rose quickly from his chair. "Your Honor, once again I object to this line of questioning. If there is such a..."

Judge Henry: "And once again I am overruling your objection. The question does not ask about content, merely whether or not Mrs. Webb kept such a chronicle. It's not unusual...many people do. Mrs. Webb, you may answer."

Mrs. Webb: "I...I'm not sure. I may have."

I may have? Mike remained stone-faced. *Never let the enemy know you're concerned about a potential bombshell.*

Attorney Vasquez: "Well, allow me to help refresh your memory."

Sofia Vasquez walked triumphantly to her counsel table. An assistant handed her a soft-covered book with a paisley pattern on its muted cover. The lawyer walked over to Mike's table, showed him her treasure, a poorly controlled supercilious expression on her face. Mike leafed through the pages and then stood.

"Your Honor, I object to the use of this...this thing Attorney Vasquez has just..."

"Attorney Lyons, what are you talking about? This 'thing,' as you put it, hasn't even been identified, let alone introduced into evidence...hasn't even been shown to the witness. You know better." The judge then turned to Attorney Vasquez, "If you intend to have the witness identify whatever this is, please proceed."

Mike shrugged his head from side to side and slowly lowered himself to his chair.

Attorney Vasquez glared triumphantly at Mike. "Are you through? May I?"

Mike: "Your Honor, if I may. I served a Notice to..."

Judge Henry: "I'm well aware of pretrial discovery requirements, Counsel. Let's get this thing identified, shall we?"

Mike: "May the Court please note my exception."

Judge: "Noted."

Mike struggled to maintain his customary cool façade.

Attorney Vasquez: "Mrs. Webb, I show you this book. Do you recognize it?"

Mike: "Objection!"

Judge: "Overruled." He turned to Sofia Vasquez: "For identification only, Counsel."

Sean turned to Mike, cupping his hand over his mouth. "If it's for identification only, then Kelvin's correct."

Danielle Webb: "Yes. It's a personal diary. I kept it in a box with other very personal things."

She looked both apologetically and triumphantly at Mike.

Taken by surprise, wary of what might be in that potential keg of dynamite, and furious that his client had never mentioned anything about a diary, Mike raised his objection once again to any use of the book other than to simply establish that Mrs. Webb did keep some sort of diary.

"Well," Judge Henry responded, "if the book will help to refresh the witness' memory of its content, and if the content is relevant to any issues in this trial, I'm going to allow questions pertaining to it."

"Your Honor, I object to any reference to the content. We haven't had a chance to examine it and I served a Notice to Produce upon Attorney Vasquez. This diary, obviously stolen from my client's personal possessions, was not included with documents Attorney Vasquez turned over to us in response. I ask..."

Judge Henry motioned Mike to sit. He then nodded to Attorney Vasquez, signaling her to proceed.

Attorney Vasquez: "Mrs. Webb, would you kindly turn to the first page on which I have placed a red paper clip. Please look at the top of that page and tell the Court what it says."

Mike: "Objection."

Judge: "Overruled."

Sean whispered to Mike: "Kelvin's dead wrong. If we lose this case, we've got excellent grounds for appeal."

Mike shook his head, mumbling: "Last thing we need is to have to appeal this thing."

Judge: "Mrs. Webb, you may answer the question."

Mrs. Webb: "Score."

Attorney Vasquez: "Score? And just what does that mean?"

Holy shit, Mike thought. "Your Honor, I must object."

Judge Henry: "No, no. Let's probe a little further and see whether or not there's anything relevant here."

Mike: "Your Honor, may I approach?"

Judge Henry: "No you may not. Let's get on with this. This trial has dragged on long enough. Let me hear the witness's answer."

Attorney Vasquez: "Mrs. Webb, would you please explain use of the word...*Score*...at the top of the page?"

Mike: "Objection."

Judge Henry: "Overruled. The witness will answer."

Mrs. Webb: "It's just a title that suited me at the moment."

Attorney Vasquez: "Just a title? Well, can you please tell His Honor the content of that page?"

Mike: "I renew my objection, if Your Honor please. Relevancy and breach of the Rules of Discovery."

Judge Henry: "Again, until I know what the content is, I can't rule properly." He motioned for Mike to sit.

Sean whispered: "Kelvin's way off base. He shouldn't allow this. If we lose this case, he's committing reversible error. The Court of Appeals would rule in our favor. Just keep objecting so the Appellate Court won't be able to say that we ceded and allowed this stuff...whatever it may be...and I think we know what it is...into the record."

Mike's adversary repeated her prior question. And Mike was on his feet again. "Objection, Your Honor. We've not had an opportunity to peruse, let alone examine, whatever this document might be. And to repeat..."

Judge Henry: "We're not dealing with a jury here. And she's just using this, whatever it is, to refresh the witness's memory. Counsel's not attempting to put this book, document itself into evidence. Is that correct Attorney Vasquez?"

Sofia Vasquez quickly agreed with the judge's assessment.

Judge Henry: "All right now. Let's see where we go with this. Let's mark it for identification purposes only. Now, Attorney Vasquez, you may proceed."

Attorney Vasquez: "Of course, Your Honor." She turned to Mrs. Webb and asked, "Is there a list of names on that page?"

Mike: "Objection."

Judge Henry: "Overruled. You may answer."

Mrs. Webb: "Yes."

Attorney Vasquez: "And are there dates next to each name?"

Mike: "Objection."

Judge Henry merely waved his hand.

Sean leaned over toward Mike's ear: "I think I know what Kelvin's up to." Mike frowned.

Mrs. Webb: "Yes."

Attorney Vasquez: "And were those the dates on which you had sex with…"

Mike: "Once again, I object. Your Honor, this sounds like an old-fashioned smutty and irrelevant fishing expedition. In addition, as I've been arguing, not only was a copy of this book not provided to us in response to our Notice to Produce, but I'm blind as to what's contained in this thing."

Judge Henry: "All right. Let's take a ten-minute recess. Attorney Vasquez, please hand over the diary to Attorney Lyons."

As Sofia Vasquez triumphantly handed Mike the book, he glanced at Brooks Webb's smug and pallid face.

Mike said to Vasquez: "You've violated the goddamned rules and you know it. If you think for one minute you're getting away with this, think again. I loathe, understand me, loathe lawyers who cheat."

Mike, Sean, and Danielle walked toward the rear of the courtroom. The tall man stood and held the door open. Mike looked at the disheveled woman. Her eyes were trying to signal something. Mike grabbed the tall man's arm. "You, sir, whoever you are. I want to talk with you…and this woman…when we're through today. I think you know something I need to know. And I have a hunch I'm right." The tall man merely nodded… nothing more.

* * *

"Holy Christ, Sean. Kelvin's all over the place with his rulings," Mike said as they got into the elevator to go down one floor and have a confrontation with Danielle Webb, who seemed to be enjoying every moment of the tension. She signaled that she was going to use the restroom.

"And what did you mean you think you know what Kelvin's up to?" Mike asked.

Sean said, "Deliberate jarring rulings. He should have allowed us to do what we're about to do now as soon as Vasquez referenced this keg of dynamite and before she could ask any questions. If Kelvin persists and allows her to use this, I've got a suspicion Kelvin may be leaning in our direction with respect to his final decision. He just may be giving Vasquez tremendous latitude...minimizing any grounds for an appeal on their part. If Vasquez loses this case, she won't be able to argue that the diary and its probable evidence of adultery were excluded. And that would be a major argument on appeal. Kelvin's not a fool. He may think our lady's a bit on the wild side, but like me, feels there's a reason for her behavior...and that there's a responsible woman beneath the veneer."

Mike chimed in, "I like your thinking, Professor. I sure hope you're right, my optimistic friend. But Kelvin's not a fan of adultery."

"Why didn't our Mrs. Webb come clean with us about this thing?" Sean pondered.

"She probably thought that it was safely stashed away and that Brooks knew nothing about it," said Mike. "And *shame*, Professor, is a powerful force. You taught me that one. Names of men she's slept with are in this diary and she's embarrassed about it."

"Maybe not," said Sean. "Maybe now that it's out in the open..."

Danielle surfaced from the ladies room.

Mike confronted her: "No surprises? What in hell do you call this? Do you have any written records at all of anything other than financial records, I asked? And what did you tell me? What did you tell me, Madam Client?" Mike waved the diary in Danielle's direction.

Danielle threw her shoulders back, facing Mike.

"Screw this bullshit," she said. "It's a goddamned diary. Okay? Personal. I didn't even know it was missing. Names and dates of guys I fucked. Okay? I'm a no-good tramp, is that what you're thinking? But a hell of a better parent than that joke of a husband could ever be. That bastard went through my stuff. He fucking stole it. He had no right…"

"Terrific," Mike said with as much sarcasm as he could muster. "And what about this next page, the one entitled *Future?* Guys you want to go to bed with? For crap's sake, you've got *my* goddamn name on that page!"

"What about mine?" Sean quipped, hoping to ease the tension.

Danielle roared with alacrity: "I'll write it in now."

Mike responded: "Very funny. The two of you are a couple of comedians."

Mike was beside himself. He had been in the business of trying cases a long time, but this one was leading him straight to McLean Hospital.

"Madam Client," Mike started, "I'm so happy you find humor in this. Listen to me very carefully before our entire case is buried beneath this building. Adultery is still a crime on the books of this Commonwealth. Consequently, you will take the Fifth on any question…I repeat, any question…that asks about your having sex with anyone other than your husband. You simply say: 'On advice of my lawyer, I invoke the Fifth Amendment privilege.' Got it?"

"Did you say 'sex with my husband'?" Danielle quipped.

Mike frowned. *Well, not unusual when a marriage is going sour...sex comes to a halt.*

"But if I do that," Danielle started, "won't the judge still know I'm guilty...that I had sex with these guys?"

The lawyers looked at each other. Their facial expressions telegraphed the obvious.

"Look, Danielle, this stuff is grim when you're seeking to gain custody. And we've got a written record in this case to protect. And despite your wildness, I still believe you're the better parent. Let's at least keep admission of extramarital sex out of the official record. Please take my advice and invoke the Fifth Amendment. Even though the judge may draw inferences from your taking the Fifth, the absence of specific admissions by you still may leave the door open for him to award custody to you. Or at the very least, joint custody. We'll talk about that possibility later. For now, if you admit that you committed adultery, our task becomes formidable. Get it?"

"I hear you," she whispered. "But..."

* * *

Court was back in session. Judge Henry resumed his place on the bench and motioned for all to be seated. "Attorney Lyons, have you and your client had an opportunity to look at the diary?" Mike said that he had. The judge gestured for Danielle Webb to take the stand. "You may proceed, Attorney Vasquez."

To no avail, but all part of fulfilling his duty to represent his client in a zealous manner, Mike objected to any reference whatsoever to the diary. Judge Henry continued to overrule the objections.

Attorney Vasquez: "Mrs. Webb, I notice that there are three consecutive names with the same last name? Does that refresh your memory?"

Mike flashed his hand toward Danielle with all five fingers upright. He intentionally signaled so that the judge and his adversary knew that he was reminding his client of her right to invoke the privilege against self-incrimination. She didn't take his advice.

Mrs. Webb: "Yes. Father, son, and grandfather. I was trying for a triple play, but granddad wasn't...*up*...to it." Her grin was as triumphant as that of an infielder completing a triple play.

The courtroom spectators failed with their efforts to suppress laughter, including the court officer and His Honor. It did release tension...with the exception of the anxiety gripping Attorney Michael Lyons.

Mike slouched back in his hard-backed chair. As he had when other cases went sour, Mike imaged a bucket of seaweed being dumped all over his body. It was the stuff that emptied out onto him on those rare but real occasions when a trial didn't turn out favorably. Sometimes "they" continued dumping the imaginary stuff after he left the courthouse. Sometimes it was piled up on the roof of his car for all to see what a loser he was when he poked along the Mass Pike on his way home.

He turned to Sean. "Pearl Harbor Day. What better day than this to get torpedoed right out of the water?"

CHAPTER THIRTY
DANIELLE

The *SS Danielle Webb-Mike Lyons-Fight-for-Custody-Of-Her-Children* was more than listing. A self-inflicted explosion sent it plummeting to the depths of the Suffolk County Probate and Family Court.

Plain and simple, thought Mike, *some clients are designed to be self-destructive. And they couldn't care less about taking their lawyer down with them. Right now the only thing thinner than my case is the air atop Mount Everest.*

The Honorable Kelvin Henry regained his composure. "Ladies and gentlemen, I think this is a good place to recess for the balance of the week. We'll convene Monday morning. Ten o'clock sharp, everybody."

"ALL RISE." Before leaving the bench the judge, wide-eyed, cast a look in Mike's direction...*Counsel, I thought that I had heard it all, but this piece of testimony? Colorful, to say the least.* Mike read the judge's thoughts and answered with a shrug, maintaining his usual steady temperament. He could feel and hear his intestines growling. *I don't even know whether or not Scotch and Maalox will calm this unmoored gut of mine.*

Mike signaled to Danielle to wait. He glanced at his adversary's table. Sofia Vasquez flashed a pompous victorious grin. "Have a splendid weekend, Counsel," she said.

I haven't fouled out of the game, lady. You've committed a blatant foul...failing to produce that diary before trial...and a diary your sanctimonious client stole. I have a long memory.

Mike nodded, feigning affability. He turned to Sean.

"I hope I'm right about Kelvin," said Sean. "But if I'm not, then as your old professor and sixth man off the bench, maybe we should consider proposing settlement based upon joint legal custody, shared physical custody and a decent percentage of the assets." He raised his eyebrows, but not getting a response, Sean continued. "Have a long talk with Danielle. Let her know that she may well have destroyed any chance to get sole custody."

"No way. I'm not folding. Iron sharpens iron," Mike responded as he gathered his papers. "I'm gonna figure something out, Professor. I'm not gonna let Danielle's outrageous testimony on that stand eclipse the fact that after all is said and done, she's the better parent. There's something complex behind her brazen behavior." Mike shrugged. "And I think you said the same. Trust our instincts. I'm not quitting. I'm not quitting on those kids or this case. Joint custody doesn't feel right…not in this one."

Sean sighed. "Through all the craziness, I admit there's a special charm about her…some depth…and I like the fight in you, Mike. Always did."

"Thanks to my folks, you, and the Corps." Mike managed a smile. He stuffed his papers into his briefcase.

He added: "I'm telling you again, Sean. There's something creepy about Mr. Brooks Webb. He's pompous and a coward. And there's something else. I just can't put my finger on it, but I will. And I know when I get my chance to cross-examine him, we're going to bounce back."

"Well, she may be sex-crazy but at least she told the truth on that stand…my God, went for a triple play!" Sean roared. "What a scenario for a law school exam question!"

"And as I said before, if she's lying about that bed scene and he did find her in the sack in their bedroom, then he's a gutless moron…punches her instead of taking on the stud. Lets the guy stroll out scot-free? No, sir. She may have screwed up big time on that stand today, but I'm not done. That son-of-a-bitch had no business whacking her—no matter how angry he was. And I think you're perfectly right about Kelvin. He's either going to realize he made some bad rulings or he did it intentionally, so if he finds for us, Vasquez will not have a basis for appeal regarding the diary and Danielle's liaisons."

Mike suddenly remembered the tall man and disheveled lady. He was anxious to talk with them—find out, finally, what the hell they were all about and why they were attending the trial. He turned around. His client was waiting for him, but the tall man and lady were gone. He slapped himself on the forehead.

"Where are they?" he asked Danielle.

"Who?"

"You know damned well 'who.' The tall guy and the woman who was with him. I told them I wanted to talk with them."

"I wish you had told me," Danielle said. "They've obviously left. And what do you think's so important about them? I told you about..."

"Nothing, Danielle. At this point in time, there really isn't anything important except your dumbass performance today. 'Triple play.' Very clever. You just might have played your way out of any chance at custody. My office, madam," he ordered, not hiding his fury. "And I hope you have your checkbook with you. The very least I can get out of your nightmare performance is combat pay."

"Yes, sir," she said, offering a salute.

Shaking his head, Mike turned to his colleague. "Sean, I'm goin' back to the office with her. Get her ready for Monday's cross. And try to figure something out. Paint him as a sleaze...going through all her stuff. But I want you to track down that tall guy and the woman. Get Billy Donovan to help if you have to."

"Donovan? The ex-cop? Is he off the sauce?" Sean asked.

"Hope so. Here's his number and his girlfriend's number. He's good. Still plugged in at headquarters. They've gotta have something on those two."

"Never thought it was going to be this much fun when you were yawning in my class back at BC Law, did you?" Sean quipped.

* * *

Mike Lyons and Danielle Webb walked, mostly in silence, to his office. Silence, that is, except for Danielle's repeated apology. She made note of the grim set of Mike's jaw.

When they stepped off the elevator, Danielle said: "I know I owe you, Mike." She pulled her pocket-sized checkbook from her handbag and waved it. "I'm going to use the girls room. I'll be right in."

Mike's secretary greeted him. "Well, how'd it go? Oops, you look like you got the good ole seaweed treatment, or even worse, as though someone plopped a plate of creamed chipped beef in front of you."

"That bad?"

"You look awful. Was it a disaster?" she asked.

"Let me put it this way. Korea was like summer camp compared to this crazy-ass case. You, Miss Jane Donnell, and I are pulling up stakes. We're gonna open that corner variety store way up north in your beloved state of New Hampshire."

"I know the bit well. Each morning we'll take inventory of Royal Crown Cola, read the paper, chew on some Tootsie Rolls, and just sit and laugh."

"Sounds idyllic," Mike said.

"You never told me how Ali and my Phil fit into all this."

"Oh, that's easy. Unlike us, they'll have real jobs. Support us."

Mike then related his client's testimony about the diary. "Slept with a father, son, and then wanted to pull off a triple play by sleeping with the grandfather."

"On the stand? She said that on the stand?" Jane asked.

Mike, aware that his client was walking down the hallway toward the office, nodded and mouthed the words "and it gets worse; said the grandfather wasn't... are you ready for this?... *up* to it. "

Jane held her hand to her mouth, shook her head.

"Hi, Jane," Danielle said.

"Mrs. Webb," Jane responded.

Mike gestured toward his office.

Danielle sat in front of his desk, pulled out her checkbook, pen in hand. "How much?"

"Jane tells me that you're five thousand behind. Let's get caught up, shall we. And I want another five up front."

"Ten grand? Can't we get it from Brooks?"

"You're joking, right? After today's testimony you want me to present a motion asking the court to order that Brooks start paying your fees? I can just hear my plea: 'Your Honor, having admitted to adultery with multiple men, my client and I think it only just and appropriate that her husband now start paying her legal fees.' And with the balance of assets and cash you already have in your own name? No way, Mrs. Danielle Webb, no way. Ten, please."

Danielle smiled, leaned forward, wrote a check with an additional thousand and handed it to Mike. "I guess my trying to turn a triple play was expensive, huh?" she quipped.

"You should've left the triple play to the Red Sox," Mike said. He stepped out of his office to bring the check to Jane.

"Deposit it... now," he whispered.

"Absolutely," Jane said. "God knows we need this. Account's getting very low."

When he returned to his office, Danielle was smoking a Cigarillo, feet propped up on Mike's desk.

"Comfortable?" he asked. "That thing stinks. And I'm concerned that you may be out of your mind."

He noticed that her propped ankles were crossed. He shoved an ashtray toward her, opened one of his windows overlooking Court Street, and then plunked himself onto his desk chair. He leaned back, stretched, and then crouched forward. His client's ankles were no longer crossed. She placed her hands on either side of her pleated skirt...a conspicuous movement upward.

"Oh, my good God. You're enough to make a combat Marine blush. Cigar?!...No underpants?!...O...U...T!"

He stood, head down, pointing to his office door.

"O...U...T...NOW!"

Hot color suffused her cheeks.

"Come on, Mike, you need some levity. Lighten up. Your client made things very tough on you today," Danielle said.

"She sure did," Mike said. "And you know what I think? I think she's got a death wish. And you know what else? I think she...you...are certifiable. You need a shrink, not a lawyer. Lady, I'm in no mood for this craziness."

"You're not quitting on me? I just gave you a check. All paid up plus an additional six...not five like you asked."

"And I should be asking for even more after today's bullshit."

"The tall man and the lady. I think I can tell you some stuff about them," she said.

"I'll bet you can. Like this whole case, there's something awfully weird about them. But not now. I'm spent. Tomorrow, with as much information as you can give me about them...10 a.m. And with your underpants ON. Go, GO!"

He pointed toward the reception area and then closed his office door.

Danielle shrugged her shoulders as she waved at Jane and left the reception area.

Jane gently nudged Mike's door. "Whoa. I heard that. No panties. Mike, she's trouble with a capital T."

"That, my dear friend, is an understatement. You and Ali were so right. I surrender. But right now I've got to crash. I'm wiped out. Sean thinks I should pull my platoon out of the battle, wave the white flag."

Jane commented, "But I know what's inside…you're a Marine."

"I can't just fold. Not when I still believe she's absolutely the better parent."

"It's getting late," said Jane. "I'm going to the bank and deposit her check, and then run a couple of errands. Should be back by six. I'll wake you then."

With that, a totally spent Attorney Lyons closed his office door, kicked off his shoes, tossed his jacket and necktie to the floor, and stretched out on his couch.

* * *

His door opened. It creaked. He thought about the need to ask the maintenance man to oil the hinges. The tall man and unkempt woman stood over the prone Mike Lyons. They were armed. She held a 12-gauge shotgun. He was toting an automatic revolver with a long silencer. They each grinned. The tall man said something barely audible: "You wanted to see us?" The two intruders laughed. Mike became aware that one had several teeth missing; the other with stained and large crooked front teeth. They stared as he tried desperately to get up from the couch. He wrestled with himself but utter panic overcame him. He, Mike Lyons, war hero, was frozen, unable to speak or move. He lay helpless. He smelled the all too familiar odor of oil from the barrel of one of their weapons. Horrified, comprehending what was about to happen, he felt one gun touch his lips and the other flick across the top of his forehead. He saw Ali and his kids. He heard his mother scream. He saw his father flailing as he tried to get up from the railroad tracks, wanting so desperately to help his son. And then the blasts rang out directly at Mike's mouth and head. There were streaks of purple and silver. Then everything went blank.

CHAPTER THIRTY-ONE
DANIELLE

Ali, Hillary, and Michelle gathered in the kitchen to start preparing dinner.

"So, Mom, what're we having tonight?" Hillary asked.

"Lamb chops."

"Lamb chops? Pretty special for a Monday night."

"You're right. But Dad's been grinding away at that awful trial. Thought I'd uplift him a bit with one of his favorites," Ali said.

"You know, Mom, I think I'm going to become a vegetarian," said Hillary.

"Oh?"

"Yeah. I don't feel so great when I think about those lambs and cows getting slaughtered."

"I respect that," said Ali, her tone both challenging and skeptical about whether or not this transformation would actually take place.

"Why not get started tonight by helping to make a salad," Ali said. "And, if you like, you can have just salad with some protein. See how it feels."

"Yup. By the way, Mom, they talked in school today about it being the anniversary of the start of WWII," said Michelle.

"Indeed. I'm happy to hear it was discussed. It's a very important date in our country's history," Ali said. "What was said?"

"Well, Mr. Morehead, in History, said that the Japanese did a sneak attack at some place in Hawaii and sunk our entire Navy fleet and killed a lot of sailors," said Michelle.

"Was that the war Dad was in?" asked Hillary.

"No. Your father was too young at the time. 1941. He was just a little kid. But later, when he was eighteen he fought in the Korean War," said Ali.

"How come he never talks about that, Mom?" Michelle asked.

"It was such a horrible experience that it's too painful for the men and women who participated to really talk about it. Every once in awhile, your dad opens up and tells me bits and pieces."

"I once asked him. He looked sad, turned away from me for a second, and then leaned over and kissed me," said Hillary.

"I'm sure Dad was touched that you asked, but just couldn't bring himself to talk about it. Let's turn on the six o'clock news. I expect there'll be reference to Pearl Harbor. That's the place in Hawaii where the attack took place. It's important. I want the two of you to listen."

Mike Lyons' office was eerily silent. Jane returned after having made the bank deposit just before closing time. She ran some errands and then picked up coffee and a snack for her beleaguered boss, fortify him for his drive home.

The door to Mike's office was closed. Jane knocked.

"Mike?...Mike?"

Silence.

Jane slowly opened the door. Mike Lyons was prone—stomach down on his couch—right arm draped lifelessly over the edge—tips of his still fingers touching the surface of the carpet.

"Mike? You asleep? MIKE?"

Mike pivoted, sat upright.

"Oh, my god. Jane. I just got shot. That tall dude...the strange woman...an unbelievable nightmare. They came right into this office. They were armed. I was frozen...couldn't move. So real. Wow. I really went out. How long was I asleep? Sean call? Billy Donovan call? What time is it?"

"Almost six thirty. Mr. Lawyer, you need to get home. You're drained. Slow down. Let yourself recover. I don't know whether or not they called. I ran some errands and went to the bank, remember? If they did call, you didn't hear…too busy having a nightmare about getting shot. I'll check for messages. And, yes, I made the deposit…into *my* very own account." She grinned. "Phil and I are running off. No more Legal Secretary. No more Star Salesman. He and I are going to my hometown to open that General Store you and I have always dreamed about. But no worries; we'll name it Lyons Den in your honor."

"Don't forget…plenty of Royal Crown and Coke," Mike quipped.

"And Fleer's *Dubble Bubble* gum," she added.

Mike sat on the edge of the couch. He ran his handkerchief across his damp forehead.

"I can't believe it. So damned real. They shot me in the head." He ran a hand through his full head of black hair.

"Just a trial lawyer's nightmare," Jane said. "Now, get out of here."

Mike said: "I'm getting my stuff together. Homework tonight. Get ready for our outrageous client. She's comin' at ten tomorrow. And I'm gonna call Sean. I asked him to see what he could learn about the tall guy and that bedraggled looking woman who keeps showing up in court. I want to compare whatever he learns with whatever Danielle tells me."

"See you tomorrow, boss. And if Danielle Webb is coming in to play baseball, I hope you'll chase her out with a bat. Triple play," she said mockingly. "Sorry, Mike, but she's a wild one."

"Go home," Mike admonished.

And there they were. As Jane opened the main office door, the tall man and disheveled woman, although she looked less unkempt than she had during her court appearances, were standing in the hallway just outside Mike's suite.

"We're looking for Attorney Lyons, ma'am. Is that his office?" the man asked. Jane was immediately aware of his unusual gray eyes.

"I'm Jane, Mr. Lyons' secretary." She surprised herself by not asking that they step in. Instead, she said, "Why don't you wait here for a moment. I think Mr. Lyons may still be on the phone…a personal call. Who shall I say is asking to see him?"

Mike heard Jane and stepped into the reception area. Still hung over from the nightmare in which he was obliterated, he observed with relief that the real-life characters were unarmed and anything but menacing.

"I can't believe this. You're actually here." He shook his head, not unlike his standard poodle when emerging from a seagull-chasing episode off the shores of Nauset Beach. "I've been wanting to talk to you for weeks. Come on in."

He mouthed the words to Jane: "It's okay. You can go. See you tomorrow."

Mike shook hands with each of the two strangers, a welcoming smile on his face. He was enjoying the relief that his having just been murdered was only a dream.

He thought to himself: But was there a message in that nightmare? Is somebody in this case about to be taken down? Am I a real target? Was I a target that morning…the morning of the shooting in front of the courthouse? Or maybe Danielle? These two know something. I can feel it. And her face. I know that face.

"Let's get started with names, shall we?" Mike asked.

"Take a good look, Mr. Lyons," the woman said. "Surely you remember me. You're my hero…the hero of Louisburg Square."

"I knew I knew you. Damn it. I just couldn't place where we'd met. Louisburg Square. Of course. Last spring."

"Those snotty security jerks tried to chase me. Couldn't stand riff-raff in their sacred domain. Might contaminate their turf. And you, sir, came to my rescue. Told those suits where to get off."

"And you told me your name was Proudfoot, or something like that."

The woman, probably in her early fifties, laughed.

"But I let you in on my real name. Hoda. And, by the way, I said *Proudfoto*, not *Proudfoot*. And someday I'll tell you the story of getting the boot from Radcliffe."

"Hoda. Of course. Radcliffe! Now that's a story I need to know."

"Someday. Promise. I'm an outlier…was then…am now. We're here to help. One good turn, as they say," Hoda said.

"I'm happy I was able to be of assistance that day. Tell me, does Hoda have a last name?"

"Some days."

"How about today?"

"John."

"Hoda John. Nice. Real?" Mike asked.

"For real. Ask any narc cop in the city," she responded.

"Narcotics?"

"We'll get to that," she said. "My friend here is Mr. Rockwell Severance. How's that for a handle?"

"Mr. Severance, a pleasure. I've been curious about you for months. Got a lot of questions to ask you. Please." Mike gestured toward his office.

"What is it you'd like to know?" Mr. Severance asked.

Mike launched into a series of questions about Rockwell's presence at the hospital emergency room the day of the courthouse shooting, his familiarity with Mrs. Webb, his appearing later that day outside Mike's office building, and then most every day in the courtroom during the trial.

"Why?" Mike asked. "What's your connection, Rockwell? I assume it's okay if I use your first name?"

"His friends call him 'Rock,'" Hoda said.

"And you, Mr. Lyons, feel free to call me 'Rock,'" he said.

"Thank you, I'm Mike."

"Mike, let me get to the point. Your client, Danielle Webb, has not been forthright with you," said Rockwell.

"Now that's an understatement."

"Sir," Rockwell said, "your client is married to a homosexual drug addict and dealer."

"A drug addict! A dealer! Homosexual? Hold on. This is too much. Let me get my head around this. Where do you come up…"

Hoda interrupted. "Mike, you know that club on Cambridge Street…the one across from MGH…not far from where you park your car everyday? The place they call *The Window*?"

"Sure. That's the place where the windows have been painted for years. A homosexual hangout." Mike paused. "And how, may I ask, do you know where I park my car?"

"And a cave for drug deals…some straights, but mostly gays," Hoda said. "Oh, your car? I've seen you leave it at that gas station a few times."

Rockwell added, "And Mr. Brooks Webb? That deadbeat is a regular at *The Window*."

Mike's head was spinning. Forty-five minutes ago these people killed him. Now they're feeding him some startling information. Was it true?

And if they know where I park my car, what else do they know about me? Do they know where I live…my kids…Ali? This is all over the top.

"I know," Hoda said. "Webb seems like such a square…a straight arrow, so to speak. But the fact is he's up to his eyeballs in cocaine…using and selling…and he has a thing for young guys."

Mike stared.

Hoda continued, "The guy he caught in bed with Danielle?"

The lawyer raised his eyebrows.

"Oh, that was the truth all right," said Hoda. "Danielle's story that Webb came home and whacked her because he had a bad day at work is nonsense. She was lying…she was in the sack, just like the scumbag husband said, but the stud was a plant. The whole thing a setup."

"A plant? Hired by Brooks Webb?"

"Bingo. The stud goes both ways," Hoda said. "Likes women, likes men."

Mike's mouth was wide open.

"Wait a minute, wait a minute. Slow down. You're telling me that Brooks Webb is homosexual, buys, sells and uses drugs, *and* hired someone to have sex with his wife in their condo?"

"That's exactly what we're telling you, Mike," Rockwell said. "He knows Danielle frequents the Ritz Bar, has a martini, maybe picks up a guy. Planted by Webb."

"Danielle was afraid to tell the truth about bedding down with this lad...we know him real well. I'm guessing she thought that'd kill her chances of getting the kids," Hoda said.

Mike raised his eyebrows.

"Hey," Hoda said, "her so-called husband's queer. She's gotta get some lovin' someplace."

Mike nodded as if to say, *I got it. Too scared...too embarrassed to level with me. Thought she could get away with it. Deception rarely works.*

"As we said, the stud Webb hired is our friend...someone he met at *The Window.* He's smart and insisted on gettin' his cash up front. It just so happens that he's very loyal and friendly to us. Told us that Webb had him hang out at the Ritz Bar. Sure enough Danielle walks into the trap. Our friend is there and comes on to her as orchestrated by Mr. Brooks Webb. It was a sting. Makes it look like he's surprised catching his wife screwin' some guy in the marital bedroom. All part of his master plan: file for divorce, paint her as a whore, he gets the kids even though he doesn't give a damn about them...just wants to keep Danielle from having the pleasure of custody and deny her a just piece of the family fortune. He's devious and a cheapskate. He figures the judge will punish her by low-balling any alimony and splitting of the assets," Hoda said.

"The Webb fortune is immense. The Webb ancestors were slave traders," Rockwell said angrily.

"And we mean they are L...O...A...D...E...D," Hoda said.

"But why does she take the plant back to her own place? Why not the Ritz where he came on to her?" Mike asks.

"Got the answer," Rockwell says.

Mike nods.

"'Pretty Boy,' that's the stud's name, was paid extra to persuade Danielle that he wanted to see her place and that it would be a lot more fun than any old hotel room, particularly when her hubby was off to work. Scripted by Webb," said Rockwell.

"He felt it would be a hell of a lot more powerful catching his wife having sex with some pickup in his own home," Hoda added.

"But Danielle? Would she take such a chance? Taking this gigolo to her own place? The kids..."

"She called Webb at his lab under the guise of asking what time she could expect him for dinner. Fell right into his trap. Pretty Boy tells us that Webb said something about being late that night," said Rockwell.

"And Webb had already convinced Danielle to take more time for herself...to try for awhile having the nanny pick up the kids from school instead of her...take them for after school activities...see how it works out," said Hoda.

"And in addition, we think Danielle's so fed up with Brooksie that if she gets caught, so be it. Bring her rotten marriage out in the open and force Webb's hand," Hoda added.

"I knew there was something sleazy about that guy. What a scheme. But why are you two telling me all of this? And how do I know you're not giving me a line, trying to set me up...for what, I'm not sure?" Mike asked.

"Let me spell out another word," said Hoda. "M-O-N-E-Y."

"Uh, now I get it. Shakedown time. And, my good friends, shakedown without a shred of evidence. And you think I'd be desperate enough to blow my ticket to practice..."

"Mr. Lyons...Mike...we're not looking for a dime from you, sir. Brooks Webb is playin' us. We're his source. He keeps cryin' that the family trust money comes into him in dribs and drabs. He runs behind. I'm advancin' him good, clean, top of the line, absolutely pure dust…Why? Because I know all about his family fortune. He owes us some serious greenbacks. I've done more than one favor for this low-life," Rockwell said.

"And Rock likes Danielle, feels bad for her and the kids. That's the real reason he hustled to the MGH on the day of the shooting. Cops told us that's where you were taken," Hoda said.

"And I just didn't know about you, Mr. Lyons…Mike…so I did follow you around some. Got some information from the cops. Needed to see you in action in court. Needed to get a measure of you. Needed to know Hoda and I can trust you," said Rockwell.

Mike nodded. "And Webb…he uses and he sells this coke?"

"Both. Big time," Hoda added. "Uses and sells at *The Window* and to his big shot fancy friends. That little lab of his in Kendall Square, where God only knows what in hell they're supposedly researching…Six users! And he charges five times what he owes us."

"And Danielle, she knows about all of this?" Mike asked.

"Not about the drugs. I can assure you I would know if she knew," said Rockwell. "I never said a word to her. And, Mike, I know she's a bit loosey-goosey, but she's great with those kids. He doesn't give a damn about them," said Rockwell.

"Webb was worried that Danielle might sue him for divorce. So, he decided to set up the sting, make her look like a harlot and get the upper hand in court," said Hoda.

"What a sleaze, but let me get this straight," Mike said. "I'm supposed to put the two of you on the stand, have you testify about this drug connection, which Webb will no doubt patently deny. And I know zero about your respective records regarding drugs or God knows what else. You could get hammered on cross. And wind up with the judge feeling he's got to blow the whistle to the DA, put the two of you in the proverbial slammer."

"Rock, show Mike my work," Hoda said, flashing a self-satisfied smile.

Rockwell Severance opened a clasped envelope and laid out several eight by ten black and white photos on top of Mike's desk.

Mike cupped his hand over his mouth. He was stunned. He pointed to one of the photos.

"That's you?" Mike asked Rockwell.

"Yup. That's me at *The Window* sitting in the booth, the one whose face is blurred. Look, two different dates with Webb. See this one? That's me handing him a baggie. The white powdery stuff? It ain't soap powder. And here, look at this. That's his hand under the table pushing a roll of 'mister green' into my hand. Two grand short that time. Son-of-a-bitch. But we got him cold."

"And take a gander at these amazin' shots," said Hoda. "That's 'Pretty Boy,' the stud Webb hired to pick up Danielle at the Ritz. And here's her hubby Webb holding hands with 'Pretty Boy.' Look at the expression on Webb's face...he's droolin'," said Hoda.

"Recognize the guy leaning over and snorting in that far booth?" asked Hoda, holding up another photo.

"That's him...no mistaking it...Mr. Brooks Webb," said Mike. "Oh, my good god. What a goddamned fool...right out in the open. This is dynamite. But who? Who took these? I'll need to put him on the stand."

"You're lookin' at her," said Hoda. "I got this wonderful Pentax. Drape it around my neck under my jacket, and secretly shoot away. Stay real unobtrusive like. Got some pretty nasty stuff from that place. These losers think it's a no-tell zone. That's why the narcs love me. Remember my last name? *Proudfoto?* Get it now?" she said.

The trial lawyer shook his head. *And I thought I had seen and heard it all.*

"Once it was clear that Webb didn't have the proper respect for us...stalling, haggling, trying to wear us down and then make a deal for less, Hoda and me…we're trusted partners…we decided it was time to nail him. Webb used me for all kinds of stuff. Said I was a friend. But when it came to paying? Talk about respect? Zero respect. Always dragging his heels when it comes to his wallet. Insulted us. Enough. And Hoda just loved your Superman act in Louisburg Square last spring. Every good turn,…" said Rockwell.

"And Mike, take a gander at this one. That's Webb's hand on 'Pretty Boy's' rear-end."

"And what's that in, as you say, 'Pretty Boy's' hand that he's opened up obviously for your camera? Bag of coke?" Mike asked.

"Absolutely," said Hoda.

"Okay. You got me. What's the deal?"

"Simple. Once you do your lawyering stuff and get these photos before Brooks Webb and his lawyer, they'll wave the white flag. Danielle gets the kids and she gets her just share of the trust."

"It's not a crime to be a homosexual. But the liar kept it from Danielle. Married her. And then humiliates her, making her think the lack of sex is her fault…that something's wrong with her. But the cocaine? Hanging out in that sordid place? Dynamite," said Mike.

"He's a dishonorable and destructive man," said Rockwell.

"And now what?" Mike asked. "You shake *her* down for the dollars Webb owes you?"

"Never," said Rockwell. "We would never do any such thing. We'll collect fair and square from Webb. He'll be so scared that we'll come up with tons more photos that he'll fork over fast. All we want is what he owes us. Nothing more."

"And if he does try to find a new source, trust us, we'll get the word out. The price for Mr. Brooks Webb to score snow would skyrocket. And besides, he wants to keep that rich ass of his out of prison," Rockwell added.

"And one day his kids are going to grow up and he'd never risk their learning about this and seeing the pictures. Tell me, does Webb know anything about these photos?" Mike asked.

"Not a clue," said Rock. "He goes into that place and gets high just whiffing the atmosphere. Hoda's a master photographer. Flips open her jacket, shoots away, closes the jacket. Music blasting, drugs, booze, smokin', sex goin' on full blast. No one knows a damn thing except the two of us, our detectives and Bruce...Pretty Boy. We thought about going directly to Webb...shake him down, face-to-face. And it might work, but we ain't gonna risk his tryin' to yell 'extortion.' And we like Danielle. Oh, she can be...wild, playful. No drugs for this lady. She's a good person," said Rockwell.

"Did you say 'detectives'?"

"We're informers, Mike. Plain and simple," said Rock.

Hoda nodded. "You had no idea you came to the rescue of a favorite of the Boston PD!"

"Mike," she continued, "let Danielle, via you, have the pleasure of sweet revenge. He was never straight with her...pun intended. Never let on that he was queer until long after they were married. Thinks he can get away with anything because he was born into a fortune. She hasn't a clue that he's a user and a dealer. And for us? We'll have the pleasure of collecting every dime he owes us."

"Either one of you want a drink? I've gotta give this some thought," said Mike. He removed a bottle of Scotch from his credenza. The three of them leaned back, listened to Mike sigh, and then each enjoyed a shot glass full of Scotch.

Mike said, "You realize, of course, that if this stuff goes before Judge Henry, he may feel obliged to refer purported crimes to the DA. Webb goes off to jail and your source for payout is gone. Why wouldn't you then turn to Danielle for the drug money that Webb owes?"

"We gave you our word. And, besides, Mr. Scumbag has the means to hire all kinds of legal eagles. Lots will go down before he does time. En route, he's going to want us out of the picture. Once he sees those photos, he won't be able to pay fast enough," said Rockwell.

"I've got two calls to make," said Mike.

Hoda and Rockwell started to get up.

"No, stay. It's okay." Mike observed that neither one reached to retrieve the photos. *Maybe I can trust them. I like them. I can vet them with the guys at Narcotics.*

"Hi Ali. How are you?"

"Fine, Mike. When you expect to leave?"

"That's why I'm calling. I'm running late. Weird day in court. Got slammed. But now something wild is percolating. What? No, no…wild as in good. Might not get home until nine. I'll explain later. You and the kids get started without me. Next life I'm gonna be a shoe salesman."

Mike then called Sean and gave him a nutshell version of what had just unfolded.

"I told you, Sean. I knew there was something creepy about Brooks Webb. And I don't give a rap about his being a homosexual other than deceiving Danielle. It's the drugs. A real low life. And with all that money."

"Are these two characters still with you?" Sean asked.

"Yup. Sitting right here. But it's okay. We've formed a mutual trust society," Mike said.

"It doesn't sound as though we can use them as witnesses. They'd both wind up in jail. Drugs, possible extortion…for beginners," Sean said.

"Absolutely. No way I'd put them on the stand in any courtroom and run that risk. Here's what I have in mind. First, I'll explain all of this to Danielle. Then try to arrange a session with Vasquez and Webb. If she ducks my call, then when we get to court on Wednesday, I'll open up…in open session…tell His

Honor that something urgent has come up…that a meeting with the enemy camp could result in a quick resolution of the entire matter."

"Excellent. Kelvin will give us all the time we need, which shouldn't be more than ten minutes once Sofia and her client take a look at what you've described. The judge would love to see this thing get settled," Sean said.

"Can you imagine the look on their smug faces when I drop the photos…one by one…on Vasquez's lap," said Mike.

"The lady…Hoda? You say she's the one who took the photos? Bring her to the conference with you. I want shots of Vasquez's and Webb's mugs when they take a peak," said Sean facetiously.

"I'd so love to do that, Sean. Once they see these photos, they'll have heart attacks," said Mike. "And then I'll simply drop our written settlement proposal right on top. Need you to burn the midnight oil, Professor. Full custody to Danielle. Review all the numbers and come up with a sixty-five to thirty-five asset split plus alimony plus major league child support. And don't forget the education trusts, including grad school," said Mike.

"Feels like we're going into full courtroom press, Mikey."

"Professor, let's face it, we're always in full…as you would say…courtroom press. I appreciate your tackling the Agreement."

"I'm already making the Maxwell House. No worries, former student. I'll have the Agreement on Jane's desk by nine. Wow! This is one hell of a turn of events."

"Sean, once they see these photos, this will become a slam dunk. Oh, before I forget, did you get hold of Billy Donovan?"

"He's at his girlfriend's. Sober. Seemed to know exactly who I was talking about when I described the tall guy and the lady. Said they are good people. Furnished the cops with a lot of good leads. Savvy about the drug underworld. He knows where they hang out. But you don't need him since we now know who these two godsends are plus the trove of photos," said Sean.

"I do need him. Hear me. I'm gonna have Rockwell and Hoda arrange to set up a sting…get Webb to *The Window*…the club on Cambridge Street. Billy, having worked in Narcotics, knows it well. Hold on a sec, Sean."

"Webb is going to meet me at eight tonight," said Rockwell.

"Great. Could you hear that, Sean? Rockwell and Hoda are way ahead of me," said Mike. "I'll ask Billy to go there, observe, take some photos…cocaine to Webb, cash to Rock or a stand-in." Mike looked up at Rock, who gestured that it was just fine if he was the one to be photographed making the deal. Mike furrowed his forehead.

"You're a genius strategist, Michael Lyons, and not a bad trial lawyer. Vasquez and her client wouldn't dare muck around with our proposal. It'd be suicide. But great that we'll have Donovan and new photos as a backup."

"Exactamente, Professor. We're going to hit them with a barrage of long-range jump shots. Just in case they're arrogant and dumb enough to blow off a reasonable settlement and we go back to trial, Billy will be our point guard. He can testify with all his surveillance expertise as an ex-cop…and an ex-Narc squad guy, to boot…as to what he saw and can ID the photos he takes. Keep my sources far from the courtroom. I don't think we'll ever have to get that far, but, as you always lectured, you can't be prepared enough in this trial business. Sean, can you believe this?"

"Poetic justice, Mike. And I'll bet Danielle will keep that fabulous nanny on her payroll. Danielle's not been totally straight with us, but now I can understand why. And I have a feeling she's probably pretty forthright with her kids. Open and honest with them. Wow. This baby's one for the books," said Sean.

"Talk to you later," said Mike.

"Hoda, Rockwell. I need to *buy* these photos from you," said Mike.

"No way," said Rockwell. "Hoda and me…we trust you."

"And I've got the negatives," Hoda added.

"Thanks. I appreciate your trust. But that's not the point. I want to keep this ethical, totally above board. If it should become necessary, I want to be able to represent that I purchased them for a fair and reasonable price."

After Mike gave Hoda a check, the three of them walked to the elevators.

"You look worried," Hoda observed. "About us, I'll bet. You're that kind of man. Don't fret. As we told you, we're informers. Billy Donovan and the entire Narc crew hold an umbrella for us. We've given them some great information these past years. We're safe, Mike. When it's time for us to check out of Boston town, we'll know and we'll be outta here," Hoda said. She then leaned forward, stretched up, and kissed his cheek. "My Louisburg Square hero."

* * *

7:50 p.m. A retired Boston police officer stood across the street from *The Window,* near Fruit Street, gateway to the Massachusetts General Hospital. Billy Donovan loved being back in the saddle. *Feel like Shane,* he thought to himself. *Haven't been in action and certainly not at The Window for what...three years now? Nabbed some serious dealers here.*

Hoda stood just ten feet away to the right of Billy.

"There he is...that's him," she pointed to her right as Webb approached, about three hundred feet from the entrance to *The Window.*

* * *

Mr. Brooks Webb paused outside the entry, glanced around, as he always did...a useless gesture because he was desperate...an insatiable need to step into his world of depravity. He was oblivious to being photographed, with more to come once he was inside.

Brooks Webb entered. His gut begged for the thrill of using, buying, selling. And he craved sex. Moments later Billy Donovan and Hoda made their unobtrusive entrance. Billy, disguised with a fake mustache, positioned himself at the end of the bar. Neil Young, The Carpenters, The Stones, David Bowie blasted away. Patrons were deep into dance, sex, and the drug scene. Webb spotted Rocky at a booth, as promised. The setup was on. Donovan inconspicuously clicked away as he observed Brooks Webb pass some cash to Rocky in exchange for two ski bags of cocaine. He snapped photos of Webb selling to a patron and then leaning over a table and snorting. To finish things off, the ex-police officer snapped Pretty Boy and a sky-high Brooks Webb participating in sexual contact.

Gathering evidence can be a sordid business. But it often tells reams about a principal's character. And this may lead to justice and make the difference in people's lives. In this case, the lives of children.

CHAPTER THIRTY-TWO
KATHERINE

The Archbishop's residence and chancery in Brighton, just over the Newton line and modeled after an Italian palazzo, was opulent and inconsistent with the Archbishop's stated mission to serve the poor and needy.

The lawyers agreed that John and his client would go ahead and meet with the Archbishop at noon while Mike, Sean and Katherine would arrive at one.

As Attorney Colello and Father Riley entered the Archbishop's office it was readily apparent that His Excellency was distressed. And he had not yet heard the actual tape. He had been told about its content during the phone call that Attorney Colello made from the courthouse. The Archbishop gestured to John to take a seat.

Without even a glance at him, the Archbishop directed that Father Riley leave his office and wait in the lobby.

"John, I can't tell you how betrayed I feel. Not by you, my good friend, but by our incorrigible priest and this unexpected turn of events. May shame be with him for the rest of his days for his wretched behavior and having lied to us about this most significant piece of evidence."

"I share your shock and disappointment, Your Excellency."

The Archbishop leaned into his intercom. "Father de Blasio, would you please bring in the cassette player."

"Father de Blasio, I'm fully aware of the friendship between you and Father Riley. But nevertheless I need you to hear this. I'll require your counsel regarding this sordid turn of events."

The three sat in silence listening to the complete recording. When it finished the Archbishop stood and walked to one of his windows. Viewing the landscape of the multi-acre campus was always a sense of solace to him.

Angry with his friend and dismayed at the turn of events, Father de Blasio exchanged knowing looks with John Colello.

The Archbishop turned to the archdiocese's attorney of many years. "How much?"

"Two hundred thousand dollars, Your Excellency."

The Archbishop sighed and raised his arms in a gesture of surrender. He turned to Father de Blasio. "I know how unfair I am, Anthony…asking that you participate. But I value your wisdom and I'm going to need your help in dealing with Father Riley. It's a great deal of money. Any doubt in your mind?"

"None, Your Excellency. As you say, it's a great deal of money. But if John feels that's what it takes…well, we have no choice. We've got to rid ourselves of this case. And then we must deal with disposition of Father Riley."

"Indeed."

"Any thoughts you care to offer, John?"

"I feel terrible about all of this. My lawyering…"

"Stop, John. You're an outstanding lawyer and have always represented the church in an excellent and honorable manner. Do not blame yourself for Father Riley's unspeakable sins of betrayal and deception."

"My best advice is that we pay what Attorney Lyons assures me is their low take," said John.

The Archbishop placed a hand over his mouth, thought for a moment, then gestured toward Attorney Colello. "It's an incredible amount of money, John. But we have no choice. I can appreciate that we are without leverage at this point. However, I would like to impose some conditions."

"Your Excellency?"

* * *

Katherine, Sean, and Mike got out of their taxi about a mile from their destination. They had time to enjoy the benefits of a walk and fresh air.

"You know, Mike and Sean, as daunting and uncomfortable as it was knowing that you-know-who was staring me down, I did experience some relief while testifying. I felt that the jury was attentive and sensitive to my story."

"You were a very impressive witness, Katherine," said Sean.

"No doubt about that," Mike added.

"But I'm thrilled that there is now the real possibility that this will get settled. The shame and embarrassment of it all is far greater than anything else. If the Archbishop and Mr. Colello agree to our settlement figure, will it get into the press? Does the public have to know about it? And the tape…is that also available to the press? I couldn't bear this all being out there. The coverage to date has already been upsetting enough."

"Katherine, Sean and I appreciate your relief. I have no doubt that they will agree to pay the amount we have demanded and I also have no doubt that they will want this kept from the press and public even more than the three of us do," Mike said.

"Having said that, I need you to know I rarely, if ever, agree to a confidentiality requirement in a settlement, which is the mechanism used to keep things private," Mike said.

"And why is that?"

"A fundamental belief in the need for absolute transparency throughout our judicial system," Mike responded.

"To elaborate a bit, Katherine," Sean started, "secrecy within the justice system is antithetical to our democracy. Trials, hearings of any kind, excepting with respect to juveniles, must be open to the public as well as all case-related documents filed in court."

"Transparency eliminates chicanery that might occur when justice is not open to the public. And," Mike continued, "many of us believe that publicizing settlements and jury trial verdicts may act as a deterrent in certain kinds of cases, such as yours."

"Ah," said Katherine, "send a message to other priests."

"Precisely," Mike said.

"But haven't we already sent enough of a message with our day-plus on trial? I'm sickened at the thought of any of this having further attention. I respect your reasoning, but I think I'm best served if this is all kept as private as possible," Katherine said.

"We get that, Katherine. We're prepared to make an exception if that's your wish. And I fully expect that the Church will request confidentiality," Sean said. "They've already been burned enough by the newspaper stories."

"Will my tape be returned?"

"Absolutely," said Sean. "Today."

"I'm going to destroy that thing," Katherine said, tears obvious. "I want it out of my life forever."

The lawyers nodded and as they approached the gated entrance to the estate in which the archdiocese offices were located, they stopped. "Over there," Mike said, looking at Katherine and pointing across the street. "BC Law. That's where I first came upon Sean. Best damned professor on that faculty."

"Quite true," Sean said while smiling.

* * *

The Archbishop stood, sweeping his robes behind him and fixating on Attorney John Colello.

"I think I know what you're thinking about, Your Excellency. Confidentiality."

"Precisely, John. Any possibility that they might agree?"

"For the most part, many of the better lawyers are averse to including confidentiality in a settlement agreement. Others are looking for bragging rights...publicity. Mike and Sean do not fall in the latter category. They're principled about not agreeing to confidentiality. I've discussed this issue with Mike in past cases. We did have a matter where he agreed to keep the amount paid confidential, but to make the case details available to the public. Ms. Hennessey is a private woman. Despite having already testified in open court, I rather suspect that she has loathed the publicity to date and would wish to keep any terms of the settlement out of the press. I'll bring this up with Lyons."

The Archbishop nodded.

"And the tape, John. Must we return it or may we destroy it?"

"Definitely cannot destroy it. This copy belongs to them. But we'll get the original from Father Riley and do away with that. I'll discuss disposition of their copy with Mike."

* * *

The three lawyers sat in a conference room, and engaged in limited small talk. Mike morphed into the business at hand.

"Well, John, I assume His Excellency has listened to the tape?"

"He certainly has," John responded, clasping his hands as though in prayer.

"I can only begin to imagine his reaction."

"As you might expect, Mike. In a word, horrified."

Mike sat silently, sending a message with his inquiring facial expression.

"His Excellency certainly wants this mess to go away, Mike. But two hundred thousand dollars? He feels that's a bit rich. After all, with inflation and other factors, that amount now, in 1972, is likely to grow well in excess of a million dollars. And keep in mind, he's being generous not instructing me to invoke the statutory limit. But I think he'll be willing to go slightly north of one-fifty." Despite authorization to pay the two hundred thousand, the negotiator in John Colello dictated that he make one last effort to test the waters and see if Mike and his client would entertain something less than their alleged bottom line.

Even the very best can't resist a last ditch effort, Mike quipped to himself. An equally adept negotiator, he knew precisely what his adversary was attempting to do. Mike rose from his chair and extended his hand. "Well, John, I guess we go back to court tomorrow. Perhaps we should call Judge Giordano and let…"

"Hold on, Mike," Colello said while raising his arms.

"John, I'm not about to bid against myself. You asked before meeting with your client what it would take to make the case go away. I conferred with Sean and Katherine. I gave you THE number, making it clear that it was our absolute bottom line…that it was not open for discussion. Is that not accurate? Is that not what I said? No dancing, John, this is too tender a matter for that."

"It'll be a tough pill for His Excellency to swallow. If we pay two hundred thousand…"

"Not *if,* John. The Archbishop either agrees to that amount or we're walking."

"Let me step out for a few moments."

"Of course," Mike said. "Take all the time you need."

After his adversary left the room, Mike thought, *Can't blame him for a last minute try. He's already got authority to pay the full amount. And I think he knows that I know it. All part of the world of negotiating. Probably going to the men's room.*

Colello returned. "Mike, we'll pay the two hundred."

The two men shook hands.

"I know that generally you have no use for confidentiality requirements. But this is certainly an unusual matter…one that I think cries out for privacy on behalf of both sides," Colello said.

"Let me guess. You're looking for confidentiality regarding all terms including the amount, and including a request to the Court to seal the filed Agreement. Anything else?" Mike asked.

"The tape," John said.

Mike was not the least bit surprised. Infused with levity, he leaned toward his adversary. "We've already made a deal with *The Globe* and if I'm not mistaken Sean has an arrangement with some well known paper in New York."

"Just got off the phone with them not an hour ago," quipped Sean.

"You realize if you clowns joked around like this with the Archbishop he'd have a heart attack. He's a serious man," said John.

Such jocularity during settlement discussions was not uncommon amongst litigators. "Humor relaxes the soul," Mike said. "This case is most unusual. Confidentiality is appropriate. We agree."

"So," Sean started, "what does His Excellency have in mind about the love tape?"

"That the Agreement include a provision whereby the original and all copies be surrendered to the archdiocese, whereupon they will be destroyed by the archdiocese."

"Forget it, John. No way," said Mike. "No requirement that she surrender her copy to anybody…certainly not the archdiocese."

"Well, how about an alternative? A provision whereby Katherine must destroy her copy within seven days of execution of the Agreement. Why would that be unreasonable?"

"The answer, John, is another emphatic no. I would not permit anybody to impose such a dictate upon Katherine. She's told us that she intends to destroy it. But that has to be done on her own terms, when she sees fit. I believe Katherine will do whatever is necessary to rid herself of any reminder of this destructive chapter in her life. This must be her own decision; not one imposed upon her."

Attorney Colello sighed and nodded in capitulation.

"Just as I have every reason to believe the archdiocese will destroy Riley's original," Mike added.

John Colello said. "I hear you. His Excellency will have to understand. I'll pass on your belief that Ms. Hennessey will destroy her copy, but when and as she sees fit. I was totally wrong about your client, Mike. She hardly fantasized about anything other than her belief that my client truly loved her. Obviously, the tape recording was not a figment of her imagination. And I think that fact together with the powerful forces of shame and embarrassment will result, as you say, in her destroying the tape in her own good time."

"And we'll want verification that the original has been disposed of," Mike said.

"Mutual verification," said Colello.

"Agreed. When Katherine has destroyed it, I'll let you know. Let's inform our clients that we have agreed upon a settlement."

On his way toward the room where Katherine was waiting, Mike turned toward John Colello. "Oh, I almost forgot. Most important. An apology from Riley...today...now...in that room," Mike said, pointing toward the Archbishop's office.

"Agreed," said Attorney Colello.

The lawyers and clients gathered in the Archbishop's office. After an exchange of pleasantries and affirmation of the settlement, Father Riley remained stoic as he uttered the words, "I apologize." He did not look at Katherine.

When everybody stepped outside, Mike was aware of Father Riley lagging behind, gazing upward with intense passivity. No effort to make contact with Katherine. *Son-of-a-bitch. Haughty to the end.* As they were about to go their separate ways, John Colello extended an arm, gesturing that he and Mike step aside.

"Great work, Mike. And my apologies for Riley's...what shall I say...lack of anything resembling remorse. And I again apologize to you for my arrogant and failed strategy...not taking your calls and avoiding you in the courthouse. Sophomore shit. And it backfired...big time."

Mike nodded. "Yes. Riley's a you-know-what. I hope His Excellency defrocks the bastard. But your apology accepted. Dinner? Next week at Locke-Ober? You, Sean, and me?"

Colello replied, "Winners pay. Wednesday at 7:30?"

"See you then."

CHAPTER THIRTY-THREE
DANIELLE

Danielle Webb bounded into Mike's reception area carrying a peace offering.

"Morning, Jane," she said loudly enough for Mike to hear from his office.

"Good morning, Mrs. Webb."

"Hope your boss man is in a good mood today. Look, coffee and his favorite coffee rolls…sooo f…r…e…s…h."

"Aren't we the clever one," said Mike, emerging from behind his desk. "Your offering, while an obvious ploy, hits a weak spot."

"And look, Counselor, slacks!" Danielle brushed her hands along the sides of her charcoal gray pants.

"And blouse. Buttoned to the top. I'm all business today."

Jane turned toward her typewriter, concentrating on absolutely nothing but her desire not to be an eyewitness to the client's flirting.

Mike shook his head as he plucked a container of coffee and bun from the cardboard tray.

"I know," said Danielle, her face etched with shame. "I'm absolutely insane. But trust me, if you had been married to Brooks Webb for twelve years you, too, would be certifiable."

"Well, step into my office before Jane and I make a call to have you shipped off to McLean Hospital…where the very best of shrinks in the entire USA practice," said Mike. "And even they would have a challenge on their hands."

"Mike, a zillion apologies for my being such a smartass yesterday, both on the stand and later in your office. I'm a bit wacky, I know that, but please understand, I adore my kids. I'm a damned good mom despite my off the chart antics. I was up all night thinking about what a jerk I've been. Something happened when I took the stand and looked at the know-it-all expressions on their faces," she said.

"And how about when you decided to flash...right here in my office? Something, as you say, *happened?"*

"Thanks to your good judgment, nothing happened. You're a together man...a loyal husband," she said.

"Well, Mrs. Danielle Webb..."

"Ugh. I can't stand that 'Mrs.' title. I'll behave. Just tell me what to do and I'll do it," she said.

"There has been an amazing twist in your case," Mike said. "Sit."

Carefully and methodically, Mike related all that Hoda and Rockwell had revealed.

Danielle sat frozen. "Oh...my...God."

Nodding his head, Mike added: "I have zero quarrel with Brooks being homosexual. But loathe his deception about it and lowlife drug capers. And you? Why didn't you tell me about him being queer? That could have been used to mitigate your diary and your...to use your own description...wacky testimony."

Sean stood at the entry to Mike's office. "Okay for me to come in?" he asked, waving documents he had prepared through the night.

"Sean, good morning. Yes, by all means come in."

Danielle turned and extended a hand to Sean, adding a subtle squeeze. The pleasure of being touched by her did not escape Sean.

"Always so comforting to see you, Sean," she said.

Waving a large clasped envelope, Mike said, "As I was saying, fortunately Hoda and Rockwell came forward with a treasure trove of information and hard evidence." He spread the photos on top of his desk.

Danielle's mouth dropped open, her face flushed. She stood and peered down at the pictures, staring, shaking her head.

"I can't…you will pardon me…fucking believe what I'm looking at…what you just told me. Drugs? Cocaine? Set me up with that stud? Sean and Mike, I'm ashamed I lied…that I deceived you with my bogus story about his hitting me because of a work problem. I was afraid you wouldn't take my case if I told you the truth. And I actually thought I could get away with it. My word over his. The more time that went on, the more ashamed I was to come out with the truth."

"Why am I not surprised?" said Mike. "You're impossible. You know that, don't you?"

She leaned back, turned her head toward the ceiling, and then tears began to flow.

Mike stepped out and removed a box of Kleenex from Jane's desk. Before Danielle arrived he had shared all the details and photos with Jane.

"A little drama?" Jane whispered.

"I think this may be for real."

"For such a smart lawyer, some of the time you're so gullible."

"For such a not so smart paralegal or legal assistant…or whatever it is I'm supposed to call you…you are one tough Granite Stater," said Mike. "Wow, Jane. What an unbelievable reversal in this goddamned case. I kept saying it, didn't I? That there was something way off kilter about that holier than thou Brooks Webb."

He returned to his office. Danielle, while brushing the back of her hand across her cheek, pored over the photographs.

"Danielle, we've got him. You're…"

"Mike," she interrupted, "you can't use this stuff. Not what they told you and not these photographs."

"Are you nuts? You are nuts. You can't let him have custody. This man is a drug addict and a dealer, for God's sake. He's a danger to your children. Now hear me out," Mike said.

Danielle shook her head, stretched her arms and held her palms toward Mike fending him off.

"It took awhile, but I learned after the kids were born that Brooks is homosexual. For a long time I thought it was me. I couldn't figure out what I was doing wrong…why I couldn't turn him on. Sex came to a halt. And it was never any good to begin with. He always blamed me. Finally, I began to suspect…I had a hunch. I confronted him. At first he denied he was gay, but after awhile, during one of his rare moments of honesty, he told me. He begged me not to leave him and not to say anything to his family, to anyone. He was too embarrassed and afraid of his family."

Sean said, "It must have been quite a blow. But why on earth didn't you let us know? And that's why you had a need to…" Sean stopped himself.

"It's okay, Sean. You can say it. A need to run around, sleep with other men. Dumb, maybe. But I needed to prove to myself that I'm a woman."

Mike sighed and walked to the other side of his office.

"That explains so much. It would have given me something to mitigate your dalliances," Mike said.

"Now you know why I got so crazy and started screwing around. He made me feel like a failure."

Turning toward Sean, she said: "I was starved after being made to feel so inadequate. I was furious. When he finally let down his guard and told me the truth, I threw him out of the bedroom."

"Danielle, please, we're almost at the finish line. Be up front and honest with us. Trust us. What about the drugs?" Mike asked.

"You could knock me over. I swear, guys, not a clue. Oh sometimes he would act strange but I thought it was all about his being homosexual." She raised her right hand. "On the souls of my mom and dad, I never knew about the drugs until this moment. It explains the many times he suddenly left the apartment in the middle of an evening…during Thanksgiving, for God's sake. He must have run over to that creepy *Window* to score some stupid dope. How could I have been so blind?"

Sean sighed. "I can't imagine what this revelation must be like for you. And how awful that he didn't come clean and let you know before any marriage that he's homosexual. Shameful and deceitful."

"I felt so much like a failure. Sexually incompetent. And now this...cocaine...using...selling...hanging out at *The Window* all the goddamned time."

Mike, rattling one of the photos, stood and faced Danielle. "This man is toxic. He's a danger to your children. Not because he's gay. But because he's a goddamned druggie. You would harm your children by prohibiting us from using this critical and damning evidence. It's more than a game-changer. It's the unvarnished truth about Brooks Webb. It goes to the heart of this case: the best interest of your kids."

"I hear you," Danielle said.

"I hope so. And you? Are you being straight with us about the drugs?" Mike asked.

"Drugs? Me? Absolutely not. Booze? Too much at times. Experiment with pot years ago? Absolutely. And that was eons ago...when I was barely sixteen."

Mike looked at his client skeptically.

"I swear on the lives of my children," she insisted, raising her right hand.

Sean leaned forward looking into Danielle's eyes. "I believe you."

"No more surprises, Danielle. The diary and your bullshit story about the black eye are enough," said Mike.

"I'm sick about this drug thing. I don't want him near the kids. But I don't want them to learn about their father being queer until they're older, until he's ready to tell them himself. I'm so afraid that it would leak; might hit that rag, the *Boston Record American*, or some teacher or kid might say something. And if the family were to learn that their Brooks is a fag and using their trust money for drugs? They'll shut off the faucet faster than..."

"But just bear in mind that in the event the trustees learn about Brooks and his drug life, they have the power to eliminate him as a beneficiary but under the terms of the trust as amended after you were married, they have the obligation to continue to provide for you and the children," Mike said.

"And that would be in accordance with the terms of the Settlement Agreement which will become a Court Order," Sean added. "So, financially, you and the children will be more than secure."

"We can use this information, Danielle, without exploiting it in open court," Mike advised. "They'll fold and settle quickly when they see these photos. We'll ask the judge for an order to seal the settlement papers. That way the Agreement will be kept confidential, not available to any reporters, not available to anyone except you and your soon to be ex-husband. In personal matters like this, with children's emotional lives at stake, I urge confidentiality. I'm certain the judge will go along with both sides' plea that the papers in the case be sealed for the protection of the children. You'll have sole custody. His visitation with the kids will be supervised by a court-appointed guardian ad litem. No overnighters."

Danielle Webb stood, walked over to the windows overlooking the traffic below, her back to the lawyers. "How did the Celtics do against the Bulls the other night?" she asked.

Sean swallowed hard at the mention of the Celtics.

"Celtics?" Mike frowned. "They won...by two. They're still on the road. Up in Buffalo tonight. The Braves shouldn't be a problem. Didn't know you were a fan." Mike understood his client's need to divert. The news about her husband was a lot to take in. He was also aware of Sean's reaction.

She turned around. "Amazing the prick didn't take a picture of me in that bed with…what did Hoda and Rockwell call him? 'Pretty Boy?'"

"Yup."

There was a long silence. Mike stood, staring at his client, his expression stoic. Finally, she sighed and looked at Sean, who nodded reassuringly.

"Okay," she said.

"Smart decision." Mike extended a hand and touched his client's shoulder. It was instinctual, a gesture of encouragement and support. Nothing more. She knew.

"I'm so relieved, Mike. To know that this will finally be over…that I'll have the kids…that this will all be kept from the public…the drug thing, his homosexuality, the money. And you're right. When Brooks hears what we know and sees the photos, he'll fold in a second."

"Yup. They'll cave in to the hard reality of our discovery, thanks to Hoda and Rockwell," Mike added.

* * *

"ALL RISE." The lawyers, witnesses, and spectators stood as the Honorable Kelvin Henry entered the courtroom and gestured everyone to sit.

"Your Honor, may counsel approach?" Mike requested.

Judge Henry beckoned them forward. Mike noted the imperious look on Sofia Vasquez's face. *I can't wait,* he thought.

"Your Honor, I think…in fact, I'm sure…that we have come up with a way to resolve this case. I suggest a conference with all counsel and clients…"

Sofia Vasquez interrupted: "Your Honor, if I may… this would be no more than a stall tactic. As I've said before…"

Pious and condescending. You're in for a big shock, Attorney Vasquez, Mike said to himself.

"Attorney Vasquez, I cannot think of one reason that Attorney Lyons would be seeking to, as you put it, stall. What

harm is there to sit down and see if you can't come to terms?
Frankly, I don't see any harm. Attorney Lyons, are you requesting
my presence?"

"I don't think that will be necessary, Your Honor. And I
think we'll all know within no more than twenty minutes whether
or not this case can be quickly settled. My colleague, Professor
Murray, and I have prepared a Separation Agreement with
exceptionally reasonable terms," Mike said while handing a copy
of the multi-page document to his adversary.

Sofia Vasquez took the papers, a look of triumph on her face.
They've decided to capitulate. The diary did them in.

Judge Henry and Mike pretended to ignore Brooks Webb's
utterance directed toward Danielle: "No deal, no way."

"Sounds encouraging. Report back in an hour," said the
judge. "Let me know how you're doing. And Attorney Vasquez, I
suggest you listen to whatever it is that Lyons has in mind. Your
respective clients *and the children* may be well served to get this
matter settled."

"Of course we'll listen, Your Honor," Attorney Vasquez
said, her facial expression one of bored insolence.

And listen she did…as did her associate…and her client. And
look they did as Mike slowly dealt his winning hand, one photo
after another.

"Irrefutable evidence…wouldn't you say?" Mike said.

Absorbing the expressions on the faces of Brooks Webb and
Sofia Vasquez, Mike thought: *this is what it must feel like when
you win the lottery.*

The smug looks evaporated. Brooks Webb was soaking wet,
his mouth open in shame. Sofia Vasquez was grim. She swallowed
hard, unsuccessfully tried clearing her throat and could barely be
heard as she asked to have a few moments with her client.

"By all means," said Mike. "And while you're talking I
suggest you take a hard look at this settlement proposal. Under the

circumstances you'll be surprised at just how generous Mrs. Webb is being."

* * *

They returned. Attorney Vasquez avoided Mike's smiling eyes. Trying to mask her shock and sudden defeat, she managed just three words: "My client accepts."

Mike thought, *I'm surprised she didn't ask that we remove reference to addiction and requirement for rehabilitation. But, then again, she knows what our response would be and she has zero leverage.*

Danielle did not smile. She glared at her husband. "This Agreement calls for you to start immediately with drug counseling," she said. "No kids until you get that right. Cold turkey. Off the drug shit. Understood?"

Consumed with shame, disgrace, and fear, Brooks Webb nodded.

Danielle stood, her arms crossed, her head shaking from side to side.

Her husband turned to Mike and Sean and, barely audible, asked: "Will I go to jail?"

Mike loved seeing the pompous, lock-jawed Brahmin brought to his knees. Mike could have just let it go, but after all the emotional beating he had endured during this trial, and out of a sense of his own outrage as a human being...*we lawyers are, after all, nothing more or less than human beings...* he couldn't pass on the opportunity to slam Webb.

"Let me just say this, Mr. Webb. There is a retired narcotics police detective, two highly regarded informants, and this trove of photos that could put you away for a long time. And that's saying nothing about some of the regulars at *The Window* who would love to save their own hides by testifying against you. You fail to heed Danielle's advice...you fail to push the behavioral reset button and stay away from drugs, your children will become lost to you forever. They'll learn the truth as they grow older."

Danielle burst out: "Why the fuck didn't you tell me before we married that you wanted men? You son-of-a-bitch. Always making me feel that I was a failure sexually. And now...cocaine...!"

Mike placed his hand on his client's shoulder, interrupting her: "I don't know what your lawyer knew, but..."

"Mike, I, I...trust me, I never knew anything about Mr. Webb's addiction...I..." said Sofia, her voice trembling.

Don't overdo this, Mike. She hasn't the stones to even make a pretense of standing up for her client. And look at him...like a frightened little boy about to receive a beating behind the shed. And she...that sorry excuse for a lawyer...can't look me in the eye. Lady, had you been the least bit cooperative, we could have saved this couple a ton of money in legal fees and made a deal. But you needed to milk this thing dry...log in as many billable hours as you could. Look at what your greed and your client's depravity and dishonesty have netted him.

Mike said: "I find that what you've done...what you're doing...and I'm talking about the drugs and lying to your wife and trying to make her feel worthless as a woman and setting her up for a fall by hiring that...that gigolo...That, sir, is a crime in and of itself. I find it all repugnant, and until you straighten out, sir, you're not getting near those children without the presence of a court-appointed guardian ad litem to supervise."

Sofia Vasquez was mortified. A product of Harvard Law School and a member of one of the paramount old-line Boston law firms that ordinarily didn't sully their corporate chambers with divorce cases, but made an exception in this matter because they saw it as a slam-dunk for their client and a sizable fee, she struggled to maintain a semblance of composure.

"Mike," Sofia started in a phony, sweet tone, "do you intend to ask the judge to report this...to the District Attorney?"

Mike didn't answer. *Let them sweat,* Mike thought to himself. *Kelvin won't blow the whistle. He'll give Webb a chance at rehabilitation, but if he doesn't turn off the drug spigot, he's done.*

After a pause, Mike said: "I suggest we go into the courtroom and report that the case is settled. To the extent the judge wants to know the details…take any kind of criminal action…well, we'll just have to see."

After entering the courtroom, Mike handed the judge's clerk the Settlement Agreement.

"We've got a deal," Mike said.

"That's great news. I'll bring the Agreement into His Honor. He'll take the bench after he reads it and will let you know his disposition," the clerk said.

* * *

Judge Henry emerged. After putting the parties under oath and receiving affirmative answers to his questions as to whether or not each understood the various terms of the written Agreement, emphasizing Brooks Webb's required treatment for drug addiction, and taking the necessary perfunctory testimony to grant what was now an agreed upon divorce, the judge issued his Order of Approval as well as a request to seal the papers "for the protection of the minor children."

"Counsel," he said. "I congratulate you both on a job well done. Mr. and Mrs. Webb, a reminder that you are each bound by the terms of this court approved Agreement. And that includes the requirement that Mr. Webb vacate the marital home and enter forthwith into an approved drug rehabilitation program. No visitation whatsoever until that happens. And when I'm assured that you are actually participating in rehab, all visits with the children will be in the presence of a court-appointed third person until I am convinced of successful rehabilitation. And a further admonition: your children always, always come first. Understood?"

The clients nodded.

"Absent anything else that anyone wishes to say…?"

The judge paused and looked at each lawyer and client.

"Your Honor," Danielle started.

Mike flashed a look: *No, no. Don't burst out, Danielle. Don't blow this deal.*

"Your Honor, perhaps if I might have a moment," Mike said clearing his throat.

But Danielle proceeded: "Your Honor, I simply want to thank you for your patience and understanding throughout the trial. And I apologize for my transgressions."

"That is very decent of you, Mrs. Webb. But it's all part of my job. Save the apologies. I think you and Mr. Webb have learned much from this experience." He stood and left the bench.

* * *

When they reached the outside of the courthouse, Danielle breathed a sigh of relief. So did her lawyers.

"You gave me one hell of a scare. Couldn't imagine what you were going to come out with," Mike said.

"I know. No way was I going to blow this great result and emphasize more about the drugs or even touch the homosexuality piece. This is all still whirling around in my head. My kids. I'm going to be the best mom ever. What about the photos?" she asked.

"They're yours. Put 'em in a safe deposit box. You never know when you may need them," Mike said.

"May I kiss you both, Mr. Attorney Michael Lyons and Professor Sean Murray?"

"It's called writing a check. That's the kiss I'm looking forward to," said Mike.

Danielle Webb grasped Mike's overcoat lapels, got up on her toes and placed a kiss on his cheek. She then turned to Sean and brought her mouth to his while slipping a piece of paper in his coat pocket. Applause rang out among the witnesses.

"You're a real warrior, Mike. Thank you for hanging in there for me...and more importantly, for my children."

"And thank you, Professor Sean Murray. And that's for more than just your legal work on my case," she said. "I appreciate how you and Mike stood tall for me, despite my craziness."

Sean smiled and looked at her quizzically.

"Like the judge said, all part of our job. But you're welcome," Sean said.

"And whatever it is I owe you, I'm multiplying by two," she said, smiling at Mike.

"Cheapskate," he yelled playfully as she made her way down the escalator to Government Center.

She turned and put up three fingers.

"A little more like it." He smiled.

"And my friend," Mike said turning to Sean, "was that not a mouth to mouth kiss I just witnessed?"

CHAPTER THIRTY-FOUR
KATHERINE

TEN DAYS LATER

"Hello, Katherine. How wonderful to see you. And if I may add, to see you looking so radiant. New coat?" Jane greeted the client, observing her use of makeup for the first time.

"Thank you, Jane. Stylish, don't you think? I finally got rid of that old rag."

Mike stepped into the reception area.

"Katherine Hennessey, what brings you to these hallowed offices?" Mike joked.

"I think, Attorney Lyons, you said something about the arrival of a check." Her tone was uncharacteristically playful.

"Indeed I did. Please come in."

"I really can't believe this is over. While riding up the elevator, it felt as though I was coming for yet another prep session."

"Sleeping any better?"

"I'm just beginning to get my head around this; that it's all over. And I'm deeply appreciative of all you've done. The settlement amount is most satisfactory, Mike. But, and we both know there's always a 'but', I felt patronized when Father Riley went through the motions of an apology, and only because he was instructed to do so. His words were perfunctory. His face cold. Nothing from his heart."

Mike responded, "He's a pathological liar. He was humiliated. He lied to you. He lied to the Archbishop and to his own lawyer. And then to face the Archbishop after he listened to the tape as well as his lawyer and his friend, Father de Blasio, he was asked to further humble himself by apologizing to you, face-to-face. Shame is a powerful force."

"What you say is partially correct. You're an insightful man. But you know, Mike, I think his coldness was by design. Deliberate. He knows how deeply that side of him wounds me. He's sadistic and hoped that his hollow delivery would hurt more than help me. He's a cruel and deceitful man. I wish we had insisted upon something in writing."

Mike leaned forward, handing Katherine an envelope.

"Madame," Mike said, "your wish…"

The former sister's mouth dropped open.

"From him?" she asked.

"Attorney Colello sent it over this morning with the check. Well? Aren't you going to open it? I'm dying to know what he said."

> *Dear Katherine,*
> *I will spend the rest of my days seeking absolution for the sins I have committed. The worst of all was the pain I inflicted upon you. And I saw it in your eyes and on your face when I was instructed to apologize to you in the presence of His Excellency. This is my non-directed repentance. It is from my heart.*
> *I am unworthy of your forgiveness.*
> *Thomas*

Mike walked with Katherine to the elevator. She looked up at him, her eyes expressing her appreciation. She tilted her head. He leaned down and placed a gentle kiss on her cheek. "I wish you well, Katherine." The elevator arrived.

CHAPTER THIRTY-FIVE
KATHERINE

"Ah, Father de Blasio, come in please." The Archbishop got up from behind his desk.

"Good morning, Your Excellency."

"Coffee?"

"You're very kind, but I've had my fill of caffeine."

"It's a beautiful morning. Are you up for a walk? I'd like to stay on campus."

"It is a sparkler out there and, yes, I think that's a capital idea," said Father de Blasio, extending a hand toward the door.

"Anthony, did you get any sleep last night?"

"I suspect not much more than you, Your Excellency."

"You and Father Riley go back such a long way. I was never much of a football fan, but your gridiron feats on behalf of Holy Cross years ago are legendary," said the Archbishop.

"Thomas is…well, I certainly thought he was a good man. He's a fine scholar, and I so enjoyed our days together at college. He was indeed an outstanding running back. Named to the Academic All-America team our senior year."

With his eyebrows alone, the Archbishop delivered the retort that Thomas Riley had tumbled from grace…his own doing.

"And such a distinguished career at Chestnut Hill. The president is beside himself about this turn of events," said the Archbishop.

"Thomas has lost his way, Your Excellency."

"I can't begin to tell you how distressed I am. He has fallen. Father Riley's sins are blatant. No need to recapitulate. Only mourn the loss of a once, as you say, 'good man.' I'm afraid his soul has been tarnished. I have a responsibility to the church. I must take some action. And I turn to you, unfairly perhaps, but you have had so much experience in dealing with our troubled priests. But as I mentioned yesterday, if you feel that your friendship with Thomas will cloud your judgment, I totally understand."

"Your Excellency, I am deeply disappointed in my friend. I feel betrayed, but am ready to forgive. I have a request," said Anthony.

"And what is that?"

"That you not ask Thomas to resign. He'll never reclaim the real soul within him if his priesthood is denied him. Order a sabbatical and treatment, just as we have done with others. And then, just as you reassigned him to St. Joseph's in Fitchburg when you first learned of the lawsuit, consider another such parish."

"John Colello is so irate at being lied to, he suggests that Thomas be defrocked. But you say no?"

"Your Excellency, that would not only destroy Father Riley, it would also bring attention to the press. His prominence at the college and indeed, storied athletic achievements, may well stoke the fires of the *Record-American* and probably the *Globe* as well. A sabbatical followed by a new assignment is unlikely to develop into a story that would sell newspapers. I hate to be so crass, but…"

"Anthony, there are many things one might say about you; 'crass' is not among them. As always, you are being forthright, wise, and honest. I shall adopt your advice. As for place of reassignment, I'm not going to burden you. I'll take that upon myself." The Archbishop paused, took a deep breath. "Well, each of us has other tasks to attend to today. Thank you, Anthony," the Archbishop said while shaking hands. "Let us pray for Father Riley."

"And for Katherine," Anthony added.

The Archbishop nodded in accord.

* * *

Following his sabbatical and psychotherapy, Father Riley left for his new assignment: St. Matthew's Church, Limerick, Maine.

The town is located in the northern central region of the state, with a population of approximately two thousand. For the most part, furniture factories were the primary means of employment. A gritty town with proud, hardworking people, St. Matthew's was one of New England's smallest Catholic parishes. From esteemed professorship and assistant to the president of Chestnut Hill College to this remote assignment…the priest had fallen. His quarters were the antithesis of the comfort of the large Tudor on Commonwealth Avenue in Newton, Massachusetts.

"I've not been sent here to rehabilitate. Realistically, it's as though I've been cast aside…excommunicated. I'm here to do penance…to suffer. My soul will suffocate in this remote…prison. Do I have the courage to resign? Leave the church? What would I do? Languish in Wellfleet? My sister despises me," Thomas Riley said to himself.

In the weeks that followed his arrival, Father Riley's alcohol intake increased and his physical exercise came to a halt. He was well aware that immorality and deceit had claimed his soul. There was little left to this one-time giant at the college and archdiocese. It was obvious that his efforts to serve his new parish were hollow.

It wasn't long before local parishioners began to gossip about why this pastor had been reassigned from a major faculty position at prestigious Chestnut Hill College to their small remote church in northern Maine.

"We're nothing more than an afterthought compared to what this man had down there in Boston. Something's not right," mused one of the regular churchgoers.

Each night while saying his prayers, Father Riley clutched a photo of Katherine Hennessey. Aging, depressed, lonely, he restrained himself from asking for forgiveness.

The priest was acutely aware that his once athletic body was deteriorating. Emotionally, he felt crushed, defeated. *Banishment to this place; it's not God's will that my mission is solely to do good here; it's the will of God that I suffer.*

On a given morning as he proceeded to a downtown coffee shop, a daily routine in an effort to connect with locals, Father Riley collapsed.

* * *

Katherine Hennessey's phone rang.

"Sister Hennessey?" It was a male voice.

"This is Katherine Hennessey. How may I help you?"

"I'm Father Anthony de Blasio, a longtime friend of Father Riley."

Silence.

"Sister Hennessey…Katherine…are you there?"

"I know who you are, Father de Blasio. Why are you calling?"

"Forgive me, Ms. Hennessey, for intruding upon you at your place of work. I learned from Thomas months ago that you were working at Rosie's Place. I'm calling to let you know that a few weeks ago Thomas suffered a major stroke. He's been moved to a rehabilitation center here in Massachusetts. I thought…"

Stunned, trying to collect her composure, Katherine could only manage a hollow "I'm sorry."

"I realize that this comes as a shock to you. Father cannot speak. That ability, I am told by the neurologist, is irreparably gone. When I recently visited, Father Riley was struggling to find something in the night table next to his bed. As I was helping him, I saw your photograph. He was reaching for it. I spoke your name and his eyes watered."

In tears, Katherine responded: "Please, Father."

"I know this is difficult. He obviously has some mental faculties intact. I just thought it might be helpful…"

Katherine finished Father de Blasio's sentence: "…if I were to visit."

"Precisely. It just might bolster his weakened spirit…his damaged mind."

"Did you say 'damaged,' Father? Father, I will be in a state of repair for the rest of my life because of that man. My very soul has been scorched with pain and humiliation. Nevertheless, I wish him no further harm. But I would be a hypocrite if I were to visit. What would you have me do, Father? Sit there and lie and pretend that I forgive him, that I care for him? That part of me was destroyed long ago. Crushed by Father Thomas Riley. For me to respond honestly and to think of my own survival, it is best for me to remain out of his life and not pretend that I forgive, because I do not forgive him."

"But Katherine, surely you recall St. Stephen, our first Christian martyr. 'He forgave, from the Cross, those who had just treated him so brutally.'"

"With all due respect, Father de Blasio, if I were to forgive Thomas Riley, and I am not prepared to do so, even such forgiveness cannot reconcile his sins. I understand your loyalty to him, but a visit is out of the question. I appreciate your letting me know. I can't even say I'll pray for him. The faith and sense of caring I once had for him were destroyed by his betrayal. No, Father, I am still struggling to salvage my own sense of worth and self-respect. I will not damage the growth and progress I have made. One day I will once again experience God's presence. Forgive me, but I must end this conversation."

Katherine closed her office door and walked to a window. *I'll struggle forever wondering whether or not I'll ever be able to recognize a genuine, caring man. My father turned his back on me. Father Riley turned his back as well. There's a fear in my head that all relationships between men and women are fraught with the danger of lying, betrayal, and abuse. I'm struggling to strengthen myself so that one day I'll be able to trust. Strange,* she thought, *but I have no tears. I'm proud of myself that I said I won't go to him, but should I be more charitable? I know Matthew's teaching: "Do not resist an evil person. If anyone slaps you on the right cheek, turn to them the other cheek also." But no, I will not turn my other cheek. Better that I be honest with myself.*

It took a couple of days but Katherine Hennessey released whatever doubts she might have had about her decision not to see Father Riley. She would continue to get on with her life. The memories would always be there, but she would not capitulate.

Katherine opened the door to the meeting room at Rosie's Place where women eager to recapture their courage and self-confidence waited for her group session to begin. She cast her soft, intelligent eyes upon the cluster of women she had come to love. Katherine had a calling here and would continue to rise to it.

CHAPTER THIRTY-SIX
SEAN AND DANIELLE

Mike, Jane and Sean stepped outside The Ritz-Carlton. They had just enjoyed their annual year-end dinner celebration. The Hennessey and Webb successes made 1972 a special year. A biting wind tore across the nearby Boston Public Garden. Mike, tugging at his overcoat collar, handed his parking voucher to the valet. He was going to drive Jane and Sean home.

A voice was heard next to a car parked just beyond the hotel entrance: "Hey, good lookin', interested in a ride home?"

They simultaneously peered in the direction of the sound. Their mouths dropped open.

Mike and Jane, each grinning, turned toward Sean.

"Me thinketh, good Professor, that it is you who just might be the 'good lookin' one in whom the fair maiden is interested," said Mike.

"You've had too much to drink," said the scarlet-faced Sean.

Within seconds Danielle Webb stood before the trio.

"Danielle, now this is a surprise. Just how did you know we were here?" Mike asked, glancing suspiciously at Sean.

"I confess to eavesdropping while I was waiting for you for one of our appointments. You and Jane were talking in your office, the door partially open. Thinking it might be about getting rid of me as a client, I was all ears. I was relieved to know the topic was plans for tonight's gathering." Danielle raised her eyebrows as if to say, *Clever of me, no?*

"Well, Mrs. Webb…" Jane started.

"Not Mrs. Webb. Danielle, please, Jane."

"Well, Danielle, I give you credit for your honesty."

"Now coming from you, Ms. Jane, that's a real compliment. Thank you. I know when I first came to the office you weren't too fond of me...and for good reason."

"And credit for your determination," Mike added. "How long have you been out here?"

Danielle turned toward Sean. "About an hour, but I cheated."

Sean raised his eyebrows as if to ask what the cheating was all about.

"I know the staff pretty well at this dining room. I lied and said that Sean was expecting me to pick him up when dinner was over. I asked for a heads-up."

"Shy and withdrawn as ever," quipped Mike.

"And as you said before, Mike, determined," Danielle responded.

Jane and Mike turned toward Sean, who was totally in shock but obviously flattered.

"Ah, here comes my car," said Mike.

He turned to his colleague. "See you soon, Professor. You won't be needing a ride from me," said Mike, struggling to withhold a knowing grin.

"No, hold on, Mike," Sean whispered. He turned to Danielle.

"Danielle," Sean began, "this is all very kind of you, but..."

Jane interrupted. "Loosen up. She's not going to bite you. Then again..." She raised her eyebrows playfully.

Danielle understood Sean's hesitancy. She stepped back toward her car, her expression one of empathy and encouragement.

Mike spoke up: "Wait, just a moment please, Danielle." He pulled Sean aside. "You deserve some fun. Case is all over. It's perfectly legit. Agreement's been filed and approved. The divorce decree has been issued. You don't have to marry her. Just have some fun for a night...or two or three." He patted his mentor on the shoulder. "And who knows, maybe it's a ride home and that's it. Whatever it is, go for it."

Sean looked at Jane as if to ask permission. She nodded, mouthing, "It's fine."

The professor took a deep breath, turned to Danielle, "Thank you. I'd be most grateful for a ride home." Sean felt a wave of excitement and pleasure he hadn't experienced since his wife and boys perished. *It must be the booze,* he thought to himself.

After they got into her car, Danielle said, "I know you think I'm wild and out of control, Sean. But I also like to think that now that you know my story, you know there's some—well, some redeeming qualities?"

Sean smiled. "Danielle, we're all imperfect beings. I'm not a judgmental man." He swallowed hard. "And I do understand."

"It's as though I've been given a new life, Sean. You and Mike closed one door and opened another for me. Being a loose Beacon Hill tramp was a dumbass reaction when I learned Brooks was queer. That he hid it from me and whipped my psyche into believing our failed sex life was all because of me only added to my anger and resentment. By sleeping around I wanted to get to Brooks…punish him for wounding me. That's over now. And so is the lying. Learning about his secret drug world was an epiphany." She started to drive toward Brookline.

Sean extended a warm smile. "I'm happy for you. So, Danielle, now that you have a new life, what are your hopes and aspirations?"

"Why did I guess you might ask me such a question? It's certainly a valid one. I want to be the best mother I possibly can be." She turned toward Sean. "And I want genuine happiness…for the first time in my life."

"Eyes front, please, madam. That's a noble ambition. But I must say, Danielle, once Hoda and Rock revealed just what kind of life your husband…'

"Ex, if you please," Danielle interrupted.

"Well, what I want to say...and yes, I'm a little bit drunk...is that all things considered, you've been doing one hell of a job with those children."

"Thank you. I'm already spending more time with them and enjoying every morsel. They're terrific kids. And you, Professor, do you intend to continue working with Mike? The two of you are a great team. I'll never hesitate to recommend you."

"We try. Yes, I like working with Mike. And since we don't have any kind of formal arrangement, it's a good place for me. A shelter. When Mike needs me, I enjoy being there for him. He's a good person and a damned good lawyer."

They arrived at the apartment complex in Brookline Village where Sean lived. After pulling over to a curb, Danielle turned and fixed her eyes directly at him.

Sean thought to himself: *Those beautiful limpid eyes. Her expression is soft. Nothing flirtatious. Something so appealing...I've got to stop this. I'm much too old for her. Perhaps it will be a fatherly friendship I can offer her. Yes. That's much more appropriate than...*

"Sean," Danielle started, "can we see each other? Dinner? A movie?"

He surprised himself with his quick answer: "That would be lovely. But Danielle..." He paused and swallowed. "Strictly as friends."

As he opened the car door and stepped outside, she responded, "Yup. Just friends."

Sean turned and looked directly into her eyes.

Appealing. There's depth there. A real person.

"Professor, aren't you forgetting something?"

Sean bent his head toward the open passenger door.

"Oh, my, forgive me. Of course. Thank you so much for the lift, Danielle. I'm flattered that you surprised me...us."

Danielle shimmied from behind the wheel toward the passenger seat. She beckoned to him and gently tapped her cheek.

"This is what I meant that you forgot. And, yes, strictly platonic," she said.

He craned his neck and leaned into the car. Self-consciously, Sean put a hand on one side of her face, then a soft kiss on the other. He smelled her perfume. And loved it.

As he straightened, he mimicked her: "Strictly platonic." They both grinned.

When Sean entered his apartment he leaned back against the door and tried to process what was going on inside his soul. *There's something...something electrifying going on.* He moved into the living room, went to the large picture window and looked upward. It was a nightly ritual. Comforting. He spoke his wife's name and imagined her saying *it's okay sweetheart. It's okay.*

This is crazy, he said to himself as he started toward his liquor stash. He nudged the handle on the cabinet door. *Hold on, Sean. You don't need this. You've had enough. It's time. Time for you to turn the corner.*

The murder of his wife and sons had fueled a sense of emotional apathy. For the first time since that personal holocaust he allowed a jolt of pleasure that surged from his heart. He gave himself permission to feel something other than pain. And maybe, just maybe, the desire for companionship and perhaps even love of a woman. Not another meaningless one-night stand. Those escapades always left him feeling even lonelier.

* * *

As part of the process of unfolding her new life, Danielle decided to rid herself of much of her material belongings that represented, in her words, a *phony past.*

On a given day while making a delivery of clothing and accessories to Rosie's Place, she observed a notice on the lobby bulletin board: "*ABUSED? PHYSICALLY OR EMOTIONALLY? You are welcome to join free group sessions here at Rosie's Place under the leadership of Katherine Hennessey.*" Katherine's credentials were posted as well as a schedule and sign-up sheet.

I could run to a fancy shrink. But I don't want fancy anymore. Why not try this? What have I got to lose? I'll give it a shot. I'll be with some real down to earth women, not the well-heeled country club set. I can learn from these people. And I can be myself, the real me. No one will know me. No need to hide from myself anymore. I'm going to unlock that box, let the real me out. And Sean...I can't get him out of my mind.

* * *

Danielle responded to Katherine's warmth and ability to help the women in the group feel that they were in a safe place. She quickly found Katherine to be nonjudgmental, never condescending, and a woman who obviously knew firsthand the pain and degradation of physical and emotional abuse. Danielle respected the women who participated and she worked hard to bridge the racial and economic gap that existed. They were, for the most part, poor African-American and Hispanic women. Each with a story of abuse, poverty, abandonment, or degradation. Danielle was the sole white participant. The same women tended to meet weekly. At first, they openly resented Danielle's presence. In fact during one meeting a participant burst out at Danielle: "What in hell do you know? You're white. And you look rich to me, lady. Like some rich bitch trying to play poor. What's your gig? You writing a book?"

Another picked up the baton. "White folks don't know about *it*. You haven't a clue. *It* is shit. Drugs and booze and beatin's. You know nada."

Calmly, Katherine seized upon these moments to guide a discussion about Danielle's presence and the undercurrent of hostility. She turned to Danielle, who had not said anything about herself during the prior meetings but had occasionally offered comments about issues the women raised.

"Perhaps, Danielle, you might share your story? Whenever you're ready. Today or maybe next time?" Katherine looked at Danielle with encouragement.

"If folks would like me to leave, I certainly understand. But I want everyone to know that I'm not writing a book. I'm not writing anything. Just trying to be whole again. You don't have to be Black or Hispanic or poor to feel broken," she said softly. The room was silent. Dramatically, the woman who had made one of the disparaging remarks leaned toward Danielle and apologized. Another said: "I hear you. Whenever you're ready, we're ready…sister."

"Thank you. You've no idea what that means to me," Danielle responded.

"I was married to a very rich man. I could have anything I wanted. But he was a liar. He lied to me. He should have told me that inside he was queer when we were dating. Instead, he hid it, asked me to marry him, and then just kept blaming me for spoiling our sex life. He's a queer, goddammit, and never fucking told me. I felt awful and couldn't figure out what it was I was doing wrong. When I asked, he'd get mean and say, 'Everything. You don't know anything about sex.' Finally out of desperation, I started to screw around…just to prove to myself that I was a normal, healthy, desirable woman." She looked around the room. Most of the women nodded knowingly. Danielle was relieved at being able to dig down, be open and candid about what she had experienced.

One of them casually asked whether or not Danielle liked her lawyer. "I'm kinda in the market for one," a woman said. "But I'm guessin' your lawyer cost plenty? Maybe I'll just go to Volunteer Lawyers."

"His name's Mike Lyons. He's a good man and I know he takes on some cases for free…no fee. I would be happy to ask…"

Katherine started to blurt out, "Mike…" But then stopped herself. At the conclusion she asked if Danielle would mind waiting for a minute.

After the others left, Katherine shared the fact that they had each been represented by Mike Lyons. Danielle was speechless. "It's okay," said Katherine. "Just one of those coincidences. He's a good man. And I imagine you also met the professor?"

"This is just amazing, Katherine. The professor and I are seeing each other. I told him about you, about this program. He never uttered a word," said Danielle.

"He's an honorable man. The issue of confidentiality, no doubt," said Katherine. This exchange paved the way toward the development of a friendship between the two.

* * *

There were dinners, theater, movies. Danielle made a point of emphasizing that the difference in age was perfectly comfortable for her. Sean accepted her reassurances as their relationship morphed from one of friendship to romance and authentic love. He marveled at his capacity to actually love a woman after losing Adele. He was moved by a kindness that emerged from Danielle. And Danielle was thrilled to cherish and admire a man, and just be herself for the first time in her adult life. She abandoned the lifestyle she had created during her marriage to Brooks. She sold the opulent apartment on Beacon Hill and bought something much more modest in Boston's gentrifying South End. Danielle began to heal from the wounds of betrayal and shame. Sean would never heal from the wounds of his tragedy, but his attachment to Danielle allowed a new layer to form in his life. They each became beloved to the other.

Danielle was aware that Sean had lost his family tragically and suddenly and felt that he would benefit from some professional help. On a given evening she broached the subject.

"Sean, you know, at least I hope you know, how much I adore you. I care about you. There's something wonderful happening between the two of us. But there's also something I think you need to do before we can get to the next level."

"Uh, oh," Sean responded, "I think I know where you're going."

She leaned forward and kissed him softly. "I'm not ready to propose," she smiled, "not just yet."

They laughed. "I'm talking about something else."

"Adele? The boys?"

"Dear Sean, until you get that stuff out and really grieve, you and I are going to be stuck. And I think we both want more."

Sean nodded. "I certainly do. You know, sweetheart, Ali and Mike have urged me to do just what you're getting at. The thought of it has been repugnant."

"Because it's scary stuff, Sean. But…"

"Maybe I'm ready now. I care about you, about us. Please understand, Danielle, Adele and my boys will never be out of my thoughts. They are a part of my fiber. My love for my wife and boys will never diminish. But also understand that there is now, at last, space in my heart for…"

Danielle felt the tears run down her cheeks. She was moved by the hurt, by the intensity of his voice. She wrapped her arms around his neck and moved her mouth toward his. It was a long passionate and deep expression of caring and love.

Because of his new life unfolding with Danielle, Sean found the strength to seek professional help to confront the crushing tragedy that had ripped his heart. It took a number of sessions before he was able to open up emotionally, allow the tears and gut-wrenching howling to escape as he related the horror that stole his wife and boys.

EPILOGUE

In mid-January, Mike received a typewritten letter with an obvious phony return address:

Hi Mike,

Thought you'd like to know. Shooter in front of courthouse, ex-cop. Desperate coke-head. Regular at the you know where. After retired from Boston PD worked as maintenance guy at Webb's lab. Reliable friend told H and me that he heard Webb at the "place" telling ex-cop that he'd fix him with good supply of dust if he could help get Danielle off his back...and out of family fortune. Was worried about D filing for divorce, getting big share of trust. And kids. Her going for kids would mean giving up even more Mr. Green. Worried about being found out as druggie. And having trusts cough up millions to her instead of him. Friend says he heard all of this and saw Webb pass bag of dust to cop. Thought he heard Webb mention something about heavy-duty cash...delivering it maybe. To the cop. To someone else. Wasn't sure. Remembers hearing Webb say to cop, "just do it." Gigolo sting wasn't enough for that scumbag Webb. Do what you will. H and me are gone. Trust you. Burn this.

R.

Mike shared the letter with Sean. "It's obviously from Rock," Sean agreed.

The two of them morphed into a debate as to whether or not to bring this to the attention of the DA.

"Could it be?" Mike asked. "That Brooks Webb actually hired that former cop to try to kill Danielle...and me?"

"Scary. It sure smells like that," Sean responded.

Shaking his head, Mike said, "But without Hoda and Rock and the no doubt druggie who gave them this info, the DA wouldn't have enough to go for an indictment."

"But Mike, we've got an obligation…"

"Hold on, Professor. No one knows where Hoda and Rock have disappeared to. Rock drove some place far away from wherever he's living and mailed it. He's too savvy."

"The DA should at least conduct an investigation. Track them down. They might reveal the source in exchange for immunity."

"I wouldn't want to take that chance. They sold too much coke even if it was to inform and give the Boston PD some coke-heads to arrest."

"Mike, my friend, Webb may well have tried to have Danielle killed. And you. We've got an ethical obligation as lawyers to turn this in. Let the DA make the decision."

"Ethics? What about loyalty and trust? I seem to remember a professor in law school who more than once talked about protecting a valuable witness. If he/she doesn't want to be exposed, or might be in danger if exposed, honor that. Unless, of course, the witness is talking about committing a crime. Rock trusts me to burn this note. He and Hoda came to the rescue of our case…and more importantly, the rescue of those kids."

"I plead guilty. But I think it's clear what Webb was up to," said Sean.

"Maybe not. Maybe he was going to offer Danielle a bundle of cash to leave quietly with the kids, and the ex-cop was drugged up and went further than Webb intended. It's all conjectural. Let's sleep on it," said Mike.

It would become moot.

* * *

Brooks Webb paid his debt to Hoda and Rock. However, consumed with shame, he was unable to contain his desire for drugs. His cocaine habit morphed into heroin. When his parents and siblings became aware that he prematurely left a rehabilitation program and once again resorted to drugs, they directed that the family trusts no longer provide him with funds; that it continue to honor the terms of the divorce agreement so that the children and Danielle would be financially secure. Brooks failed to keep scheduled supervised visits with the children. Having lost his birth and nuclear families, his job, and having fallen into debt, Brooks Webb took his life.

* * *

The wedding was simple. It took place at the Lyons home. The Honorable Colleen Murphy officiated. In addition to the Lyons family, the wedding party included Sean's brother and sister, Danielle's children, Katherine and a close friend, Jane and her fiancé. The honeymoon would include Danielle's children. It was a total sabbatical from the lives they had been living. A year on Monhegan Island off the coast of Maine turned out to be an utter joy, despite the island's eternal wind. Sean wrote the novel he had been longing to write. Danielle volunteered at the island's only school and proved to be a revered teacher as well as a talented student of an accomplished artist. The children thrived on a simpler, less posh, less structured life. Monhegan would become their summer refuge for years to come, and Katherine's annual visit always a highlight.

* * *

Hoda returned to her native South Dakota and its poverty-stricken Pine Ridge Reservation. In addition to helping young Native Americans learn about photography, she volunteered for programs aimed at curbing alcoholism.

Rockwell ultimately landed in Miami Beach where he entertained himself romancing wealthy divorcees and widows, hoping to find the one who might provide an annuity for his future. Whether or not he was successful is conjectural.

Jane married Phil. She became pregnant and worked with Mike up to her delivery day. She would return to the office once her daughter and son were of school age.

As for Ali and Mike, they continued to be caring and nurturing parents. Hillary and Michelle would excel in high school and move on to Brown University and Vassar College, respectively. Ali left the world of school psychology and became a full time guardian ad litem, assisting Family Court judges with challenging child custody cases. Mike's practice grew to the point where he moved to a larger space and hired three young lawyers to assist him and Sean with their growing inventory of cases.

On the day after the new sign, *Lyons & Murray, Attorneys at Law,* was placed on the suite entry, Mike paused to take it in. His eyes moistened.

ACKNOWLEDGMENTS

My wife, *Ellen,* complimented my writing style and for years urged me to consider writing a book. Her steadfast encouragement, praise, and deep listening inspired me while I regaled her with a myriad of possible scenarios and dialogue. Her meticulous copyediting of many drafts and constructive suggestions were of immeasurable help in the development of this novel.

My daughters, *Tracey Aronson*, superb lawyer, and *Jennifer Parker*, extraordinary library scientist, patiently listened during their teen years while I burdened our family with endless stories of cases. Their very presence in my life and limitless love continue to inspire me daily.

Myrna, my late wife and mother of our daughters, from the very beginning supported, stood by me and encouraged my development as a trial lawyer.

Eric Parker, son-in-law and exceptional litigator, kept me informed of the constant changes in the world of civil litigation.

Larry Armour, friend since Dartmouth days and former editor at Time Inc., generously served as editor of this book. Larry's experience and talent as a writer and editor resulted in meaningful improvements and adjustments.

Harriett Galvin, good friend and an assistant district attorney in Manhattan, took time to research applicable questions of law, read multiple chapters, and offer constructive modifications.

Suzanne Pemsler, study group leader at the Harvard Institute for Learning in Retirement (HILR), stoked the fires within me to pursue writing as a hobby in retirement. Her writing classes were exceptional and style of communicating encouraging. Suzanne persuaded me that there is a writer in my soul.

The *Writers Group at HILR* provided thoughtful critiques and helped me to hone my writing skills. I am grateful to each member for chapter-by-chapter suggestions. Special thanks to the originals of the group: *Dolores Murphy, Jane Weingarten, Bob Kinerk, Judy Uhl, Ross Neisuler, David Rich,* and the late *Stan Davis*.

Special thanks to *Karen Wilder* for her superb formatting, attention to detail, patience and encouragement.

I also deeply appreciate the expertise contributed by other professionals and friends: *Kathleen Lynch, Debra Englander, Rachel Shuster, Val and Bob Marier, Marilyn Gottlieb Levy, Babs Armour, Kelli Parker, and Jeff Soloway*.

And lastly, *Macbeth and Sky,* our family's successive standard poodles in the seventies, eighties, and nineties. Each was inundated with opening statements and closing arguments as we took our late night walks through our suburban and Cape Cod neighborhoods.